Tibet

WORLD BIBLIOGRAPHICAL SERIES

General Editors:
Robert G. Neville (Executive Editor)
John J. Horton

Robert A. Myers   Ian Wallace
Hans H. Wellisch   Ralph Lee Woodward, Jr.

John J. Horton is Deputy Librarian of the University of Bradford and currently Chairman of its Academic Board of Studies in Social Sciences. He has maintained a longstanding interest in the discipline of area studies and its associated bibliographical problems, with special reference to European Studies. In particular he has published in the field of Icelandic and of Yugoslav studies, including the two relevant volumes in the World Bibliographical Series.

Robert A. Myers is Associate Professor of Anthropology in the Division of Social Sciences and Director of Study Abroad Programs at Alfred University, Alfred, New York. He has studied post-colonial island nations of the Caribbean and has spent two years in Nigeria on a Fulbright Lectureship. His interests include international public health, historical anthropology and developing societies. In addition to *Amerindians of the Lesser Antilles: a bibliography* (1981), *A Resource Guide to Dominica, 1493–1986* (1987) and numerous articles, he has compiled the World Bibliographical Series volumes on *Dominica* (1987) and *Nigeria* (1989).

Ian Wallace is Professor of Modern Languages at Loughborough University of Technology. A graduate of Oxford in French and German, he also studied in Tübingen, Heidelberg and Lausanne before taking teaching posts at universities in the USA, Scotland and England. He specializes in East German affairs, especially literature and culture, on which he has published numerous articles and books. In 1979 he founded the journal *GDR Monitor*, which he continues to edit.

Hans H. Wellisch is Professor emeritus at the College of Library and Information Services, University of Maryland. He was President of the American Society of Indexers and was a member of the International Federation for Documentation. He is the author of numerous articles and several books on indexing and abstracting, and has published *The Conversion of Scripts* and *Indexing and Abstracting: an International Bibliography*. He also contributes frequently to *Journal of the American Society for Information Science, The Indexer* and other professional journals.

Ralph Lee Woodward, Jr. is Chairman of the Department of History at Tulane University, New Orleans, where he has been Professor of History since 1970. He is the author of *Central America, a Nation Divided*, 2nd ed. (1985), as well as several monographs and more than sixty scholarly articles on modern Latin America. He has also compiled volumes in the World Bibliographical Series on *Belize* (1980), *Nicaragua* (1983), and *El Salvador* (1988). Dr. Woodward edited the Central American section of the *Research Guide to Central America and the Caribbean* (1985) and is currently editor of the Central American history section of the *Handbook of Latin American Studies*.

VOLUME 128

Tibet

John Pinfold

Compiler

CLIO PRESS

OXFORD, ENGLAND · SANTA BARBARA, CALIFORNIA
DENVER, COLORADO

British Library Cataloguing in Publication Data

Pinfold, John
Tibet. — (World bibliographical series; v. 128).
I. Title   II. Series
016.9515

ISBN 1-85109-158-0

Clio Press Ltd.,
55 St. Thomas' Street,
Oxford OX1 1JG, England.

ABC-CLIO,
130 Cremona Drive,
Santa Barbara,
CA 93117, USA.

Designed by Bernard Crossland.
Typeset by Columns Design and Production Services Ltd., Reading, England.
Printed and bound in Great Britain by
Billing and Sons Ltd., Worcester.

THE WORLD BIBLIOGRAPHICAL SERIES

This series, which is principally designed for the English speaker, will eventually cover every country in the world, each in a separate volume comprising annotated entries on works dealing with its history, geography, economy and politics; and with its people, their culture, customs, religion and social organization. Attention will also be paid to current living conditions – housing, education, newspapers, clothing, etc.– that are all too often ignored in standard bibliographies; and to those particular aspects relevant to individual countries. Each volume seeks to achieve, by use of careful selectivity and critical assessment of the literature, an expression of the country and an appreciation of its nature and national aspirations, to guide the reader towards an understanding of its importance. The keynote of the series is to provide, in a uniform format, an interpretation of each country that will express its culture, its place in the world, and the qualities and background that make it unique. The views expressed in individual volumes, however, are not necessarily those of the publisher.

VOLUMES IN THE SERIES

1 *Yugoslavia*, John J. Horton
2 *Lebanon*, Shereen Khairallah
3 *Lesotho*, Shelagh M. Willet and David Ambrose
4 *Rhodesia/Zimbabwe*, Oliver B. Pollack and Karen Pollack
5 *Saudi Arabia*, Frank A. Clements
6 *USSR*, Anthony Thompson
7 *South Africa*, Reuben Musiker
8 *Malawi*, Robert B Boeder
9 *Guatemala*, Woodman B. Franklin
10 *Pakistan*, David Taylor
11 *Uganda*, Robert L. Collison
12 *Malaysia*, Ian Brown and Rajeswary Ampalavanar
13 *France*, Frances Chambers
14 *Panama*, Eleanor DeSelms Langstaff
15 *Hungary*, Thomas Kabdebo
16 *USA*, Sheila R. Herstein and Naomi Robbins
17 *Greece*, Richard Clogg and Mary Jo Clogg
18 *New Zealand*, R. F. Grover
19 *Algeria*, Richard I. Lawless
20 *Sri Lanka*, Vijaya Samaraweera
21 *Belize*, Ralph Lee Woodward, Jr.
23 *Luxembourg*, Carlo Hury and Jul Christophory
24 *Swaziland*, Balam Nyeko

25 *Kenya*, Robert L. Collison
26 *India*, Brijen K. Gupta and Datta S. Kharbas
27 *Turkey*, Merel Güçlü
28 *Cyprus*, P. M. Kitromilides and M. L. Evriviades
29 *Oman*, Frank A. Clements
31 *Finland*, J. E. O. Screen
32 *Poland*, Richard C. Lewański
33 *Tunisia*, Allan M. Findlay, Anne M. Findlay and Richard I. Lawless
34 *Scotland*, Eric G. Grant
35 *China*, Peter Cheng
36 *Qatar*, P. T. H. Unwin
37 *Iceland*, John J. Horton
38 *Nepal*, John Whelpton
39 *Haiti*, Frances Chambers
40 *Sudan*, M. W. Daly
41 *Vatican City State*, Michael J. Walsh
42 *Iraq*, A. J. Abdulrahman
43 *United Arab Emirates*, Frank A. Clements
44 *Nicaragua*, Ralph Lee Woodward, Jr.
45 *Jamaica*, K. E. Ingram
46 *Australia*, I. Kepars
47 *Morocco*, Anne M. Findlay, Allan M. Findlay and Richard I. Lawless

48 *Mexico*, Naomi Robbins
49 *Bahrain*, P. T. H. Unwin
50 *The Yemens*, G. Rex Smith
51 *Zambia*, Anne M. Bliss and J. A. Rigg
52 *Puerto Rico*, Elena E. Cevallos
53 *Namibia*, Stanley Schoeman and Elna Schoeman
54 *Tanzania*, Colin Darch
55 *Jordan*, Ian J. Seccombe
56 *Kuwait*, Frank A. Clements
57 *Brazil*, Solena V. Bryant
58 *Israel*, Esther M. Snyder (preliminary compilation E. Kreiner)
59 *Romania*, Andrea Deletant and Dennis Deletant
60 *Spain*, Graham J. Shields
61 *Atlantic Ocean*, H. G. R. King
62 *Canada*, Ernest Ingles
63 *Cameroon*, Mark W. DeLancey and Peter J. Schraeder
64 *Malta*, John Richard Thackrah
65 *Thailand*, Michael Watts
66 *Austria*, Denys Salt with the assistance of Arthur Farrand Radley
67 *Norway*, Leland B. Sather
68 *Czechoslovakia*, David Short
69 *Irish Republic*, Michael Owen Shannon
70 *Pacific Basin and Oceania*, Gerald W. Fry and Rufino Mauricio
71 *Portugal*, P. T. H. Unwin
72 *West Germany*, Donald S. Detwiler and Ilse E. Detwiler
73 *Syria*, Ian J. Seccombe
74 *Trinidad and Tobago*, Frances Chambers
76 *Barbados*, Robert B. Potter and Graham M. S. Dann
77 *East Germany*, Ian Wallace
78 *Mozambique*, Colin Darch
79 *Libya*, Richard I. Lawless
80 *Sweden*, Leland B. Sather and Alan Swanson
81 *Iran*, Reza Navabpour
82 *Dominica*, Robert A. Myers
83 *Denmark*, Kenneth E. Miller
84 *Paraguay*, R. Andrew Nickson
85 *Indian Ocean*, Julia J. Gotthold with the assistance of Donald W. Gotthold
86 *Egypt*, Ragai, N. Makar
87 *Gibraltar*, Graham J. Shields
88 *The Netherlands*, Peter King and Michael Wintle
89 *Bolivia*, Gertrude M. Yeager
90 *Papua New Guinea*, Fraiser McConnell
91 *The Gambia*, David P. Gamble
92 *Somalia*, Mark W. DeLancey, Sheila L. Elliott, December Green, Kenneth J. Menkhaus, Mohammad Haji Moqtar, Peter J. Schraeder
93 *Brunei*, Sylvia C. Engelen Krausse, Gerald H. Krausse
94 *Albania*, William B. Bland
95 *Singapore*, Stella R. Quah, Jon S. T. Quah
96 *Guyana*, Frances Chambers
97 *Chile*, Harold Blakemore
98 *El Salvador*, Ralph Lee Woodward, Jr.
99 *The Arctic*, H.G.R. King
100 *Nigeria*, Robert A. Myers
101 *Ecuador*, David Corkhill
102 *Uruguay*, Henry Finch with the assistance of Alicia Casas de Barrán
103 *Japan*, Frank Joseph Shulman
104 *Belgium*, R.C. Riley
105 *Macau*, Richard Louis Edmonds
106 *Philippines*, Jim Richardson
107 *Bulgaria*, Richard J. Crampton
108 *The Bahamas*, Paul G. Boultbee
109 *Peru*, John Robert Fisher
110 *Venezuela*, D. A. G. Waddell
111 *Dominican Republic*, Kai Schoenhals
112 *Colombia*, Robert H. Davis
113 *Taiwan*, Wei-chin Lee
114 *Switzerland*, Heinz K. Meier and Regula A. Meier
115 *Hong Kong*, Ian Scott
116 *Bhutan,* Ramesh C. Dogra
117 *Suriname*, Rosemarijn Hoefte
118 *Djibouti*, Peter J. Schraeder
119 *Grenada*, Kai Schoenhals
120 *Monaco*, Grace L. Hudson
121 *Guinea-Bissau*, Rosemary Galli
122 *Wales*, Gwilym Huws and D. Hywel E. Roberts
123 *Cape Verde*, Caroline S. Shaw
124 *Ghana*, Robert A. Myers
125 *Greenland*, Kenneth E. Miller
126 *Costa Rica*, Charles L. Stansifer
127 *Siberia*, David N. Collins
128 *Tibet*, John Pinfold

To J. with love

Contents

INTRODUCTION xiii

THE COUNTRY AND ITS PEOPLE 1

GEOGRAPHY 6
    Maps and gazetteers   8
    Guidebooks   9

TRAVEL AND EXPLORATION 11
    General accounts   11
    Pre-1900   13
    1900–1950   19
    1950–   24

FLORA AND FAUNA... 27

HISTORY 30
    General   30
    Early and medieval   33
    16th to 19th centuries   36
    1900–1950   38
    1951–   45

POPULATION 54
    Extraterritorial population   56
    Women   59

ANTHROPOLOGY AND ETHNOLOGY 61

LANGUAGE.. 65
    Dictionaries   65
    Grammars and phrasebooks   66
    Phonology   68
    Tibetan script   68

RELIGION 70
    General   70

Contents

Bonism 71
Buddhism 72
Christian missions 84

SOCIAL CONDITIONS 87

TIBETAN MEDICINE 90

POLITICS AND GOVERNMENT 93

HUMAN RIGHTS 100

FOREIGN RELATIONS 103

ECONOMY 108

EDUCATION 112

LITERATURE 115
General 115
Poetry 116
Drama 117
Prose 119

ART 120
General 120
Painting 122
Architecture 123
Crafts 124
Printing and book production 125

MUSIC 126

FOLKLORE 128

PHILATELY 130

ASTRONOMY AND ASTROLOGY 131

FOOD 132

PERIODICALS 133

BIBLIOGRAPHIES 135

INDEX OF AUTHORS 139

INDEX OF TITLES 143

Contents

INDEX OF SUBJECTS 155

MAP OF TIBET 161

Introduction

'Tibet the mysterious', 'The roof of the world', 'The land of snows', 'The jewel in the lotus', 'The lost world': these epithets clearly indicate the sense of mystery and fascination which has always characterized the Western view of Tibet. Until this century, the number of European or American travellers who had visited Tibet was very few, and of those only a mere handful had set eyes on the capital, Lhasa, whose very inaccessibility and remoteness gave it the legendary allure which was also, in earlier times, attached to Timbuktu. Even in these days of package tours, which have penetrated to Lhasa itself, Tibet remains, for most people, a distant, legendary land which retains the glamour and fascination which other, more accessible, places have lost. It also remains one of the world's flashpoints. The border with India is disputed, and demonstrations within Tibet itself in recent years have indicated that Chinese rule is still not accepted by many of the Tibetans, despite some attempts by the authorities to make their rule more palatable.

Geography

Tibet covers an area of 1,228,000 sq. km. and lies at the heart of the Asian land mass. It is bounded on the east by the Chinese provinces of Qinghai and Sichuan, on the south-east by Bhutan and the Indian states of Arunachal Pradesh and Sikkim, on the south-west by Nepal, on the west by Ladakh (Indian or Western Tibet) and on the north by Xinjiang. Geographically, Tibet consists of a high plateau, its average altitude being as high as 5000 m. On the south it is bordered by the world's highest mountain range, the Himalaya, and the northern side of Mount Everest (called in Tibetan Qomolangma) is in Tibet. The principal river is the Tsangpo, which flows roughly east to west and becomes the Brahmaputra; this rises in the sacred Mount Kailas, which is also the source of two other major rivers of Asia, the Sutlej and the Indus. The Tsangpo has a number of important tributaries, including the Kyi Chu, which is the river on which Lhasa stands, and the Nyang Chu which flows through Shigatse.

Tibet can be divided into three geographical regions. In the south, where the rivers flow parallel to the Himalaya, there is a reasonably fertile and prosperous zone. This is where the major towns of Lhasa, Shigatse and Gyantse are situated. To the north of this area is the high plateau area which is largely desert, and to the east is the district of Kham where the mountain ranges run north to south and which is the area of the nomadic pastoralists.

Like many high desert regions, Tibet has little rainfall and the climate is characterized by dry, thin air. Temperatures are subject to violent fluctuations depending on whether the sun is shining or not. In Lhasa the temperature ranges from 26 degrees centigrade in the summer to −15 degrees in the winter. The total rainfall and snow in most of Tibet is as little as 254 mm per year; in the south it is greater than this, the annual rainfall in Lhasa being about 358 mm. During winter many of the passes are blocked with snow. Spring and summer tend to come almost together.

History

The early history of Tibet is shrouded in mystery. Neolithic remains, dating from around 50,000 years ago, were discovered near Chambo in 1977. By the 2nd century BC the area was occupied by nomadic tribes who also roamed over what is now Xinjiang and Mongolia.

The origins of the Tibetans themselves is also obscure. Tibetan tradition suggests that they are the result of a union between a monkey and a she-devil; more recent research indicates that they emerged from among the ancient tribes who inhabited the eastern borderlands between present-day Tibet and China.

The 7th and 8th centuries saw the establishment of a strong military empire based on Tibet. The principal architect of this development was the king Songtsen Gampo who reigned around the period 627–650. It was during his reign that the Tibetan alphabet was conceived and the first code of laws drafted. The various Tibetan tribes were unified into a strong military state and the Tibetan empire began to expand into the neighbouring territories of Kashmir, Nepal, Sikkim, Bhutan and parts of Turkestan. By the end of the 7th century Tibet controlled many of the most important trade routes of central Asia.

It was also during this period that Buddhism came to Tibet. Amongst his other brides Songtsen Gampo had married a Nepalese princess, Bhrikuti Devi, and a Chinese princess, Wen Cheng, and traditionally it was through their efforts that Buddhism was introduced to Tibet. Hardly surprisingly, the native Bon priests did not regard this development very favourably and the struggle for supremacy between the two religions lasted for several centuries. This struggle intensified during the reign of Trisong Detsen (755–797). The Bon priests, allied to members of the aristocracy, scored a number of successes, but the arrival of the Indian Buddhist teacher Padma Sambhava signalled the resurgence of Buddhism in Tibet. Padma Sambhava can in many ways be regarded as the true founder of Tibetan Buddhism. A tireless traveller and evangelizer, he was also astute enough to incorporate a number of features of Bonism into his brand of Buddhism, the use of oracles for example, and, with royal support, the new religion began to flourish. However, the struggle was far from over. King Tri Ralpachen, who reigned during the first half of the 9th century, attempted to impose Buddhist orthodoxy by force and provoked a rebellion. He was eventually assassinated by his brother Lang Darma who then attempted to suppress Buddhism through relentless persecution. Buddhism was not to re-establish itself finally in Tibet until the 11th century, partly as a result of the teachings of Atisa.

These internal disputes weakened the kingdom considerably and with the rise of other powers in central Asia, Tibet became increasingly isolated and a prey to invaders from elsewhere. By the early 13th century Tibet had become a vassal state of the great Mongol conqueror Genghis Khan. Under Mongol patronage the Sakyapa school of Buddhism became predominant in Tibet, but their power was challenged in the following century by the new reform movement led by Tsong-ka-pa. This led to the founding of the Gelukpa (or Yellow Hat) school and it was this sect which was eventually to gain power. In 1578 the Mongols gave the title of Dalai Lama (Ocean of Wisdom) to Sonam Gyatso who was the third high priest of the Gelukpa school, and this title was also given posthumously to his two predecessors. It was the 'Great Fifth' Dalai Lama, Lobsang Gyatso (1617–82), however, who was responsible for the extension of the Dalai Lama's temporal power and the establishment of the unique form of centralized theocratic government which was to prevail in Tibet until the Chinese Communist invasion in 1950. He was a skilled politician as well as a great theologian and Tibet's greatest building, the Potala Palace in Lhasa, is his creation. It was also during this period that the office of Panchen Lama was established and rivalry between the two supreme lamas has been a feature of Tibetan history and politics ever since. Both lamas are reincarnations, the Dalai Lama of Avalokitesvara or Chenrezig, the patron saint of Tibet, and the Panchen Lama of Amitabha or Opame, the Buddha of Boundless Light. The Dalai Lama is supreme in temporal and spiritual matters and the Panchen Lama in spiritual matters, the first Panchen Lama having been the tutor of the 'Great Fifth'. [This dilemma has never been resolved, hence the constant conflict between the two Lamas.]

The following is a list of the Dalai Lamas to date:

I	Gedun Drub	1391–1474
II	Gedun Gyatso	1475–1543
III	Sonam Gyatso	1543–1588
IV	Yonten Gyatso	1589–1617
V	Lobsang Gyatso	1617–1682
VI	Tsangyang Gyatso	1683–1706
VII	Kesang Gyatso	1708–1757
VIII	Jampel Gyatso	1758–1805
IX	Luntok Gyatso	1806–1815
X	Tshultrim Gyatso	1816–1837
XI	Khedrup Gyatso	1838–1856
XII	Trinle Gyatso	1856–1875
XIII	Thupten Gyatso	1876–1933
XIV	Tenzin Gyatso	1935–

The 6th Dalai Lama has the reputation of having been something of a libertine with a partiality for wine and women. He is best known for his poetry, at once both mystical and erotic. His death remains a mystery and he is the only Dalai Lama whose tomb is unknown.

The 7th Dalai Lama was uninterested in affairs of state and he delegated his temporal duties to the Regent and the Panchen Lama. It was during this period that both the Chinese and the Mongols once again began to exert considerable influence on Tibetan affairs. In 1720 a Chinese army demolished the walls of Lhasa and a garrison was stationed there. The Imperial Viceroy or Amban became the symbol of Chinese suzerainty over Tibet and after the death of the 7th Dalai Lama the Chinese appear to have conspired with certain elements in Tibet to ensure that few of the succeeding reincarnations reached the age of majority. Some of them were poisoned, but the means used were sometimes more exotic; the 12th Dalai Lama, for instance, died as a result of the collapse of his bedroom ceiling.

During the 19th century Chinese influence over Tibet declined as Manchu power perceptibly weakened in China itself. The rising powers in Asia were seen to be the British in India and the Russian Empire, and Tibet's strategic position bordering on to the area where the three empires met came to play an increasing part in the calculations of those who played the 'Great Game'. Tibet's isolation served only to increase the curiosity of the outside world and one theme of the 19th century is of persistent Western attempts to open up Tibet and equally persistent attempts by the Tibetans to repulse them. Tibet appears to have been perceived as fair game by all manner of adventurers, spies, military surveyors and genuine explorers and one can feel a certain amount of sympathy with the Tibetans who, desiring only to be left alone, set themselves the task of preventing them from reaching Lhasa and expelling them from the country.

In fact Westerners had reached Tibet considerably earlier. Christian missionaries, mainly Jesuits, were the first to penetrate the country. Stephen Cacella and John Cabral's journey of 1626–32 had taken them to Gyantse and Shigatse and they had been followed later in the 17th century by John Grueber and Albert d'Orville who had travelled from China through eastern Tibet to Lhasa itself before going on to India. In 1716 the Jesuits Ippolito Desideri and Emmanuel Freyre entered Tibet through Kashmir and Desideri stayed in Lhasa for three years, later producing a comprehensive survey of Tibet and its culture which remained unpublished for two centuries afterwards. The first Englishman to visit Tibet was George Bogle who was sent as an envoy in 1779 to establish relations between British India and Tibet and open up the country to trade. Bogle spent some time at Shigatse and became friendly with the Panchen Lama, but this early promise of Anglo Tibetan friendship was not fulfilled and later contacts between the two countries proved to be far less easy to establish. The second English visitor to Tibet could hardly have been more different. Thomas Manning was an eccentric and an individualist who travelled to satisfy his own intellectual curiosity and seems not to have been unduly concerned about making his experiences known to the rest of the world. The race to be first to Lhasa which developed amongst Western travellers and explorers in the second half of the 19th century seems strangely futile when it is remembered that this solitary eccentric had been there more than half a century before.

A more intellectual exploration of Tibetan culture was begun in the first half of the 19th century by the Hungarian scholar and traveller Kőrösi Csoma Sándor (usually known in English as Alexander Csoma de Kőrös), who studied at a monastery in Zanskar and produced the first Tibetan dictionary. His pioneering research laid the foundation for academic study of Tibet in the West, and he can justly be described as the first Tibetologist.

Western pressure on Tibet undoubtedly increased towards the end of the 19th century. The opening up of Africa had left Tibet as one of the last blank spaces on the map and the imperialism of both Russia and Britain in central Asia meant that before long one or other of these powers would seek to establish some sort of control over Tibet, if only to deny it to the other. Alongside the genuine explorers, adventurers and missionaries who continued to probe Tibet, there appeared the Indian pandits such as Sarat Chandra Das who were essentially spies. Nevertheless, for the time being, the official policy of the British government was to retain the status quo, and it is noteworthy, for example, that they refused to intervene directly in the war between Tibet and Nepal in 1855–56, but worked to localize the conflict and prevent any change in the balance of power in the Himalayan region.

Lord Curzon's appointment as Viceroy of India in 1899 heralded the beginning of a new phase in Anglo-Tibetan relations. Unlike many previous viceroys he had already travelled extensively in Asia and he had strong views on the necessity of curbing Russian expansionism to preserve the British Empire in India. Given this background, it was perhaps inevitable that he would soon turn his attention to Tibet. Disputes over trade, a series of border incidents and (probably ungrounded) fears over increasing Russian influence in Lhasa all played their part in leading to increasing impatience with the Tibetans on the part of the Indian government and in 1904 Colonel Francis Younghusband was despatched with a military escort to compel the Tibetans to negotiate. The story of the Younghusband Expedition has been often told. The ill-equipped Tibetans were no match against the modern weaponry of the British and the indiscriminate slaughter of hundreds of Tibetans by machine-gun fire shocked both members of the Expedition themselves and public opinion at home in Britain. Younghusband pushed on to Lhasa, which was thus finally opened up to the West, but the Dalai Lama had fled to Mongolia and the agreements which Younghusband signed with the Tibetan government were later repudiated by the British government in London. Despite this inauspicious beginning, however, many of the English and the Tibetans appear to have got on well together, and it is significant that when the Chinese invaded Tibet in 1910, on that occasion it was to India that the Dalai Lama fled.

In October 1911 a revolution in China swept away the Manchu dynasty and Chinese soldiers stationed in Tibet also revolted. The Tibetans seized their opportunity and managed to expel the disorderly and demoralized Chinese troops out of the country. By 1913 there were no Chinese troops remaining and from then until 1950 Tibet enjoyed a *de facto* independence. The Dalai Lama returned from exile in India and set about establishing a government which would have effective control over both domestic affairs and foreign relations. The Simla Convention of 1914, although only initialled by Britain and Tibet and never agreed to by China, gave Tibet some kind of international standing and settled the question of the border with India for as long as there was no power able or willing to challenge its provisions. The British maintained formal diplomatic relations with the government of the Dalai Lama and, with China in a more or less permanent state of turmoil, the Tibetans were able to enjoy three decades of stability and independence – in fact if not in any strict interpretation of international law.

The 13th Dalai Lama was a strong leader who saw clearly that there was a need to introduce reforms and modernize the country. During the 1920s and 1930s some reforms were indeed introduced and the country began very slowly to open up to Western influences; a few Tibetans were even sent to study in England. But in retrospect it can be seen that these reforms were too few to prepare the country for the troubled times that lay ahead. To all intents and purposes Tibet was still a feudal society ruled by a theocracy unwilling and perhaps unable to come to terms with the modern 20th-century world outside. The death of the Dalai Lama in 1933 came at a critical time and was accompanied by disturbing omens. The political testament of the Dalai Lama himself, for example, can now be seen as a prophecy of the terrible events to come: 'It may happen that here in the centre of Tibet the religion and the secular administration will be similarly attacked from without and within, and the holders of the Faith, the glorious Rebirths, will be broken down and left without a name. As regards the monasteries and the priesthood, their lands and their properties will be destroyed. The officers of state, ecclesiastical and lay, will find their lands seized and their property confiscated, and they themselves made to serve their enemies or wander about the country as beggars do. All beings will be sunk in hardship and fear and the nights will drag on slowly in suffering.' After his death his body was found turned facing towards the east as if to indicate that it was from that direction that the danger threatened.

At first, however, little appeared to change. An attempt by the Chinese nationalist government to use the interregnum to their own advantage was unsuccessful, and the Tibetans were able to discover and instal the new Dalai Lama without outside interference.

Following the victory of the Communists in the Chinese civil war, it soon became apparent that the new Chinese government was seeking to re-establish control over Tibet. By the end of 1949 editorials were appearing in the Chinese press which suggested that the time for Tibet's 'liberation' was soon approaching. In November 1950 the Chinese People's Liberation Army moved into eastern Tibet. The Tibetan government appealed to the United Nations for help, but the response of the Western powers and of India was at best lukewarm. The British, for example, despite the fact that they had treated Tibet as an independent country for many years, argued that Tibet's international status was unclear, and the newly independent Indian government, seeking to maintain good relations with China, suggested that negotiations were the best way of assuring some form of autonomy for Tibet. Both the Soviet Union and the Chinese Nationalist government in Taiwan supported the Chinese government's position that Tibet was an integral part of China and the United Nations decided to take no action to support the Tibetans. Faced with this lack of resolve on the part of her supposed friends, Tibet had no alternative but to negotiate from a position of weakness. On 21 May 1951 an agreement on the peaceful liberation of Tibet was signed, and a few months afterwards the Dalai Lama, who had fled to Yatung near the Indian border, returned to Lhasa. In an attempt to maintain appearances, both the Dalai Lama and the Panchen Lama were invited to become members of the National Committee of the Chinese People's Political Consultative Conference and in 1954 they both attended the Chinese National People's Conference in Beijing.

The next few years were characterized by an awkward compromise as the Chinese attempted to consolidate their hold over the country and to introduce the reforms which they were implementing in the rest of China, whilst the Dalai Lama and his advisers attempted to retain as much autonomy as possible and to frustrate those reforms which they saw as harmful to the country. However, real power lay with the Chinese, and in 1956 they began to introduce land reforms and set up cooperatives. A partial stay of execution was gained by the Dalai Lama when he persuaded Chairman Mao to declare that reforms would not take place during the 1958–62 five-year plan, but in practice plans for the new order and establishing the Autonomous Region of Tibet continued to go ahead.

Dissatisfaction with Chinese rule culminated in the revolt of March 1959. The immediate cause was an invitation by the Chinese to the Dalai Lama to attend a theatrical performance in the Chinese military compound. Fearing that he would be arrested when he got there, the Tibetans persuaded the Dalai Lama to refuse. There then followed some fighting in and around Lhasa in the course of which both the Potala and some of the major monasteries were shelled. Later, a full-scale revolt broke out and there was serious fighting in the east of the country. The Tibetans were no match for the better trained and equipped Chinese forces and the revolt ended in total defeat. Perhaps as many as 100,000 Tibetans died during the revolt and its immediate aftermath. The Dalai Lama, along with approximately 80,000 of his people, fled to India where he was granted political asylum. Eventually he settled in Dharamsala in the small hill-state of Himachal Pradesh, and this has now become the centre of the Tibetan communities abroad and the base of the Dalai Lama's Government-in-Exile. There he has occasionally been an embarrassment to his Indian hosts, and indeed it is noteworthy that, despite there being much sympathy for the Tibetans in the non-Communist world, Western governments, anxious not to offend the Chinese, have tended to avoid having any official contact with him. In March 1991, for example, neither the British Prime Minister nor the Foreign Secretary would receive him during his visit to London, although the Prince of Wales, to his great credit, did.

In Tibet itself, following the defeat of the 1959 revolt the Chinese established complete political and military control over the country. Large numbers of Chinese troops were deployed in Tibet and its strategic importance to China was greatly increased following the deterioration of relations with India and the border war of 1962. Perhaps as many as 300,000 Chinese troops remain in Tibet today. Civilian Han Chinese have also been encouraged to settle in Tibet and, together with the military, they now form probably as much as 20% of the population. Their presence is especially noticeable in urban areas, and some foreign travellers have remarked that Lhasa is beginning to look increasingly like a Chinese rather than a Tibetan town.

In 1965 Tibet was declared an Autonomous Region but there is little doubt that effective power remained with the Chinese. The Dalai Lama was declared a traitor in 1964, and the following year the Panchen Lama who had remained in Tibet and who was generally more sympathetic to the Chinese view, was dismissed from his post. The Cultural Revolution (1966–76) was an economic, social and spiritual disaster for the country as Red Guards swept through the country leaving a trail of destruction in their wake. Most of the surviving monasteries were closed down and many were totally destroyed. Following the fall of the Gang of Four, however, the new more pragmatic leadership in Beijing began to introduce a degree of liberalization. As in the rest of China, this was more successful in the economic than the political sphere. There is little doubt that, freed from the constraints of Maoist dogma, farmers have been able to restore the country's agriculture, and that living conditions generally have improved over the last decade. At the same time a certain amount of religious freedom was allowed and a number of monasteries re-opened. Tourism from the West was encouraged and even a number of the Tibetan exiles in India were invited to return. Welcome as these reforms were, however, they served not to stifle discontent, but rather to whet people's appetites for more far-reaching change, something the Chinese government has, up till now, refused to contemplate.

In September and October 1987 there were pro-independence demonstrations in Lhasa. These were followed in March 1988 by a further demonstration at the end of the Great Summons prayer meeting. Western reports suggest that as many as 10,000 people took part in the demonstration which turned to violence with a police station coming under attack. According to the Chinese, one policeman was killed and around 300 injured, and the response of the authorities was to clamp down hard. Lhasa was sealed off from the outside world and a large number of arrests were made. A large military presence prevented any further demonstrations on 10 March, the anniversary of the 1959 revolt. However, a number of smaller demonstrations continued through the summer and on 10 December there were further violent disturbances which, according to Chinese sources, left one person dead and thirteen injured; Western sources put the figures at eighteen dead and fifty injured. In March 1989 more violence on the streets led the Chinese to impose martial law, but smaller demonstrations have continued to take place and were reported in Shigatse and Gyantse as well as in the capital during the autumn of 1989.

The role of the Dalai Lama during this period has been a difficult one. Recognizing his unique spiritual authority over all Tibetans, the Chinese have tried on more than one occasion to come to an agreement with him and pave the way for his return to Tibet. However, all these negotiations have so far been abortive. China has refused absolutely to discuss the key question of sovereignty, whilst for many of the Tibetans in exile nothing less than complete independence would satisfy their aspirations. Seeking a middle way between these two extremes, the Dalai Lama has developed a five-point plan. In essence, this proposes a 'self-governing democratic political entity' for Tibet, with China retaining a measure of control over defence and foreign policy. The Dalai Lama first outlined these proposals before the United States Senate Foreign Relations Committee in 1987 and developed them further in a speech to the European Parliament in June 1988. After an initially hostile response, the Chinese did offer to negotiate with the Dalai Lama but later pulled out of the proposed talks on the grounds that the Dalai Lama's position was 'insincere'. The situation worsened after the crushing of the pro-democracy movement in China itself in June 1989 and there has been no further attempt at negotiation between the Chinese government and the Dalai Lama since then. Tibet's future thus remains very uncertain at the time of writing; at least one commentator has warned of Tibet becoming prey to the kind of political violence and alienation that has plagued Northern Ireland for the last twenty years. For the sake of Tibet's long-suffering people one hopes that this is a false prophecy, but the omens are not good.

Religion

Religion dominates Tibetan culture and society to a degree unparalleled elsewhere in the world with the possible exception of the Vatican City, and no introduction to the country would be complete without mention of the Tibetan form of Buddhism.

Buddhism reached Tibet in the 7th century and after a long struggle replaced the native Bon religion. Although the first contacts with Buddhism were made through China, it was from India that Tibet was to receive the forms of Buddhism which were ultimately to prevail. In the 8th century the famous Buddhist teacher Padma Sambhava was invited to Tibet and it was under his influence that the first monasteries were founded. In 1042 another famous Buddhist scholar Atisa came to Tibet and further influenced the development of the religion there. Despite the influence from India, however, Tibetan Buddhism developed a number of unique features. Perhaps inevitably, elements of Bonism survived in many of the popular forms of Buddhism; more important were the rise in influence and power of the large monasteries, and the absorption of many Tantric ideas and rituals. Reincarnation also came to dominate Tibetan monasticism to a degree unknown elsewhere. The use of spells and divination are also common.

Tibetan Buddhism recognizes three spiritual ways: Theravada or the way of elders, Mahayana or the greater vehicle and Vajrayana or the diamond-like way. Of these, Mahayana Buddhism is predominant in Tibet; it is a form of Buddhism that appeals particularly to the heart rather than the mind, and one of its principal features is the cultivation of Bodhisattva, or the wisdom which comes from an understanding of the truth and the renunciation of Nirvana with the aim of helping others reach that state themselves. There are also several different monastic orders and schools. The most important sects are known as the Nyingmapa, Kagyupa and Sakyapa (all of whom are sometimes referred to as the 'Red Hats') and the Gelukpa (the 'Yellow Hats'), founded in the 14th century by Tsong-ka-pa; the Dalai Lama is a member of the Gelukpa sect so it is not surprising that they became the dominant sect.

Almost all Buddhist practice is aimed at the acquiring of merit. Compassion is the ideal Buddhist virtue and its practice is the highest method of acquiring merit, but, as any visitor to the country will have observed, there are many more mechanical means that can be employed: the turning of a prayer wheel, the fluttering of a prayer flag, the constant intoning of the famous Buddhist prayer 'Om mani padme hum', the addition of stones carved with this prayer to the 'mani walls' which dot the landscape and lead to holy places, the circumambulation of monasteries and other holy places, and pilgrimages to Lhasa, the sacred Mount Kailas, and elsewhere, are all common means of acquiring merit.

The Communist Chinese occupation of Tibet spelt disaster for Buddhism within Tibet. What happened after 1959, and more especially during the years of the Cultural Revolution, has been described as nothing less than 'religious genocide'. Yet it is also during these years that more and more people in the rest of the world, and especially in Western Europe and the United States, have come to know of Tibetan Buddhism and to accept its teachings and precepts. It might even be said that the Dalai Lama has lost a kingdom but gained the world, thus fulfilling the prophecy made by Padma Sambhava himself as long ago as the 8th century: 'When the iron bird flies and horses run on wheels, the Tibetan people will be scattered like ants across the world and the Dharma will come to the land of the Red Man.'

About the bibliography

In compiling this bibliography my aim has been to present material which will provide an understanding of Tibet and its people. Following the general style of the World Bibliographical Series, books have been preferred wherever possible to journal articles, but many of the latter have been included where book titles alone provide insufficient coverage of an important subject. A clear preference has been made to include as much recently published material as possible, but a large number of the classic historical works on Tibet are still of great value and have therefore been listed as well. I have examined all the items listed in the bibliography; regrettably, some potentially very useful titles, both old and new, have had to be excluded as I was unable to locate copies. The majority of the titles are in English, but some foreign-language material has been included where it has been felt appropriate. Entry within each section is alphabetical by author or compiler, and, where these are absent or unclear, by title. Tibetan names present a particular problem. There is no standard form of transcription and I have therefore not attempted to be completely consistent, but have tended to follow the styles within each publication.

I cannot stress too strongly that this is a selective and not a comprehensive list of literature on Tibet. It is aimed not so much at the specialist, who is already familiar with the sources of information on his subject, but at those people, be they students or researchers or simply intellectually curious individuals, who may be approaching the subject for the first time and want to know where to start. I hope, nevertheless, that specialists will also find some value in this compilation. Anyone seeking more comprehensive lists should consult the bibliographies listed in the final section of this book which will guide them towards the more specialist writings they may need.

Professor Melvyn Goldstein has justly observed that 'The literature on Tibet suffers from chronic religious indigestion.' In this bibliography I have, quite deliberately, attempted to redress this balance, and, whilst giving Tibetan Buddhism its due weight, to emphasize other areas of Tibetan studies which have received less attention in the past. Even so, there are many areas of study which have received attention in other volumes of the World Bibliographical Series which find no place in this volume simply because they are inappropriate in the Tibetan context or because there is no relevant literature available.

A further problem is that much of the writing on Tibet is highly polemical in character. Tibet's status in international law and the exact nature of its relationship with China have never been wholly clear, but the Chinese occupation of Tibet since the 1950s, their repression of the 1959 uprising, and the cultural and political oppression that has followed have brought these questions into much sharper focus. Both the Chinese authorities in Beijing and many of the Tibetans now living abroad have strong views on the present and the future status of Tibet, views which have remained wholly irreconcilable up till now. Whilst holding my own views on these questions, I have decided that, in the interests of balance, both viewpoints should be represented in this volume, and that the reader should make up his or her own mind as to their relative validity.

Acknowledgements

In compiling this bibliography I have drawn on the collections of the following libraries: School of Oriental and African Studies (University of London), British Library of Political and Economic Science (London School of Economics), Hoover Institution on War, Revolution and Peace (Stanford University), Stanford University Libraries, and University of California at Berkeley; thanks are due to the members of staff of all these libraries for their assistance. My thanks are also due to the Drawing Office of the London School of Economics for preparing the map. The staff of Wisdom Books in London generously allowed me on more than one occasion to make a detailed examination of their very extensive stock of books on Tibet and Buddhism in general. I have also made considerable use of the previously published catalogues and bibliographies listed in the final section of this book, and of on-line bibliographical databases, especially *Historical Abstracts*, *Public Affairs Information Service*, *Social Sciences Citation Index*, and *Sociological Abstracts*.

I should like to thank Dr Robert Neville of Clio Press for his support and encouragement throughout, and Anne Wilcock for her editorial expertise. Any errors or omissions that remain are naturally mine.

John Pinfold
Baldock, Herts.
March 1991

The Country and Its People

1 **Altar of the earth: the life, land and spirit of Tibet.**
   Peter Gold. Ithaca, New York: Snow Lion, 1987. 222p.

This is an impressionistic evocation of the sights and sounds of modern Tibet which concentrates on the principal sacred and natural places of central Tibet, including Lhasa, Shigatse and Gyantse and some of the mountain areas of southern Tibet.

2 **Meine Tibet Bilder.** (My Tibet pictures.)
   Heinrich Harrer, text by Heinz Woltereck.   Seebruck im Chiemsee,
   Germany: Heering Verlag, 1960. 202p.

Heinrich Harrer is one of the most noted travellers in Tibet, and his books *Seven years in Tibet* and *Return to Tibet* (q.v.) have become modern classics. This book presents many of the photographs he took in Tibet and is particularly useful to those studying the art, architecture and material culture of the country. Costumes and jewellery are especially well covered.

3 **The monasteries of the Himalayas: Tibet, Bhutan, Ladakh, Sikkim.**
   Suzanne Held.   Lausanne, Switzerland: Edita S.A., 1988. 149p. map.

This sumptuous volume contains 147 outstanding colour photographs of Buddhist temples, their life, their art and their rituals. Religion is all-pervasive in Tibetan culture and society, and this is a fine visual introduction to that religion.

4 **A general survey of Tibet.**
   Heyu.   Beijing: New World Press, 1988. 111p.

A short introductory survey of Tibet's history, religion, and social customs and conditions is followed by a more detailed description of the events of the last thirty years and the implementation of regional autonomy. Although less overtly propagandist than some of the publications on Tibet which have emanated from Beijing, this book nevertheless reflects the official Chinese view on Tibet and should therefore not be read in isolation.

The Country and Its People

5 **Hidden Tibet: the land and its people.**
Roger Hicks.   Shaftesbury, England: Element Books, 1988. 480p.
This is primarily a photographic introduction to Tibet with many of the photographs being drawn from the archives of the Library of Tibetan Works and Archives in Dharamsala and from the Dalai Lama's own collections; a good proportion of them have never been published before. The author provides a readable accompanying text which forms a good introduction to both the culture and religion of the old Tibet and of the new Tibet of 1959 and afterwards.

6 **Tibet: a handbook.**
Helmut Hoffmann.   Bloomington, Indiana: Indiana University Publications, 1975. 246p. bibliog. (Indiana University Asian Studies Research Institute. Oriental Series, vol. 5).
Intended to be used as an introduction to Tibet by students in higher education, this book is different from many in this section. It is not a general, impressionistic, account of the country but a more academic presentation of the facts of Tibet's geography, history, politics, religion, social and economic structure, and literature. Carefully researched and drawing on a wide range of sources, it is notable for the amount of information it contains and for the extensive bibliographies which accompany each chapter. It can be highly recommended as an introduction for the serious student.

7 **Tibet.**
Kevin Kling.   London: Thames & Hudson, 1985. 1 vol. [unpaginated]. map.
Contains ninety-six photographs, ninety-one in colour, which were taken by the author during his visit to Tibet in 1980. A short introduction places the pictures in context.

8 **The land of the lama: a description of a country of contrasts & its cheerful, happy-go-lucky people of hardy nature & curious customs; their religion, ways of living, trade & social life.**
David Macdonald.   London: Seeley, Service, 1929. 283p. map.
Of mixed Scottish and Sikkimese parentage, David Macdonald had already lived for eleven years in Tibet, mainly as British Trade Agent in the Chumbi valley, when he wrote this book. It is one of the most readable and also one of the most comprehensive introductions to the old Tibet, ranging through a broad spectrum of subjects from history, politics and religion to the position of Tibetan women, birth and death ceremonies, dress, Tibetan food, the coinage, Tibet's trade and commerce and Tibetan literature.

9 **Tibet.**
David Macdonald.   London: Oxford University Press, 1945. 32p. map. bibliog. (Oxford Pamphlets on Indian Affairs, no. 30).
This short survey still provides a valuable introduction to many aspects of Tibet including its history, culture, religion, society and art. The author had lived for over twenty years in Tibet by the time he wrote it.

10 Tibet: its history, religion and people.
Thubten Jigme Norbu, Colin Turnbull. Harmondsworth, England:
Penguin, 1972. 359p. map.

Thubten Jigme Norbu is the elder brother of the Dalai Lama, and this book is
therefore of importance in providing an insider's guide to the history, culture and
religion of Tibet. The viewpoint is often quite different from that of Western writers,
with, for example, a mingling of legend and factual history which scientific historians
might find unacceptable but which provides a most valuable insight into how Tibetans
view themselves and their country.

11 Tibet: the lost civilisation.
Simon Normanton. London: Hamish Hamilton, 1988. 190p.

A profusely illustrated introduction to the history of Tibet. The text is compiled from
the writings of some of the explorers and other Western visitors to Tibet including Sir
Charles Bell, Edmund Candler and Heinrich Harrer. Their impressions of Tibet are
probably best read in the original works; what distinguishes this book are the
illustrations which include many early colour photographs.

12 Proceedings of the Csoma de Kőrös memorial symposium held at
Mátrafüred, Hungary, 24–30 September 1976.
Budapest: Akadémiai Kiadó, 1978. 586p.

The reader who already has some knowledge of Tibetan history and culture will find
much of value in the forty-one papers contained in this volume, covering a wide variety
of topics relating to Tibetan culture, language, literature, philosophy, religion and
history. A further collection of papers on similar themes can be found in the
proceedings of the succeeding seminar, published as *Contributions on Tibetan
language, history and culture: proceedings of the Csoma de Kőrös symposium held at
Velm-Vienna, Austria, 13–19 September, 1981* and *Contributions on Tibetan and
Buddhist religion and philosophy: proceedings of the Csoma de Kőrös symposium held
at Velm-Vienna, Austria, 13–19 September, 1981* (Vienna, 1983).

13 Tibet: a geographical, ethnographical, and historical sketch, derived from
Chinese sources.
William Woodville Rockhill. Peking: [Wen tien ko shuchuang], 1939.
291p. maps.

This work was originally published as a series of articles in the *Journal of the Royal
Asiatic Society* in 1891. Its interest lies in the fact that it is drawn almost entirely from
Chinese sources of the 18th and 19th centuries and thus presents Tibet from the
traditional Chinese perspective. It is a mine of information, but is best approached
only after some of the more modern Western introductions to the country. The colour
plates and maps, reproduced from old documents, are charming as well as being of
historical interest in themselves.

14 Western Tibet and the British borderland: the sacred country of Hindus
and Buddhists.
Charles A. Sherring. London: Edward Arnold, 1906. 367p. map.

This book is considerably wider in scope than its title suggests. It is a mine of
information on the religions, ethnology, geography, history, social customs and

traditions, and the forms of administration of the western areas of Tibet. There is a special section on Mount Kailas, the sacred home of the gods; and all sections are exceptionally well illustrated.

15 **Silver on lapis: Tibetan literary culture and history.**
   Edited by Christopher I. Beckwith. Bloomington, Indiana: Tibet
   Society, 1987. 220p. bibliog.

This volume contains a collection of scholarly papers which were presented at a conference held to mark the 200th anniversary of the birth of the Hungarian Tibetologist Alexander Csoma de Kőrös. They cover a range of subjects including the early history of Tibet, Tibetan medicine, philology and Tibetan thought. The authors are some of the most eminent present-day Tibetologists. This is not a book for the newcomer to the subject, but one which a reader with some background knowledge will find stimulating.

16 **Tibetan civilization.**
   R. A. Stein. London: Faber & Faber, 1972. 334p. maps. bibliog.

First published in French in 1962, Stein's book has become a classic introduction to the civilization of Tibet, equally accessible to the serious scholar and the general reader alike. Using a large number of primary Tibetan and Chinese sources, Stein approaches the subject thematically rather than by period or region and covers such topics as Tibetan history, religion, social structure, customs, literature and art; the section on Tibetan literature is especially valuable as this does not receive such detailed attention in most of the other general introductions to Tibet. Although the imposition of Chinese rule after 1951 is given some coverage, this book's value lies in the portrait it paints of the country's traditional culture and society as it existed before the enormous and damaging changes of the last forty years.

17 **Tibet.**
   London: HMSO, 1920. 75p. bibliog. (Handbooks prepared under the
   direction of the Historical Section of the Foreign Office, no. 70).

This pamphlet, which was prepared for the Paris Peace Conference of 1919, provides in relatively few pages an impressive amount of information on the physical and political geography, the history and the economic conditions of Tibet as it was in the early 20th century. There are even details of the coins in circulation and of the telegraph system.

18 **Tibet.**
   New York: McGraw-Hill, 1981. 296p. map. bibliog.

An illustrated introduction to Tibet, this is the product of a team of Tibetan authors, scholars and men of affairs and eighteen of China's top photographers. There are 237 colour plates, making this an ideal book for the armchair traveller. A brief textual introduction precedes each of the sections.

19 **Tibet, the sacred realm: photographs, 1880–1950; . . . photographs from
   the archives of the Academy of Natural Sciences, Philadelphia (et al.);
   chronicle by Lobsang P. Lhalungpa.**
   [n.p.]: Aperture, 1983. 159p. bibliog.

This selection of photographs forms the catalogue of an exhibition held at the Philadelphia Museum of Art. It contains some 100 black-and-white pictures taken during the period 1880–1950 by some of the well-known Western explorers and travellers, including Sven Hedin, Alexandra David-Neel, George Roerich, Heinrich Harrer and Ilya Tolstoy.

20 The splendour of Tibet.
Audrey Topping. New York: SINO Publishing, 1980. 185p. map.

The author and her husband visited Tibet in 1979 on assignment for *The New York Times*. The resulting book is fair-minded in its attempt to find a middle way between the propaganda put out by both the Chinese authorities and the more extreme members of the refugee community. The text includes descriptions of visits to some of the major temples and museums and to an agricultural commune. The excellent photographs, taken by the author, include interior views of the Potala Palace and Jokhang (cathedral), and a rare set of pictures of the controversial series of clay sculptures representing the former feudal oppression of the serfs; the originals are in the Museum of the Revolution.

21 Tibet: land of snows.
Giuseppe Tucci, translated by J. E. Stapleton Driver. New York: Stein & Day, 1967. 216p. map. bibliog.

This comprehensive survey of Tibet's spiritual, artistic and social achievements emphasizes the 'old' pre-1959 Tibet which the author knew well, having visited the country eight times between 1927 and 1948. It provides an authoritative introduction to the history, religion and daily life of Tibet, and also covers the art and literature of the country. There are over 100 illustrations, many of them in colour.

22 A portrait of lost Tibet.
Rosemary Jones Tung. New York: Holt, Rinehart & Winston, 1980. 224p. map. bibliog.

A photographic evocation of Tibet as it was before the Chinese invasion, this book contains 131 photographs taken by Ilya Tolstoy and Brooke Dolan as they travelled through Tibet for ten months in 1942 on a diplomatic mission. This is one of the best pictorial studies of Tibetan life and culture, complemented by Rosemary Tung's text which describes the society of the time.

Geography

23 **A sketch of the geography and geology of the Himalaya mountains and Tibet.**
S. G. Burrard, H. H. Hayden, 2nd ed. revised by Sir Sidney Burrard,
A. M. Heron.   Delhi: Manager of Publications, 1932–33. 4 parts. maps.
bibliog.
The four parts of this important reference source, which was first published in 1907–8,
cover the high peaks of Asia, the principal mountain ranges of Asia, the rivers of the
Himalaya and Tibet, and the geology of the Himalaya. There are numerous plates and
maps.

24 **Tibet: continents in collision.**
Nigel Harris.   *New Scientist*, vol. 124, no. 1694 (9 Dec. 1989), p. 34–8.
This useful article for the non-specialist reviews the current state of knowledge of
Tibet's geology following the 1985 Tibet Geotraverse expedition which was composed
of both Western and Chinese scientists. The results of the expedition suggest that the
Tibet plateau has risen to its current height in two distinct phases as the land mass of
India has moved further north and collided with the continent of Asia. The first phase
saw the plateau rise to a height of 3000 metres over twenty-five million years ago; more
recently it has been lifted to a height of 5000 metres over the last five million years.

25 **Southern Tibet: discoveries in former times compared with my own researches in 1906–1908.**
Sven Hedin.   Stockholm: Lithographic Institute of the General Staff of
the Swedish Army, 1916–22. 11 vols. maps.
Sven Hedin sometimes comes across as a self-opinionated and difficult man, but he was
one of the leading explorers of Tibet in the early 20th century and this massive work of
reference is still indispensable. The first four volumes cover the geography and
exploration of southern and western Tibet; volume 5 covers geology, and volume 6
meteorology. There is also an illustrated volume of 'Tibetan panoramas' and two

volumes of maps; these are particularly useful as detailed and accurate maps of Tibet are still hard to find. Parts of the text are only in French or German. For Hedin's account of his own journey see his *Trans-Himalaya*.

26 **The changing face of Tibet: the impact of Chinese communist ideology on the landscape.**
Pradyumna P. Karan.   Lexington, Kentucky: University Press of Kentucky, 1976. 114p. maps. bibliog.

Karan attempts to discover the effects communism has had on the geography of Tibet and how it has moulded the visible and invisible features of the landscape. This leads to an investigation of how the Tibetan economy has been transformed, an analysis of demographic changes and discussion of the strategic implications of the Chinese occupation. The author's conclusion is that China has developed Tibet using methods which combine great harshness with subtlety and flexibility. Ideological indoctrination has been successful amongst factory workers, but farmers who may originally have welcomed some of the material advances have come to resist the regimentation and all-powerful state control. The maps and bibliography are especially useful.

27 **How Tibet's climate affects other countries.**
Elmer R. Reiter.   *Tibetan Review*, vol. 17, no. 4 (April 1982), p. 11–15.

In this article Reiter demonstrates how the changing weather patterns in Tibet affect the climate not just in northern India but as far away as the North Atlantic, and speculates as to whether reforestation of Tibet would improve the climate in the Indian sub-continent.

28 **Proceedings of the Symposium on Qinhai-Xizang (Tibet) Plateau: abstracts.**
Beijing: Academica Sinica, 1980. 323p.

Provides abstracts of some 180 papers presented at the Symposium which was held in Beijing from 26 May to 1 June 1980 on the general themes of: the geophysical conditions, the geological history and the origin of the formation of the Plateau; the characteristics and evolution of the flora and fauna of the Plateau and the effects of its rise on them; the formation, evolution and differentiation of the geographical environment of the Plateau. Collectively these papers contain a vast amount of information, even though their presentation is somewhat dry and technical.

29 **On the weather and climate of Tibet.**
J. M. Walker.   *Tibet Journal*, vol. 2, no. 3 (Aug. 1977), p. 44–61. bibliog.

A general survey of the weather patterns and climate of Tibet, which includes notes on rainfall patterns, temperature, cloudiness, wind and snow conditions.

30 **The geography of Tibet according to the 'Dzam-gling-rgyas-bshad.**
Turrell V. Wylie.   Rome: Istituto Italiano per il Medio ed Estremo Oriente, 1962. 286p. map. (Serie Orientale Roma, 25).

This book contains both the Tibetan text and an English translation of an idigenous work on Tibetan geography which was compiled in the early years of the 19th century and probably completed around 1820. The original work covered the geography of the whole world, but only the part dealing with Tibet itself is included in this volume. The emphasis is on the physical description of the country, but the author also mentions important people, events and legends in the course of surveying the country.

31 **The Tibetan tradition of geography.**
Turrell V. Wylie. *Bulletin of Tibetology*, vol. 2, no. 1 (March 1965), p. 17–25. bibliog.

An interesting article which demonstrates that the study of geography as a scientific description of the physical world did not develop in Tibet as it did in other cultures. Instead there were only two traditions of geography in Tibet, religious geography and political geography. The former is unique to Tibet and is a description of the geographical location and religious history of sacred places; this dominates Tibetan geographical literature. Political geography is to be found scattered in diverse sources, and indicates that the Tibetans do have a tradition of political areas and boundaries which reflect their concept of ethnic and political Tibet.

32 **Mount Qomolangma: highest in the world.**
Zhang Rongzu. Beijing: Foreign Languages Press, 1981. 64p.

This short survey covers the physical characteristics, geology, climate, flora and fauna and agricultural development of Mount Everest. There is less emphasis on its discovery and conquest by mountaineers and climbers.

33 **Heat beneath Tibet.**
Liao Zhijie (et al.). *Geographical Magazine*, vol. 51, no. 8 (May 1979), p. 560–6.

Tibet has rich, but generally unexploited, reserves of geothermal energy which characteristically reveal themselves in the form of hot springs. This short article gives a brief description of some of the geyser areas in Tibet and discusses the initial plans by the Chinese to develop them as energy resources.

Maps and gazetteers

34 **Hong Kong, Macao, Sinkiang, Taiwan and Tibet: official standard names approved by the United States Board on Geographic Names.**
United States Board on Geographic Names. Washington, DC: United States Government Printing Office, 1955. 390p.

Contains (on p. 357–90) 2,300 entries for Tibet, covering not only towns and villages but other features such as halting places, monasteries, mountains, passes, streams and lakes. Each entry gives the latitude and longitude and the administrative area into which the place or geographical feature falls, and in many cases there is also a locational reference to one of the maps or atlases listed at the beginning of the section.

35   **The mountains of central Asia: 1:3,000,000 map and gazetteer.**
Compiled by the Royal Geographical Society and the Mount Everest
Foundation.   London: Macmillan, 1987. 98p. map. bibliog.
The large folding map contained in this volume covers the entire Himalayan range
from Chengdu in the east to the Khyber Pass in the west. The gazetteer includes a
glossary of generic terms as well as all place names with map references.

36   **South-central Tibet; Kathmandu–Lhasa route map.**
London: Edward Stanford, 1989. 2nd ed. Scale 1:1,000,000. Map size:
66 × 53 cm. (Stanfords International Maps).
This coloured, single-sheet folded map shows the principal geographical features and
main roads of the area of Tibet most likely to be visited by tourists. There is also a
simple street map of Lhasa in an inset, and other useful information given includes a
cross-section of the road between Kathmandu and Lhasa, tables of distances and
journey times between major points, and some basic meteorological data.

37   **Tibet and adjacent countries.**
[n.p.]: [n.p.], 1919. Scale 1:2,500,000. Map size: 100 × 68 cm.
Until recently, good maps of Tibet have been hard to obtain. This single-sheet
coloured map shows the principal physical features, communication routes and
settlements. Its value is indicated by the fact that reprints are still available in
bookshops in Nepal today.

38   **Tibet: carte routière; road map.**
Paris: Éditions Astrolabe, [n.d.]. Scale 1:2,000,000. Map size:
90 × 65 cm.
This modern single-sheet folded map of all Tibet indicates the major roads and
geographical features of the country in a clear, uncluttered way. Distances between the
principal settlements and road junctions are given, but generally, as one would expect,
the level of detail is less than on the larger-scale Stanfords map.

Guidebooks

39   **The Tibet guide.**
Stephen Batchelor.   London: Wisdom, 1987. 465p. maps.
bibliog. (A Wisdom Tibet Book. Yellow Series).
An award-winning guidebook, written by an expert in Tibetan Buddhism and culture
who is also fluent in both written and spoken Tibetan. He explains the land and its
people, history, religion and culture. Details are given of all the major places of
interest in Lhasa, central and western Tibet and along the road from Kathmandu.
There is also a useful iconographical guide, a glossary of terms and a phrase book. This
is probably the book which all visitors to the country should be armed with.

9

40   **A guide to Tibet.**
Elizabeth B. Booz.   London: Collins, 1986. 223p. maps. bibliog.
Some readers will find the layout of this book, with snippets of history and religion and descriptions of Tibetan symbols scattered at random through the text, somewhat irritating, but it does contain well-illustrated descriptions of the principal sights, and useful hard factual information on where to stay, where to eat, etc.

41   **Tibet: a travel survival kit.**
Michael Buckley, Robert Strauss.   South Yarra, Australia; Berkeley, California: Lonely Planet, 1986. 256p. maps.
Designed for the budget-conscious individual traveller, but of equal use to any visitor to Tibet, this guide follows the usual Lonely Planet formula of giving the hard factual information many of the glossier guides ignore. Which are the cheap hotels and restaurants? How do you find them? Where is the bus station? How much should you be paying? The answers to these and other questions like them are to be found here. In addition, of course, there are descriptions of the principal towns and monasteries and the other tourist attractions, and a general survey of Tibet's history and culture. It represents very good value for money.

42   **The power places of central Tibet: a pilgrim's guide.**
Keith Dowman.   London: Routledge & Kegan Paul, 1988. 320p. maps.
This guide describes the location, remaining relics and religious and historical significance of 170 monasteries, temples, sacred caves, lakes and mountains in Tibet. The majority of the sites are within 150 kilometres of Lhasa, but the guide also describes the major sites on the principal tourist routes into Tibet.

43   **Tibet: a guide to the land of fascination: an overall perspective of Tibet of the ancient, medieval and modern periods.**
Trilok Chandra Majupuria, Indra Majupuria.   Gwalior, India: Madhoganj, 1988. 358p. maps.
Much more than just a guidebook for the tourist, this book can also serve as a general introduction to the country as a whole. There are wide-ranging surveys of Tibetan culture, the natural history of the country and its government, economy and development. The authors have a particular interest in Tibet's natural history and this section is, in consequence, especially comprehensive. The second half of the book contains a wealth of practical information for the intending traveller and descriptions of the principal places of interest. There is also a short glossary of useful Tibetan phrases. Although harder to obtain, this book is of greater value than some of the other titles listed in this section.

44   **Trekking in Nepal, west Tibet and Bhutan.**
Hugh Swift.   London: Hodder & Stoughton, 1989. 360p. maps.
All the principal trekking routes in the area described in the title are covered in this exhaustive guide. It also includes a chapter on the natural history of the Himalaya by Rodney Jackson, a Tibetan glossary, and an impressive amount of practical advice on such questions as what clothing and equipment to take and what documents and permits are needed.

Travel and Exploration

General accounts

45 **A mountain in Tibet: the search for Mount Kailas and the sources of the great rivers of India.**
Charles Allen. London: Deutsch, 1982. 255p. maps. bibliog.
Situated in western Tibet, Mount Kailas is a holy place for both Hindus and Buddhists and close by are the sources of four of the great rivers of Asia: the Ganges, Indus, Sutlej, and Tsangpo or Brahmaputra. This highly readable book tells the story of Western exploration of this area from the time of the Jesuit missionaries through the Indian pandits to Sven Hedin (whom Charles Allen treats with more respect than most writers) and the other explorers of the late 19th and early 20th centuries.

46 **The myth of Shangri-la: Tibet, travel writing and the western creation of sacred landscape.**
Peter Bishop. London: Athlone Press, 1989. 400p. bibliog.
This book is different from the others in this section in that the author is less interested in accounts of actual exploration in Tibet than in the ways in which these accounts were interpreted in the West and the myths that developed from them. He draws on accounts, both factual and fictional, from the late 18th century to the present day, surveys the ways in which the myths have developed and changed in that time, and analyses them from a Jungian viewpoint.

47 **Tibet, the mysterious.**
Sir Thomas Holdich. London: Alston Rivers, 1904. 356p. maps. bibliog. (The Story of Exploration).
This general account of the early exploration of Tibet is old and contains a number of errors but is still readable. Holdich emphasizes the discovery and exploration of the country as a whole and not just the more glamorous 'race' to Lhasa.

11

48 **Trespassers on the roof of the world: the race for Lhasa.**
Peter Hopkirk.   London: John Murray, 1982. 274p. maps. bibliog.
Hopkirk's book is a very readable general account of the prising open of Tibet by an
inquisitive outside world. He takes up the story from the mid-19th century, and uses
the travellers' own published accounts as the basis of his narrative. The emphasis is
very firmly on European exploration of Tibet and on the race to be first to Lhasa
rather than on the exploration of the country as a whole. Nevertheless, it is well
researched and is certainly one of the first books anyone coming new to the subject or
planning to travel to Tibet themselves should read. The climax of the book is reached
with the Younghusband mission to Lhasa, but later chapters carry the story of Western
travel in Tibet on up to 1959.

49 **The western experience in Tibet, 1327–1950.**
Barbara Lipton.   Newark, New Jersey: Newark Museum, 1972. 59p.
map. bibliog. (The Museum, new series, vol. 24, nos 2/3).
The principal feature of this introduction to the subject is a useful chronological chart
which details the major European journeys of exploration in Tibet before 1950. There
is also a partially annotated bibliography which lists over 100 titles, covering both
individual journeys and more general accounts. The second part of the book contains a
more detailed account of the American missionary Albert Shelton's experience of
Tibet during the period 1903–22; it was Shelton who was responsible for collecting
many of the artefacts now held at the Newark Museum.

50 **Tibet: a chronicle of exploration.**
John MacGregor.   London: Routledge & Kegan Paul, 1970. 373p.
maps. bibliog.
This history of Western (and Japanese) travels in Tibet covers the period from the
earliest times up to the Younghusband Expedition of 1904 when 'the spell of mystery'
was finally broken. The author takes the story further back than the Jesuit missionaries
who are generally believed to have been the first Europeans to visit Tibet, and includes
accounts of medieval emissaries to the Mongols such as the Flemish friar William of
Rubruck who was the first European to refer to incarnate lamas, and the 14th-century
Franciscan Odoric who, although he personally probably never reached Tibet,
provided the first real information on Tibet to reach Europe.

51 **On top of the world: five women explorers in Tibet.**
Luree Miller.   London: Paddington Press, 1976. 222p. maps. bibliog.
The five women covered in this volume are Nina Mazuchelli, Isabella Bird Bishop,
Annie Taylor, Fanny Bullock Workman and Alexandra David-Neel. Of these, in fact,
only two (Annie Taylor and Alexandra David-Neel) reached the heart of Tibet, the
others having merely travelled on the fringes of the country (Nina Mazuchelli was the
first Western woman to see Everest). The general theme underlying the individual
stories of travel and exploration is that these were all women who, in a man's world,
ventured forth to see with their own eyes what women had previously known about
only at second hand.

52 **The exploration of Tibet: history and particulars.**
Graham Sandberg. Delhi: Cosmo Publications, 1973. 324p.

Sandberg's book was first published in 1904 when the Younghusband Expedition was still encamped at Gyantse. The introduction includes a justification of the action taken by the Government of India, and expresses the hope that the peaceful development of Tibetan resources 'under British auspices and assistance' will follow. Considerable emphasis is placed on the 18th-century Jesuit missions – at the time of writing these were only just being rediscovered – but much of the text is now superseded by Hopkirk and MacGregor.

53 **The sacred mountain: travellers and pilgrims at Mount Kailas in western Tibet and the great universal symbol of the sacred mountain.**
John Snelling. London: East-West Publications, 1983. 241p. maps. bibliog.

This book offers both a succinct explanation of the significance of Mount Kailas and its holy lakes in the Buddhist, Jain and Hindu traditions, and an account of the travels of both explorers and pilgrims in the area from the 18th century onwards. The experiences of those who were pilgrims as well as explorers, such as Swami Pranavananda and Tucci, are given greater prominence than in the book by Charles Allen (q.v.) on the same subject.

54 **Into Tibet: the early British explorers.**
George Woodcock. London: Faber & Faber, 1971. 277p. maps. bibliog.

Woodcock's survey covers the journeys of George Bogle, Samuel Turner and Thomas Manning which took place in the late 18th and early 19th centuries.

Pre-1900

55 **A világ tetején: Kőrösi Csoma Sándor nyomdokain nyugati Tibetbe.**
(The roof of the world: experiences of Alexander Csoma de Kőrös in western Tibet.)
Ervin Baktay. Budapest: Lampel, 1930. 310p. maps.

The exploration of Tibet by the great Hungarian scholar Alexander Csoma de Kőrös was primarily an intellectual one, he having been responsible, almost single-handedly, for the establishment of Tibetology as a serious subject of research in Europe. The creation of the first Tibetan dictionary was his most noteworthy achievement. This substantial biography in Hungarian is perhaps less accessible to most readers than the slighter volume by Mukherjee (q.v.).

56 Diary of a journey across Tibet.
Hamilton Bower. London: Rivington, Percival, 1894. 309p. map.

Bower's journey took him approximately 800 miles across Tibet in 1891–92; his narrative is full of information but is not amongst the more lively of the Tibetan travelogues of the period.

57 Travel and adventures in Tibet, including the diary of Miss Annie R. Taylor's remarkable journey from Tau-Chau to Ta-Chien-Lu through the heart of the forbidden land.
W. Carey. London: Hodder & Stoughton, 1902. 285p. map.

The author's introduction which gives a general introduction to Tibet's history and religion and a general account of early European exploration in the area is less important than the transcription of Annie Taylor's diary which forms the greater part of the book. Her own account of her lone attempt in 1892 to be the first European woman to reach Lhasa (ultimately foiled by the Tibetan authorities) makes for exciting reading and deserves to be better known. In recent years it has been reprinted both in India and Taiwan.

58 Ázsiai levelek és más írások. (Asian letters and other writings.)
Kőrösi Csoma Sándor (Alexander Csoma de Kőrös). Budapest: Officina Könyvtár 105, 1949. 68p.

Those who can read Hungarian will find this an interesting collection of some of the letters and other writings of Alexander Csoma de Kőrös whose researches contributed greatly to the growth of Tibetan studies in the rest of the world. His own writings have an immediacy which is necessarily missing from the biographies by Baktay and Mukherjee (q.v.). Some of them have been translated into English and published as *Tibetan studies, being a reprint of the articles contributed to the Journal of the Asiatic Society of Bengal and Asiatic researches* (Budapest, Akadémiai Kiadó, 1984).

59 Journey to Lhasa and central Tibet.
Sarat Chandra Das. London: John Murray, 1902. 285p. map.

Faced with Tibetan opposition to European travel in Tibet, the British authorities in India in the late 19th century hit upon the idea of using Indian spies to survey and map the country. Although some of the men chosen turned out to be unsatisfactory, many of the Indian pandits' expeditions turned out to be very successful and their observations and measurements (recorded clandestinely and smuggled back into India) were later shown to be surprisingly accurate considering the circumstances in which they were taken. Sarat Chandra Das was the most famous and the most successful of the pandits, and this book records his journey into Tibet in 1881–82.

60 In Tibet and Chinese Turkestan, being the record of three years' exploration.
H. H. P. Deasy. London: H. F. Unwin, 1901. 420p. map.

A readable account of the author's travels in north-west Tibet during the years 1896–99. There is a lengthy and useful botanical appendix.

61 **An account of Tibet: the travels of Ippolito Desideri of Pistoia, S.J.,**
    1712–1727.
    Edited by Filippo de Felippi. Taipei, Taiwan: Ch'eng-wen, 1971. 474p.
    map. bibliog.

The lost manuscript of the Jesuit missionary Ippolito Desideri was rediscovered in
1875, but published only many years later. This edition is a reprint of one first
published in 1932. Desideri's account is important because it gives the earliest general
Western description of Tibet and draws on both personal observation and an
investigation of Tibetan texts. A century before the great age of European exploration
of Tibet, Ippolito Desideri had already provided an accurate and complete survey of
the country and its culture, including details of folk customs, the country's natural
history, a history of the sacred mountain of Kailas and a full description of Lamaism;
and he learnt Tibetan many years before scholars in Europe had any knowledge of it at
all.

62 **Travels in Tartary and Thibet.**
    Abbé Huc.   London: Herbert Joseph, 1937. 352p. map. (Great
    Explorations, vol. 3).

This book was first published in French in 1850, was quickly translated into English,
and has been reprinted many times since. Huc and Gabet were Lazarist missionaries
whose travels through Tartary and Tibet were undertaken at the request of the
Apostolic Vicariat of Mongolia and occupied from 1844 to 1846. Dressed in the habit
of lamas, they were able to gain an insight into the lives of the ordinary people they
met along the way, and to study in detail the precepts and rituals of Tibetan Buddhism.
Ultimately they reached Lhasa and met the Regent of Tibet before returning to China.
Their account of their travels was a best-seller when it first appeared and it is still
eminently readable and enjoyable today.

63 **Tibet: the forbidden land.**
    A. H. S. Landor.   London: New York: Harper, 1899. 2 vols.

Landor's account of his 1897 journey through Tibet, made under conditions of great
hardship, and during which he was (according to his own account) captured, tortured
and fired at, is one of the most highly coloured of the 19th-century Tibetan
travelogues. Indeed, the more one reads it, the more one begins to wonder just how
much of it is fact and how much fiction invented to cater for a sensation-seeking public.
Landor was unquestionably an adventurer rather than a serious explorer, but his book
remains very readable and it includes a large number of coloured lithographs,
illustrations and line drawings.

64 **Narrative of the mission of George Bogle to Tibet, and of the journey of**
    Thomas Manning to Lhasa.
    Clements R. Markham.   New Delhi: Cosmo, 1989. 362p. maps.

This is a reprint of a work which was first published in 1876 and comprises the journals
and papers of the first two Englishmen to visit Tibet. Their journeys were quite
different in character. Bogle was sent as an envoy to Tibet by Warren Hastings in 1779,
with the object of establishing formal relations between British India and Tibet. He
became an intimate friend of the 3rd Panchen Lama and his report contains much
valuable material on the conditions in Tibet in the late 18th century. Thomas Manning,
on the other hand, was a solitary and somewhat eccentric traveller, driven on by his

own intellectual curiosity and less concerned to provide a detailed account of his journey for posterity. Nevertheless, long before the Victorian race to Lhasa began, he became the first Englishman to visit the city and the story of his travels is a fascinating one.

65   **Extracts from an explorer's narrative of his journey from Pitoragarh in Kumaon via Jumlah to Tadum and back, along the Kali Gandak to British territory.**
      T. G. Montgomerie.   London: William Clowes & Sons, 1876. 14p.
This represents the report (or at least as much of it as the authorities were prepared to make public) of one of the journeys of the Indian pandits into the unexplored area north of British India.

66   **Journey to Shigatze in Tibet, and return by Dingri-Maidan into Nepaul in 1871, by the native explorer no. 9.**
      T. G. Montgomerie.   London: William Clowes & Sons, 1876. 19p.
This report of a journey of exploration by one of the pandits is particularly interesting as it includes tables showing the results of the clandestine observations of latitudes and boiling points to determine height. The distances are also shown by the number of paces it took the pandit to traverse them. Later the data collected by these methods was shown to be surprisingly accurate.

67   **Narrative of an exploration of the Namcho or Tengri Nur Lake in Great Tibet made by a native explorer during 1871–2.**
      T. G. Montgomerie.   London: William Clowes & Sons, 1876. 16p.
A third report illustrative of the explorations carried out by the pandits.

68   **The great Tibetologist: Alexander Csoma de Kőrös, hermit-hero from Hungary.**
      Hirendra Nath Mukherjee.   New Delhi: Sterling, 1981. 102p.
The Hungarian Alexander Csoma de Kőrös (1784–1842) was a different kind of explorer from the others whose exploits are chronicled in this section, for he was a scholar who was the first in Europe to begin the serious study of Buddhism from original sources. He studied for a considerable period at a Buddhist monastery in Zanskar and produced the first Tibetan dictionary; his work can generally be said to have placed Tibetology on the map of serious research in Europe. Having done most of his research in western Tibet and Zanskar, he died in Darjeeling whilst hoping to travel on to Lhasa.

69   **A new general collection of voyages and travels.**
      London: Thomas Astley, 1745–47. 4 vols. maps. bibliog.
Accounts of the journeys of early European travellers to Tibet are included in this general collection, together with a bibliography of materials on Central Asia and Tibet known at the time.

70 **The dream of Lhasa: the life of Nicholas Przhevalsky (1839–88), explorer of Central Asia.**
Donald Rayfield.   London: Paul Elek, 1976. 221p. maps. bibliog.
Rayfield's biography is the first in English of Russia's greatest central Asian explorer. All told he made four expeditions through Mongolia, Sinkiang and the deserts of central Asia. Lhasa was his ultimate goal but he was fated never to reach the Tibetan capital.

71 **With the Tibetans in tent and temple: a narrative of four years' residence on the Tibetan border, and of a journey into the far interior.**
Susie Carson Rijnhart.   Chicago, Illinois: Revell, 1901. 406p. map.
This is a travelogue which contains a great deal of valuable material on the social conditions of the time. Susie Rijnhart's journey was one of the most tragic of all the 19th-century explorers as both her husband and her infant child died on it.

72 **Two lady missionaries in Tibet.**
Isabel Stuart Robson.   London: S. W. Partridge & Co., 1909. 160p.
Tells the story of the travels of two Christian missionaries in Tibet at the end of the 19th century. Annie Taylor's journey took place in 1892 when she attempted to reach Lhasa on her own but was turned back by the Tibetans. Later she established a mission station in Yatung and acted as a nursing sister on the Younghusband Expedition when she spoke up for the Tibetans. Susie Carson Moyes (Rijnhart) had a disastrous journey with her husband and infant child, of which she was the only survivor. She later remarried but the ordeal of her journey had its effect and she died in 1908.

73 **Diary of a journey through Mongolia and Tibet in 1891 and 1892.**
William Woodville Rockhill.   Washington, DC: Smithsonian Institution, 1894. 413p. map.
This day-by-day diary covers William Woodville Rockhill's second journey through Tibet. His aim was to travel right through the country from the north-east to the Indian border, but he was eventually turned back by the Tibetans and forced to return eastwards. Knowing both Chinese and Tibetan gave him an advantage over some of the other Western travellers to Tibet and his book contains detailed information on many aspects of Tibetan life and culture. One of his primary interests was anthropology and this book contains a considerable number of drawings of everyday objects such as saddles, boots and cooking utensils, many of which were collected by Rockhill on his journey and presented to the Smithsonian Institution. Appendices include a list of plants of Tibet and a table of latitudes and altitudes of each of the places he passed through.

74 **Relations de divers voyages curieux qui n'ont point esté publiées ou qui ont esté traduites d'Hacluyt, de Purchas et d'autres voyageurs . . .**
(Stories of several strange travels which have not been published or which have been translated from Hakluyt, Purchas and other travellers . . .)
M. Thevenot.   Paris: A. Cramoisy, 1666–73. 4 vols in 2. maps.
A contemporary account of the journey of the Jesuits Grueber and d'Orville through Tibet in 1661 can be found in this general collection.

75 **An account of an embassy to the Teshoo Lama in Tibet; containing a narrative of a journey through Bootan and part of Tibet; to which are added views taken on the spot by Lt. Samuel Davis, and observations botanical, mineralogical and medical by Mr. Robert Sanders.**
Samuel Turner. London: G. & W. Nicol, 1800. 473p.

Turner also includes a history of Tibet during the period 1785–93 and a description of the Nepalese–Tibetan war of 1788–92. This classic early Western account of Tibet was reprinted in India in 1971.

76 **The pundits: British exploration of Tibet and central Asia.**
Derek Waller. Lexington, Kentucky: Kentucky University Press, 1990. maps. bibliog.

This detailed and thoroughly researched study covers the period 1863–93 which was the period when the British were most active in the employment of native explorers (and spies) to fill in the gaps on their maps of the vast territories to the north of British India. The pandits recorded information on the topography and customs of the country and the nature of its government and military resources, and their undetected methodical work was probably of far greater value than many of the flamboyant journeyings of Western travellers engaged on the quest to be first into Lhasa during the same period.

77 **Through unknown Tibet.**
M. S. Welby. London: T. Fisher Unwin, 1898. 440p.

Welby and Nicholson, two British officers, travelled through parts of northern Tibet whilst on leave. From Kashmir they journeyed to Ladakh, Tibet, Mongolia and on to China.

78 **Early Jesuit travellers in Central Asia 1603–1721.**
C. Wessels. The Hague: Martinus Nijhoff, 1924. 344p. map.

Although few of the European travellers to Tibet in the 19th century realized it, much of the ground that they were exploring had already been traversed by the Jesuit missionaries over 100 years before. This book, based on manuscript as well as printed sources, chronicles the journeys of all of the Jesuits who reached Tibet. The most interesting journeys are those of Stephen Cacella and John Cabral (1626–32) who visited Gyantse and Shigatse, John Grueber and Albert d'Orville (1661–64) who travelled from China through eastern Tibet to Lhasa and then went on to India, and Ippolito Desideri (1714–22) who travelled from Kashmir along the Tsangpo to Lhasa; this book should be read in conjunction with his own account (q.v.).

79 **Cathay and the way thither, being a collection of medieval notices of China.**
Henry Yule, new edn. revised by Henri Cordier. Cambridge, England: Hakluyt Society, 1913–16. 4 vols. maps. bibliog.

This compilation includes the account of Friar Odoric who was supposed to have travelled to Tibet in the 14th century; this claim is now generally rejected and it is thought that he received his information from other travellers he met rather than by visiting the country himself.

1900–1950

80 **China–Tibet–Assam: a journey 1911.**
   F. M. Bailey. London: Cape, 1945. 175p. maps.
Bailey was a man of many parts, explorer, secret agent and botanist amongst them.
(The Himalayan blue poppy is named after him.) He was a member of the
Younghusband Expedition and then spent over three years as Trade Agent in Tibet.
This book tells the story of his geographical expedition in 1911 when he travelled from
China through the south-eastern corner of Tibet to Assam, seeking to establish the
course of the Tsangpo river.

81 **No passport to Tibet.**
   F. M. Bailey. London: Hart-Davis, 1957. 294p. maps.
This book tells the story of Bailey's 1913 journey with Morshead during which they
solved the mystery of the Tsangpo gorges and mapped the country forming the
geographical frontier between Assam and Tibet. During the course of their journey
they made several interesting discoveries in the realms of natural history, both flora
and fauna.

82 **Land of a thousand Buddhas: a pilgrimage into the heart of Tibet and the
   sacred city of Lhasa.**
   Theos Bernard. London: Rider, 1940. 320p.
Bernard was an American Buddhist who studied to become a lama in Lhasa in the
1930s. During his time there he met many of the leading persons of Tibet, both
religious and secular, and his book is of particular interest in describing many of the
religious shrines and ceremonies, as well as giving a more general picture of the social
conditions of the time.

83 **A stranger in Tibet: the adventures of a Zen monk.**
   Scott Berry. London: Collins, 1990. 309p. maps. bibliog.
Readers who find the account of his travels by the Japanese Buddhist Ekai Kawaguchi
(q.v.) rather hard going may find this recent biography of him more accessible. Berry
quite justifiably points out that the pearls in Kawaguchi's book can be hard to find
amongst the more turgid passages, but he is also right to stress that Kawaguchi could
also be a perceptive observer of all aspects of Tibetan society. The rumour that
Kawaguchi was a British secret agent he dismisses; rather he sees him as an inveterate
busybody and gossip.

84 **First Russia, then Tibet.**
   Robert Byron. Harmondsworth, England: Penguin, 1985. 254p.
Robert Byron's classic work was first published in 1933. In it he quite deliberately
contrasts two societies which could hardly be more different. The Russia he describes
is one in the throes of a modern industrial revolution whose philosophy represented a
challenge to the West. Tibet, on the other hand, was a pre-industrial society, 'higher
and more coloured than any country on earth'. His writing is distinguished by its
elegance and lucidity, and he proved himself to be a keen observer of both societies. In
Tibet his friendship with a number of leading families enabled him to gain a deeper
understanding of the country and its civilization.

85 **Lhasa: the holy city.**
Spencer Chapman. London: Chatto & Windus, 1938. 342p.

Spencer Chapman was a member of the 1936 expedition to Lhasa and this book provides a narrative of the journey and a detailed description of the city and its people during his stay there which lasted until February 1937. One chapter deals with Tibetan festivals and there is also some information on the flora and fauna of the country. It is profusely illustrated.

86 **Le lumineux destin d'Alexandra David-Neel.** (The luminous destiny of Alexandra David-Neel.)
Jacques Chalon. Paris: Librairie Académique Perrin, 1985. 487p.
bibliog.

A thorough and authoritative biography of the famous French traveller who became the first European woman to reach Lhasa. Chalon gives due weight to her role as a Tibetologist and promoter of a better understanding of Tibet by the West as well as an indefatigable traveller and explorer.

87 **The fire ox and other years.**
Suydam Cutting. New York: Charles Scribner's Sons, 1940. 393p.
maps.

Cutting was responsible for collecting many of the artefacts now held by the Newark Museum (q.v.). This volume gives an account of his travels throughout Asia and includes a section on the forbidden cities of Tibet.

88 **Magic and mystery in Tibet.**
Alexandra David-Neel. London: Unwin, 1984. 224p.

First published in England in 1931, this book languished forgotten for many years before being republished in a number of recent editions. It should be read after David-Neel's *My journey to Lhasa* (q.v.) which gives a chronological account of her epic journey through Tibet to become the first Western woman to reach Lhasa. This book is a collection of some of the stories of her travels and of the discoveries she made of the practices and beliefs of the mystics she encountered. Typical stories tell of how Tibetan mystics can defy the cold or travel long distances without food or drink. Instances of telepathy and psychic phenomena are also related and there is even a story of a mystic defying gravity and flying.

89 **My journey to Lhasa.**
Alexandra David-Neel. London: Virago, 1983. 310p.

First published in 1927, this has become a classic travel book. A lifelong student of Buddhism, Alexandra David-Neel outwitted officials (both Tibetan and British) and bandits to become the first European woman to enter Lhasa in 1923. She travelled on foot disguised as a pilgrim and lived in Lhasa undetected for two months. Her infectious enthusiasm for all things Tibetan comes over strongly in this vivid account of her travels and adventures, whilst the hardships she describes appear to have done her no harm since she lived on until 1969, dying at the age of 100.

90 **Tibetan skylines.**
Robert B. Ekvall. London: Gollancz, 1952. 240p. map.
Ekvall is today best known as an anthropologist, but it is worth remembering that he was originally a missionary by occupation, born of missionary parents on the Tibetan–Chinese border and brought up speaking both Tibetan and Chinese. He lived for several years amongst the Samtsa nomads of northeastern Tibet and his account of his years in Tibet from 1930 to 1935 and from 1939 to 1941 gives a rare insider's view of life on the Tibetan borderlands. The book ends ominously with Chinese communist troops skirting the fringes of Tibet during their famous Long March. Tibet was spared then but it was an omen of what was to come later.

91 **Seven years in Tibet.**
Heinrich Harrer. London: Rupert Hart-Davis, 1953. 288p.
In 1943 Heinrich Harrer, an Austrian mountaineer and skier who had been interned in India at the beginning of the war, made his escape from India to Lhasa. From being a destitute fugitive he rose to the position of tutor and confidant to the young Dalai Lama until 1950. This account of his experiences in Tibet has become a classic of travel, adventure and penetrating observation and has been reprinted many times. Unlike many European visitors, Harrer appears to have gained both the confidence and the friendship of the Tibetans and as a result he was able to present a wholly convincing insider's account of Tibet to a degree few other European writers have approached.

92 **Sport and travel in the highlands of Tibet.**
Sir Henry Hayden, Cesar Cosson. London: Richard Cobden-Sanderson, 1927. 262p. map.
This is a well-illustrated travelogue from the inter-war period. The authors' journey, which took place in 1922, covered some of the remoter areas of Tibet where they carried out a certain amount of geological exploration. They also visited Lhasa where they were received by the 13th Dalai Lama.

93 **Central Asia and Tibet: towards the holy city of Lassa.**
Sven Hedin. London: Hurst & Blackett, 1903. 2 vols. maps.
These two volumes contain a detailed account of Sven Hedin's journey of exploration in the first years of the century which took him through Chinese Turkestan and the Takla-Makan and Gobi deserts before he turned south into Tibet. He travelled through parts of northern Tibet and then attempted to reach Lhasa, only to be intercepted by Tibetan troops and turned back. He then turned south and travelled through to India via Ladakh. Although his prose style is sometimes hard going, his books are invariably rewarding; these two volumes also contain over 400 illustrations, both line drawings and photographs, and several maps.

94 **A conquest of Tibet.**
Sven Hedin. London: Macmillan, 1935. 400p.
Sven Hedin's accounts of his journeys and explorations in Tibet can sometimes be rather heavy going. This volume was aimed at a more general reader than his other books and is perhaps the most accessible of his works today.

95   Trans-Himalaya: discoveries and adventures in Tibet.

Sven Hedin.   London: Macmillan, 1909-13. 3 vols. maps.

Sven Hedin was one of the most indefatigable explorers of Tibet in the early part of this century, but, for a number of reasons, he fell foul of the British establishment and this has meant that his works have sometimes received less attention than they should. Nevertheless they are a mine of information and cannot be ignored by the serious scholar. Volumes 1 and 2 of *Trans-Himalaya* describe his journey of 1906–8; volume 3 includes an historical account of previous exploration in Tibet. There are numerous illustrations.

96   Three years in Tibet.

Ekai Kawaguchi.   Benares, India; London: Theosophical Publishing Society; Madras, India: Theosophist Office, 1909. 719p. map.

Kawaguchi was a Japanese Buddhist who reached Lhasa, disguised as a Chinese doctor, in 1901. He remained in Tibet until June 1902 and his book contains an important account of Lhasa under the 13th Dalai Lama, with whom he had several audiences. The picture he draws is largely unfavourable: he was shocked by the decadence of many of the monks, the cruelty of Tibetan punishments, the sexual infidelities of Tibetan women and the general squalor of the city. Even if he was not, as has been asserted, a professional spy, his account of Russian intrigues may have alarmed the British authorities and helped pave the way towards the Younghusband Expedition.

97   To Lhasa in disguise: an account of a secret expedition through mysterious Tibet.

W. Montgomery McGovern.   London: Thornton Butterworth, 1924. 352p. maps.

Despite the opening up of Tibet effected by the Younghusband Expedition, travel for the individual to Tibet remained fraught with difficulties in the inter-war period as Montgomery McGovern's experiences show. To reach Lhasa he disguised himself as a Tibetan coolie and succeeded in reaching the capital undetected. Once there, however, he revealed his true identity, sparking off a popular riot against him; the Tibetan government thereupon declared him a prisoner of state and escorted him out of the country. Although his contention that Tibet's policy of modernization could be compared to that of Japan reads rather oddly now, his book provides a vivid picture of Tibet in the early 1920s under the forceful, reformist rule of the 13th Dalai Lama. Although some critics have dismissed this book, like that by Savage Landor (q.v.), as fiction, this now seems unlikely.

98   Secret Tibet.

Fosco Maraini.   London: Hutchinson, 1952. 251p. maps. bibliog.

This is a good book for getting the 'feel' of the old Tibet. Fosco Maraini travelled as a wanderer and talked to people of all classes and backgrounds, both lay and religious, and, as a result, his book is especially strong on customs and folk stories.

99 Tibetan marches.
André Migot.   London: Readers Union, 1956. 303p. map.

Migot's journey took him through the eastern marches of Tibet in 1946–47. He visited Kantze, Derge and Jyekundo, and also the famous monastery of Kumbum near Sining, but he failed in his attempt to reach Lhasa. This is a very readable book by one who was sympathetic to Tibetan Buddhism and society at a time when they were both beginning to be threatened by forces from outside.

100 Tibetan journey.
George N. Patterson.   London: Faber & Faber, 1954. 232p. maps.

George Patterson was a missionary based with Geoffrey Bull in the east of Tibet. In 1950, faced by the necessity to retreat in the face of the Chinese communist troops he travelled across the southeastern corner of the country to reach India, and this is the day-by-day record of his journey.

101 Exploration in Tibet.
Swami Pranavananda.   Calcutta, India: University of Calcutta, 1939. 161p. maps.

This is a particularly interesting book. Swami Pranavananda made four journeys to the area around Mount Kailas and spent a whole year as an inmate of the Thugolho monastery, a rare privilege for a non-Buddhist at that time. His book is partly an account of his own explorations and partly a more general examination of the sources of the four great rivers that rise in the area. Like many others, he was critical of some of Sven Hedin's findings, and his book contains much information on the physical geography, botany, mineral resources, agricultural and economic life, and the peoples of the area.

102 The great plateau, being an account of exploration in central Tibet, 1903, and of the Gartok Expedition, 1904–1905.
C. G. Rawling.   London: Edward Arnold, 1905. 324p. maps.

Rawling's route took him from Gyantse along the Brahmaputra to its source and then through areas of western Tibet back to India by the Shipki pass.

103 Military report on western Tibet including Chang Tang and Rudok.
C. G. Rawling.   Simla, India: Government Monotype Press, 1905. 96p. map.

As the book's title suggests Rawling's journey was at least partly intended to provide information on the military capacity of Tibet, and his report includes details on the location of the frontier guards and estimates of the fighting strength of the areas he passed through, as well as more general information on the geography and ethnography of western Tibet.

104 In search of the mahatmas of Tibet.
Edwin G. Schary. Lucknow, India: Asia Publications, 1986. 312p.
maps.

First published in 1937, this book tells the extraordinary story of the author's lone trek west to east through Tibet, from Zanskar to Gyantse, in 1918. Schary comes across as a somewhat naive young man and as a source for the study of Tibet his book is disappointing.

105 Beyond the frontiers: the biography of Colonel F. M. Bailey, explorer and special agent.
Arthur Swinson. London: Hutchinson, 1971. 245p. maps. bibliog.

A very readable biography of one of the last players of the 'Great Game' and a noted explorer and botanist. Bailey's participation in the Younghusband Expedition and the subsequent Gartok Expedition, his time as Trade Agent in the Chumbi valley and his important geographical and botanical expeditions in 1911 and 1913 all receive detailed coverage.

106 Secrets of Tibet, being the chronicle of the Tucci Scientific Expedition to Western Tibet (1933).
Giuseppi Tucci, E. Ghersi, translated from the Italian edition by Mary A. Johnstone. London: Blackie, 1935. 210p. maps.

Giuseppi Tucci is one of the leading scholars of Tibet and this daily diary of one of his early expeditions to the western part of Tibet is as meticulous and as readable as one would expect.

107 The riddle of the Tsangpo gorges.
Frank Kingdon Ward. London: Edward Arnold, 1926. 328p. map.

Although Ward was primarily a botanist, his books contain much other information on the natural habitat and social customs of the areas through which he travelled. This book is his account of his 1924 journey through southern Tibet when he followed the spectacular route of the great Tsangpo river.

1950–

108 Flight of the wind horse: a journey into Tibet.
Niema Ash. London: Rider, 1990. 208p.

The author is not a Tibetologist or an anthropologist, but is rather a woman who travels for the sheer love of travel. Her reactions to present-day Tibet are therefore those of someone coming totally fresh to the country and her views are generally spontaneous and immediate. The picture she draws is of a civilization and a culture that are close to annihilation and she was clearly not taken in by Chinese propaganda about Tibet. Amongst other experiences, she witnessed a sky burial and ceremonies at the Jokhang. Armchair travellers with little previous knowledge of Tibet will enjoy this book; it is a pity there are no maps.

109 **Inside the treasure house: a time in Tibet.**
Catriona Bass. London: Gollancz, 1990. 221p. map.

Catriona Bass spent 16 months teaching English in Tibet during 1985–86. This account of her time there makes for enjoyable reading, and, although other recent travellers have shown greater insight into the country, she was clearly disturbed by the evidence of 'Han chauvinism' she found there.

110 **Land of the snow lion.**
Elaine Brook. London: Cape, 1987. 238p. map. bibliog.

This rather chatty book falls naturally into three sections. In the first, Elaine Brook recalls her experiences as a member of the Shishapangma mountaineering expedition; the second tells of her journey back to Lhasa, visiting Shigatse and Gyantse on the way; the third is devoted to her stay in Lhasa.

111 **Alone through China and Tibet.**
Helena Drysdale. London: Constable, 1986. 207p. map.

Approximately one-third of this book is concerned with Tibet. Helena Drysdale travelled to Lhasa from Xian through Qinghai, following a route similar to that of Alexandra David-Neel sixty years before. Her account of the journey is highly readable and displays considerable insight. Her description of a sky burial, something she is one of the few Westerners to have observed, is notable.

112 **A winter in Tibet.**
Charles Hadfield, Jill Hadfield. London: Impact Books, 1988. 226p. map.

The authors spent nine months teaching in Lhasa during the early 1980s when Tibet opened up to foreigners. People rather than places make the greatest impression in their account. They met both Chinese and Tibetans and tried to understand the feelings of everyone they came in contact with, the result being that their book appears both honest and sensitive.

113 **Lhasa, the open city: a journey to Tibet.**
Han Suyin. London: Cape, 1977. 180p. bibliog. map.

The author visited Tibet in the autumn of 1975, just before the country began to be opened up to tourism. Her book is essentially a review of the changes which have taken place in Tibet since the 1950s and she offers a generally uncritical appraisal of Chinese policies in Tibet.

114 **Return to Tibet.**
Heinrich Harrer. London: Weidenfeld & Nicolson, 1984. 184p. maps.

Unlike many other authors of recent travel books on Tibet, Harrer has an intimate knowledge of the old Tibet as well, and thus he is one of the few Westerners who can make comparisons between the old and the new based on first-hand experience of both. As one might expect, he is unsympathetic to the 'liberation colonialism' of the Chinese, and he concludes with the pessimistic view that economic and material considerations override the cultural and spiritual needs of the country and that recent concessions and promises by the authorities will not be upheld.

Travel and Exploration. 1950–

115 **Calling from Kashgar: a journey through Tibet.**
Rod Richard.   Kirstead, England: Frontier, 1990. 172p. maps. bibliog.
Having spent some time exploring China, the author travelled from Lhasa through
Tibet to the sacred Mount Kailas and then on to Kashgar and Pakistan. His book is
very much the work of someone approaching Tibet for the first time, with sympathy
and an open mind; and he rightly comments that a few apologies followed by the
imposition of martial law is not a policy sufficient to right the wrongs China has
inflicted on Tibet. The selection of black-and-white photographs, taken by the author
and chosen to illustrate this book, is outstanding.

116 **From heaven lake: travels through Sinkiang and Tibet.**
Vikram Seth.   London: Chatto & Windus, 1983. 178p. map.
In 1981 Vikram Seth hitch-hiked through Sinkiang to Lhasa and then on to Nepal. By
breaking away from the customary routes of organized travel, by travelling alone and
by persistence allied with never-failing good humour, he was able to see things not
usually on the tourist itinerary and to mix with the local people more easily than most
Western travellers. The result is a modern classic of travel, beautifully written and far
more revealing of the country than the majority of recent travelogues.

117 **To the navel of the world: yaks and unheroic travels in Nepal and Tibet.**
Peter Somerville-Large.   London: Hamish Hamilton, 1987. 225p.
map.
The journal of the author's travels from Nepal to Gyantse and Lhasa. He then
participated in a modern pilgrimage to the 1981 spring festival at Mount Kailas, the
first to take place for 20 years.

118 **Journey across Tibet.**
Sorrel Wilby.   Chicago, Illinois: Contemporary Books, 1988. 236p.
map.
Whereas many other modern visitors to Tibet have stuck to the well-travelled route to
Gyantse and Lhasa, Sorrel Wilby trekked through many of the remoter areas of the
country inhabited mainly by nomads. Starting from Mount Kailas she trekked 1900
miles eastwards towards Lhasa, having many adventures on the way, but gaining a
valuable insight into areas of the country most visitors never see or experience.

Flora and Fauna

119 **Role of the dog in Tibetan nomadic society.**
Robert B. Ekvall. *Central Asiatic Journal*, vol. 8 (Sept. 1963),
p. 163–73.
In this article, based largely on personal observation, Ekvall shows that, in contrast to
many other Asiatic societies, amongst the Tibetans the dog is honoured both in
tradition and in real life. Dogs are used both for hunting and as watchdogs; the latter
function is the more common and the more important, and in a nomadic society living
in tents they also have the valuable function of providing privacy and ample social
distance between families.

120 **A quest of flowers: the plant explorations of Frank Ludlow and George**
Sherriff told from their diaries and other occasional writing.
Harold R. Fletcher.   Edinburgh: Edinburgh University Press, 1975.
387p.
Ludlow and Sherriff were probably the greatest collectors of plants from the Tibetan
region and this book chronicles their collecting expeditions between 1933 and 1949.
There is a botanical index.

121 **Domestication and exploitation of livestock in the Nepal Himalaya and**
Tibet: an ecological, functional, and culture historical study of yak and
yak hybrids in society, economy and culture.
Richard Pietro Palmieri.   PhD thesis, University of California, Davis,
1976. 304p. maps. bibliog. (Available from University Microfilms, Ann
Arbor, Michigan, order no. AAC 768988).
The yak is a remarkable animal: it can be used as a pack animal, it provides milk, beef,
leather and cord, and its dung can be used for fuel in the inhospitable highlands of
Tibet. This study details its taxonomy, its distribution, breeding and habitat, its
products and other economic uses, and, most interestingly, its role in folklore and
religion. Yak horns, for instance, were used as fertility symbols; and the author

speculates that the yak's original domestication may have been caused by the desire to acquire sacrificial bovines for cult purposes rather than by economic pressures.

122 The abominable snowman.
Swami Pranavananda. *Journal of the Bombay Natural History Society*, vol. 54 (April 1957), p. 358–64.
Sadly for lovers of exotica, this careful investigation into the yeti or abominable snowman suggests that no such creature exists. Mistranslation of various Tibetan words for man, bear and snow, allied to a fanciful interpretation of the 'evidence' of various sightings, has led to wild and exaggerated stories of the abominable snowman, almost all on the Indian rather than the Tibetan side of the Himalayas, and the conclusion is that the yeti is no more than the Himalayan red bear.

123 Tibetan dogs.
J. Taring. *Tibet Journal*, vol. 6, no. 2 (Summer 1981), p. 64–6.
This short article describes the different breeds of dog to be found in Tibet, and their different roles as pets, watchdogs and hunting dogs.

124 Tibet and its birds.
Charles Vaurie. London: H. F. & G. Witherby, 1972. 407p. map. bibliog.
This work is divided into two parts. The first is of general interest and contains a description of geographical Tibet, a history of ornithological exploration, a history of the collections made and an account of the distribution, composition and origin of birds recorded in Tibet, with some notes on migration patterns. The second part comprises a list of all the species recorded to date, a gazetteer and a working list of Sino-Himalayan species. A total of 505 species are listed as having been seen in Tibet, and the list includes details of dates and locations of sightings. The book is enhanced by three fine colour plates.

125 The land of the blue poppy: travels of a naturalist in eastern Tibet.
Frank Kingdon Ward. Cambridge, England: Cambridge University Press, 1913. 283p. maps.
Records the author's experiences and observations in western China and eastern Tibet in 1911 when he was collecting plants for the horticultural firm of Bees Ltd. Although primarily concerned with the natural history of Tibet, the book can be read as a travelogue as it also contains many interesting comments on the social life and customs of the country. There are many photographs and a useful list of around 200 plant species collected on the expedition.

126 A plant hunter in Tibet.
Frank Kingdon Ward. London: Cape, 1934. 317p.
Provides an account of the author's 1933 journey to Tibet.

127 **Pilgrimage for plants.**
Frank Kingdon Ward.   London: Harrap, 1960. 191p. bibliog.

The autobiography of one of the most notable plant collectors whose travels in Asia took him to Assam, Burma and China as well as Tibet.

History

General

128 **Himalayan triangle: a historical survey of British India's relations with Tibet, Sikkim and Bhutan 1765–1950.**
Amar Kaur Jasbir Singh. London: British Library, 1988. 408p. maps. bibliog.
Based on source materials held at the India Office Library and Records this study presents an integrated appraisal of the three Himalayan countries and reassesses major aspects of their history. Topics covered include the policies of Britain and Russia, China's claim to sovereignty in Tibet and the consequences after 1947 of Britain's earlier policies in the area. The author argues that, without a neighbour willing to guarantee her independence, Tibet was an easy victim to her own internal weakness and Chinese expansionism.

129 **Tibet: past and present.**
Sir Charles Bell. Oxford, England: Clarendon Press, 1924. 326p. maps.
Introductory chapters outline the geography and early history of Tibet, but the bulk of the book is concerned with 20th-century events and Bell's own mission to Lhasa. Bell also outlines the main principles of British policy towards Tibet and puts forward his own view that Britain should maintain a benevolent attitude towards Tibet without becoming too involved there.

130 **England, India, Nepal, Tibet, China: 1765–1958: a synchronistic table**
showing the succession of heads of state and other political and
diplomatic personages of importance in these countries, along with
Nepali tributary missions to China, from the mid-eighteenth to the mid-
twentieth century.
Margaret Welpley Fisher, Leo E. Rose. Berkeley, California:
University of California, 1959. 17p.
This useful work of reference lists year by year the Dalai and Panchen Lamas and the
Chinese Residents at Lhasa alongside the rulers of England, India (Governors-General
and Viceroys), Nepal and China. The complete list of Chinese Residents is particularly
important as it is hard to come by elsewhere.

131 **The making of modern Tibet.**
A. Tom Grunfeld. London: Zed Books, 1987. 277p. maps. bibliog.
This refreshingly impartial account of Tibet's history examines the conflicting claims of
the Chinese authorities and the Tibetan refugees in the light of archival and
documentary evidence. The earlier periods are covered in outline with the main
emphasis given to the events of the 20th century, and the situation since the Chinese
invasion is examined both internally and in relation to external attempts to destabilize
Tibet and put pressure on China. There is a chapter on the Tibetan diaspora and a very
useful appendix which attempts to adjudicate between the conflicting figures and
determine the true size and ethnic breakdown of Tibet's population.

132 **Tibet: today and yesterday.**
Tieh-Tseng Li. New York: Bookman, 1960. 324p. map. bibliog.
The title page of the copy I read had been 'annotated' by a previous reader 'or how to
claim the world belongs to China', and this gives an accurate picture of the tone of this
book. The facts are presented in such a way as to show that Tibet has always been
subject to China and any events which could be taken to show the contrary are
misinterpreted or ignored.

133 **Dalai Lamas of Tibet: succession of births.**
Inder L. Malik. New Delhi: Uppal Publishing House, 1984. 188p.
Gives a description of the lives of each of the Dalai Lamas, devoting the most attention
to the present 14th Dalai Lama. There are also chapters on the Panchen Lamas and on
Buddhist philosophy.

134 **Tibet: heart of Asia.**
Laura Pilarski. Indianapolis, Indiana: Bobbs-Merrill, 1974. 125p.
map.
Pilarski's book provides a short introductory history.

135 **Tibet and its history.**
Hugh E. Richardson. London; Boulder, Colorado: Shambhala, 1984.
2nd ed., rev. and updated. 372p. maps. bibliog.
Richardson's standard history of Tibet from the 6th century AD to the present day is
highly regarded. It opens with a brief account of the geography, race, language,

government, economy and law of Tibet, the character of the people, their religion, culture, education and occupations. All the main themes of Tibetan history are covered: the rule of the early kings, the coming of the Dalai Lamas, and Tibet's relationships with China and the West culminating in the Chinese invasion. Less emphasis is given to post-1959 events. Richardson was head of the British Trade Mission in Tibet for 9 years, and is one of the greatest living authorities on Tibet, and this book constitutes an authoritative and accessible introduction to Tibetan history.

136 **Tibet disappears: a documentary history of Tibet's international status, the great rebellion and its aftermath.**
Compiled and edited by Chanakya Sen. London: Asia Publishing House, 1960. 473p.

This compilation presents a documentary account of the old Tibet and the consequences of its disappearance, with particular emphasis on Sino-Tibetan relations and the status of the McMahon Line. The story is told by means of treaties, extracts from debates, discussions and statements made by prominent people and organizations in India, China and the United Nations. Although going back as far as the 8th century, the great majority of the sources are from the period 1950–59, with particular attention paid to Indian sources, including speeches by Nehru and debates in the Lok Sabha. An introduction gives a general survey of Tibet's history and international status.

137 **Tibet: a political history.**
W. D. Shakabpa. New Haven, Connecticut: Yale University Press, 1967. 369p. map. bibliog.

An important contribution to the study of Tibet, this is the first account by a Tibetan lay official of high rank of his own country's political history. His sources include some rare Tibetan government records and other materials not previously cited in English-language works, as well as some of the standard Western sources.

138 **A cultural history of Tibet.**
David Snellgrove, Hugh Richardson. New York: Praeger, 1968. 291p. maps. bibliog.

This comprehensive survey, by two acknowledged experts, traces the evolution of Tibetan culture from its pre-Buddhist origins in the 6th century AD, through the arrival of Buddhism, the rise of the great monasteries, the split between the 'Yellow Hats' and the 'Red Hats', and the establishment of the Dalai Lama, up to the Chinese invasion of 1959.

139 **The status of Tibet: history, rights and prospects in international law.**
Michael C. Van Walt Van Praag. London: Wisdom; Boulder, Colorado: Westview Press, 1987. 381p. maps. bibliog.

The author reviews the history of the Tibetan state from its unification in the 7th century to its present disputed incorporation into the People's Republic of China. Amply documented from numerous sources, this book provides a basis for understanding the longstanding and unresolved problem of Tibet's relationship to China.

140 **Highlights of Tibetan history.**
Wang Fujen, Suo Wenqing. Beijing: New World Press, 1984. 206p.
(China Studies Series).
This is very much a history of Tibet from the Chinese point of view as is apparent from
the foreword which states 'All evolutions and changes that have taken place in Tibetan
society are closely related to and inseparable from the Chinese nation as a whole'.
Thus early peaceful contacts between China and Tibet are stressed and Western
capitalists' and Czarist Russia's agressions are contrasted with the 'peaceful liberation'
of Tibet by Chinese forces in 1951.

Early and medieval

141 **Ancient Tibet: research materials from the Yeshe De Project.**
Berkeley, California: Dharma Publishing, 1986. 371p. maps. bibliog.
This book provides a very useful survey of the earliest period of Tibet's history up to
the 9th century. Early chapters deal with the formation of the land and the geological
history of the Tibetan plateau, based on the most recent scientific research. Then
follows an account of the origins and development of the Tibetan tribes and the rule of
the early kings, and the book concludes with a survey of the political and cultural
achievements of Tibet in the 8th and 9th centuries, based on contemporary source
materials.

142 **The Tibetan Empire in central Asia: a history of the struggle for great**
power among Tibetans, Turks, Arabs and Chinese during the Middle
Ages.
Christopher I. Beckwith. Princeton, New Jersey: Princeton University
Press, 1987. 269p. maps. bibliog.
A detailed history of the Tibetan Empire in central Asia during the period 600–866 AD
is the subject of this important work, which challenges the view that Europe and Asia
were largely isolated from each other until the establishment of the sea routes, and
emphasizes the importance of overland contacts via the Silk Road in the early middle
ages. Tibet's history during this period is placed in the context of general conflicts in
central Asia.

143 **Four lamas of Dolpo: Tibetan biographies.**
Edited and translated by David L. Snellgrove. Cambridge,
Massachusetts: Harvard University Press, 1967. 302p. maps.
Dolpo is on the borders of northwest Nepal and Tibet proper. Three of the four lamas
whose biographies are recounted here lived during the 15th and 16th centuries; the
fourth lived a century later. The texts are more or less contemporary with their
subjects, and like all Tibetan historical writings are religious in character, but also
contain much information on the social conditions of the area and the life of the laity
during the period.

144 **The white annals.**
Gedun Chos-'phel, translated from the Tibetan by Samten Norboo.
Dharamsala, India: Library of Tibetan Works and Archives, 1978.
103p.

The author was born in 1905 and became a leading Tibetan historian and writer who developed highly nationalistic aspirations for Tibet. His incomplete *White annals* present the earliest proofs of Tibet's independent status, but the work is far from being a mere propagandist piece as the author's critical scholarship produced an intelligent appraisal of the very early period of Tibetan history and its kings. Gedun Chos-'phel died in 1951 with his work still unfinished.

145 **The Yar-lun dynasty: a study with particular regard to the contribution by myths and legends to the history of ancient Tibet and the origin and nature of its kings.**
Erik Haarh. Copenhagen: G. E. C. Gad's Forlag, 1969. 481p. maps.
bibliog.

This is a massive and scholarly study which covers the entire Imperial age in Tibet's history from the 5th to the 9th centuries AD. Haarh sets out the genealogies of the kings, analyses the different traditions, and discusses the whole prehistorical tradition of the mythical kings. His study also encompasses the traditions of death and the tombs of the Tibetan king. The style of this book does not make for easy reading, but it is one no serious student of the period can afford to ignore.

146 **Sources for a history of the bSam yas debate.**
Gary W. Houston. Sankt Augustin: VGH-Wissenschaftsverlag, 1980.
122p. bibliog. (Monumenta Tibetica Historica. Abt. 1, Scriptores Bd. 2).

The bSam yas debate was held at the monastery of that name in 792–794. Ostensibly it was a debate between the Chinese and Indian forms of Buddhism, but it was also tied up with politics and the whole question of Tibet's relationship to China and the status of royal power in Tibet. This volume contains the texts, in Tibetan and English, of some of the historical documents relating to the debate, accompanied by an introduction by Gary Houston. In this he argues that the Indian faction did win the debate and that Tibet's independence from China was thus assured for at least another century.

147 **Une note sur les mégalithes tibétains.** (A note on the megaliths of Tibet.)
A. W. Macdonald. *Journal asiatique* (1953), p. 63–76.

This article brings together the descriptions of Tibetan megaliths from many earlier works and speculates on their significance and function. It should be read in conjunction with Roerich's *The animal style among the nomad tribes of northern Tibet* (q.v.).

148 **Histoire ancienne du Tibet.** (Ancient history of Tibet.)
Paul Pelliot. Paris: Librairie d'Amérique et d'Orient, 1961. 168p.
Provides a translation of important sources covering the history of Tibet during the 6th to 9th centuries.

149 **A corpus of early Tibetan inscriptions.**
Hugh E. Richardson. London: Royal Asiatic Society, 1985. 185p.
bibliog. (James G. Forlong Series, no. XXIX).
The inscriptions included in this volume cover the years 764–840. They have all been published before but this is the first time they have been brought together and this volume therefore supersedes some of Hugh Richardson's earlier compilations. The purpose of the inscriptions varies: some deal with the maintenance of the Buddhist religion, some are charters granting privileges to meritorious persons and one concerns the building and endowment of a temple. The most well-known one is the treaty of 821/822 between Tibet and China, recorded on a stone pillar outside the Jokhang, an important event in Tibet's history and subsequent interpretations of the historical relationship with China. Each of the inscriptions is given in Tibetan and English translation, and the text is accompanied by 16 plates.

150 **The animal style among the nomad tribes of northern Tibet.**
George N. Roerich. Prague: Seminarium Kondakovianum, 1930. 42p.
Not much has been written on Tibetan prehistory. This short report presents the result of archaeological exploration of northern Tibet. It contains descriptions of graves, megalithic monuments and objects in animal style which were either discovered in the graves or still in use by the nomads. There are a number of detailed plates of some of the objects described.

151 **The blue annals.**
George N. Roerich. Delhi: Motilal Banarsidass, 1976. 2nd ed. 1275p.
This work is a translation of the original Tibetan text compiled by the Tibetan scholar Gos lo-tsa-ba-gZon-nu dpal (1392–1481). It establishes a chronology of the events of early Tibetan history and works out in detail the names of important religious teachers and their spiritual lineage. It is divided into 15 chapters, each devoted to the history of a particular school or sect of Tibetan Buddhism, and also includes the history of the early kings of Tibet.

152 **Les tribus anciennes des marches sino-tibétaines: légendes, classification et histoire.** (The ancient tribes of the Sino-Tibetan borderlands: legends, classification and history.)
R. A. Stein. Paris: Presses Universitaires de France, 1961. 105p. map. bibliog. (Bibliothèque de l'Institut des Hautes Études Chinoises, vol. 15).
A detailed examination of the ancient tribes who inhabited the region on the borders of present-day China and Tibet is the subject of this book, with extensive reference back to literary sources and linguistic evidence. Stein concludes that these tribes played a large part in the later creation of the royal kingdom based on central Tibet. There was of course much movement of peoples both from east to west and west to east, but

these eastern tribes appear to be linguistically the closest to the Tibetans of the historical era.

153 **The tombs of the Tibetan kings.**
Giuseppe Tucci.   Rome: Istituto Italiano per il Medio ed Estremo Oriente, 1950. 117p. (Serie Orientale Roma, 1).
This is a scholarly investigation, based on textual evidence and fieldwork, of the location and character of the tombs of the early Tibetan kings, which also includes some discussion of the chronology of the period and early Tibetan history. An appendix contains some of the relevant Tibetan texts, inscriptions and edicts.

16th to 19th centuries

154 **Hidden treasures and secret lives: a study of Pemalingpa (1450–1521) and the Sixth Dalai Lama (1683–1706).**
Michael Aris.   London: Kegan Paul International, 1989. 278p. map. bibliog.
This is a fascinating study, based on a detailed analysis of the relevant Tibetan texts, of the central mysteries in the lives of two of the most enigmatic figures in Tibetan history. Pemalingpa was a professional treasure hunter and discoverer of hidden texts. The 6th Dalai Lama is now best known as the author of some of the finest Tibetan poetry, but he was in his own day a controversial figure and mystery surrounds both his birth and his death.

155 **Trade through the Himalayas: the early British attempts to open Tibet.**
S. Cammann.   Princeton, New Jersey: Princeton University Press, 1951. 186p.
In the last years of the 18th century the British authorities in India sought new ways to open up the trade with China and this inevitably brought them into contact with Tibet for the first time. Cammann's study covers the period 1767–94 and tells the story of the early British missions to Tibet.

156 **Trans-Himalayan trade: a retrospect (1774–1914): in quest of Tibet's identity.**
Phanindra Nath Chakrabarti.   Delhi: Classics India, 1990. 138p. bibliog.
The scope of this book is wider than the title suggests. Its subject is primarily the relationship between China and Tibet and China's attempts to impose her authority on Tibet. India's commercial transactions with China through Tibet are also covered as are the East India Company's attempts to open up the same trade route. The author makes the interesting point that the British authorities in India were generally reluctant to intervene in Tibet, citing as proof the British refusal to come to Tibet's assistance to resist Nepalese aggression.

157 **The water horse and other years: a history of 17th and 18th century Tibet.**
K. Dhondup. Dharamsala, India: Library of Tibetan Works and Archives, 1984. 113p.

Dhondup's period is that of the first to the seventh Dalai Lamas. His book is mainly intended for young Tibetans but it could equally well serve as an introduction to the period for all readers. He covers the sectarian and regional conflicts of the era, involving Tibetan regents, Mongol chiefs and Manchu emperors, set against the background of the rise in importance as a temporal and spiritual power of the Dalai Lama.

158 **The secret deliverance of the sixth Dalai Lama.**
Piotr Klafkowski. Vienna: Arbeitskreis für Tibetische und Buddhistische Studien, Universität Wien, 1979. 93p. bibliog.

The sixth Dalai Lama was a controversial figure and his death has remained something of a mystery. This book is based on a rare text which suggests that he did not die around 1706 as is customarily stated, but lived on in seclusion and secrecy for another 40 years. The author puts the case for and against this view and leaves the question open to the reader to decide.

159 **British India and Tibet, 1766–1910.**
Alastair Lamb. London; New York: Routledge & Kegan Paul, 1986. 353p. maps. bibliog.

This is a revised and expanded edition of the author's *Britain and Chinese Central Asia: the road to Lhasa, 1767 to 1905*, published in 1960. This is unquestionably the definitive work on British contacts with and concerning Tibet from the time of Clive through to 1910 when the Chinese occupied Lhasa, following the British government's repudiation of the Younghusband Expedition.

160 **Nepal–Tibet war, 1855–56.**
Kanchanmoy Mojumdar. *Journal of the United Service Institution of India*, vol. 94 (1964), p. 175–94.

Relations between Nepal and Tibet were not good during the 19th century. This article examines the origins and course of the war which eventually broke out in 1855 following a period of rising tension. The author emphasizes that both Britain and China were keen to localize the conflict but argues that instability in the Himalayan border regions was an indication of declining Chinese control over Tibetan affairs.

161 **China and Tibet in the early XVIIIth century: history of the establishment of Chinese protectorate in Tibet.**
L. Petech. Leiden, The Netherlands: E. J. Brill, 1972. 2nd rev. ed. 309p. maps. bibliog. (T'oung Pao: archives concernant l'histoire, les langues, la géographie, l'ethnologie et les arts de l'Asie orientale. Monographie 1).

Chinese policy towards Tibet in the early 18th century can be divided into several distinct periods. At times the Manchu emperors exercised only a shadowy form of suzerainty with no military occupation and no regular Resident in Lhasa. However, in

1721–23 and 1748–50 military garrisons were posted in Lhasa and Residents with varying degrees of power were appointed. In 1751 the organization of the protectorate took the form which lasted until 1912 when the Ambans were given the rights of control and supervision; from 1792 they were also given the right of direct participation in the Tibetan government.

1900–1950

162 Tibet on the imperial chessboard: the making of British policy towards Lhasa, 1899–1925.
Premen Addy.   Calcutta, India: Academic Publishers, 1984. 364p. maps. bibliog.

This well-researched and thoroughly documented history deals with Anglo-Tibetan relations from the high peak of Curzon's 'forward policy' through the Younghusband Expedition and the Simla Conference to the beginnings of British decline in India. It is particularly important in giving due weight to the influence of international politics in both Europe and the Far East on British policy towards Tibet.

163 Adventures of a Tibetan fighting monk.
Compiled by Hugh Richardson, edited by Tadeusz Skorupski.
Bangkok: Tamarind Press, 1986. 135p.

This book is in essence the autobiography of a Tibetan monk called Tashi Khedrup which has been compiled from a series of conversations he held with Hugh Richardson. He was born in a rural village, ordained as a monk and eventually became one of the renowned *Dob-dob* or fighting monks. His narrative contains much information on the life of a monk in the old Tibet and also includes an account of the 1959 uprising following which he fled to India.

164 Dans les marches tibétaines: autour du Dokerla: novembre 1906 – janvier 1908. (On the frontiers of Tibet: around Dokerla: November 1906 – January 1908.)
Jacques Bacot.   Paris: Plon-Norrit, 1909. 215p. map.

This account of the author's travels in the eastern borderlands of Tibet includes a description of the fighting between the Tibetans and the Chinese.

165 Le Tibet révolte: vers Nepemako, la terre promise des tibétaines. (Tibet in revolt: towards Nepemako, the promised land of Tibetans.)
Jacques Bacot.   Paris: Hachette, 1912. 364p. map.

This further account of Bacot's travels along the Chinese–Tibetan border contains a description of the fighting between the Tibetans and the Chinese.

166 **Portrait of a Dalai Lama: the life and times of the great Thirteenth.**
Sir Charles Bell.   London: Wisdom, 1987. 467p. (A Wisdom Tibet
Book. Yellow Series).

Bell was a personal friend of the Dalai Lama and this book (first published in 1946)
presents a vivid picture of a powerful yet also humble man who worked tirelessly for
the good of his country. He warded off political and military onslaughts from China
and sought (ultimately in vain) for support from the outside world. Internally he
sought to introduce radical reforms to Tibetan society. The book concludes with an
account of the discovery and enthronement of the 14th Dalai Lama.

167 **The unveiling of Lhasa.**
Edmund Candler.   London: Edward Arnold, 1905. 304p. maps.

Candler was one of the newspaper correspondents who accompanied the Younghusband Expedition and his book is one of the fullest of the many contemporary
accounts by journalists and others. Like many others who were present he came to feel
much sympathy for the Tibetans and his book is notable for its fair-minded approach.
It also contains one of the best sets of photographs of the campaign.

168 **The water bird and other years: a history of the 13th Dalai Lama and
after.**
K. Dhondup.   New Delhi: Rangwang, 1986. 224p. bibliog.

This book covers the period from around 1910 up to 1959. The author views the 13th
Dalai Lama in a very favourable light and sees his death in 1933 (the year of the water
bird) as an important watershed in Tibetan history. After that, aristocratic and
monastic plots and counter-plots emaciated the natural strength and unity of Tibet just
when they were most needed. The book can be read as an indictment of this critical
period when all the achievements of the 13th Dalai Lama were lost through the selfish
and self-defeating policies of Lhasa and its politicians.

169 **Bayonets to Lhasa: the first full account of the British invasion of Tibet
in 1904.**
Peter Fleming.   London: R. Hart-Davis, 1961. 319p. maps. bibliog.

The sub-title is not entirely accurate, but this book nevertheless remains essential
reading for anyone interested in the Younghusband Expedition and is certainly the one
that anyone coming new to the subject should read first. Perhaps because they were
somewhat similar in character, Fleming seems better able to present a convincing
portrait of Younghusband than any of the other writers on the campaign.

170 **Further papers relating to Tibet.**
London: HMSO, 1904. 29p. (Cd. 2054: British Parliamentary Papers,
1904, vol. LXVII, p. 1103–35).

This second selection of official documents published by the British government covers
the period December 1903 to April 1904. See also *Papers relating to Tibet* (Cd. 1920),
and Cd. 2730 and Cd. 5240 below.

171 **Further papers relating to Tibet. No. III.**
London: HMSO, 1905. 277p. (Cd. 2730: British Parliamentary Papers, 1905, vol. LVIII, p. 433–735).

The third selection of official documents published by the British government covers the period March–December 1904. These documents demonstrate the conflict between the British and Indian governments over the terms of the convention Younghusband negotiated in Lhasa.

172 **Further papers relating to Tibet.**
London: HMSO, 1910. 229p. (Cd. 5240: British Parliamentary Papers, 1910, vol. LXVIII, p. 615–859).

This last selection of official documents covers the period from the signing of the Lhasa Convention by Younghusband up to the flight of the Dalai Lama to India in 1910.

173 **A history of modern Tibet, 1913–1951: the demise of the Lamaist state.**
Melvyn Goldstein, with the help of Gelek Rimpoche. Berkeley, California: University of California Press, 1989. 898p. maps. bibliog.

This monumental, even awe-inspiring study will unquestionably be the standard scholarly work on the subject for many years to come. Drawing on a wealth of sources including oral interviews, unpublished memoirs, government documents and Tibetan archives, many of them previously unexplored, Professor Goldstein has produced a detailed and unbiased account of modern Tibet which, whilst recognizing the importance of Buddhism, does not allow it to predominate, and which gives due weight to internal political developments as well as to international relations, thus redressing the balance of many previous works. Indispensable to a proper understanding of modern Tibet.

174 **The jewel in the lotus: recollections of an Indian political.**
B. J. Gould. London: Chatto & Windus, 1957. 252p.

Gould was British Trade Agent in Gyantse in 1912–13, and this volume of memoirs includes an account of his time there and of his visits to Lhasa in 1936, 1940 and 1941.

175 **Lhasa: an account of the country and the people of central Tibet and of the progress of the mission sent there by the English government in the year 1903–04.**
Perceval Landon. London: Hurst & Blackett, 1905. 2 vols.

Landon was the correspondent of *The Times* who accompanied the Younghusband Expedition and his book is one of the most detailed of contemporary accounts. Appendices cover such topics as the folklore of Tibet, the natural history of southern Tibet, and an essay on the government of Tibet by O'Connor (q.v.). There are many photographs and a list of all the officers who took part in the expedition.

176 **Tibetan polity, 1904–37: the conflict between the 13th Dalai Lama and the 9th Panchen Lama: a case study.**
Parshotam Mehra. Wiesbaden, Germany: Harrassowitz, 1976. 94p. bibliog. (Asiatische Forschungen, Bd. 49).

Conflict between the two supreme incarnate lamas has been a recurring feature of Tibetan history. In recent times the Dalai Lama has inclined towards support from the West or Russia, whereas the Panchen Lama has had closer relations with the Chinese. The story of this conflict is traced in detail from the time of the Younghusband Expedition to the death of the 9th Panchen Lama in 1937, four years after the death of the 13th Dalai Lama with the two leaders remaining unreconciled to the end.

177 **The Younghusband Expedition.**
Parshotam Mehra. London: Asia Publishing House, 1968. 408p. bibliog.

Mehra gives a fair-minded and objective account of an expedition that will always be controversial. Younghusband is seen primarily as 'Curzon's man', sharing with his master an overriding fear of Russian expansion in central Asia and aiming to obtain more for his country than was contained in his instructions because he knew that, although unspoken, that was what the Viceroy wanted too. The generally favourable impression made by the British troops on the Tibetans paved the way towards the good relations between the British and Tibet in the inter-war period.

178 **To Lhassa at last.**
Powell Millington. London: Smith, Elder, 1905. 200p.

Written in a 'ripping yarn' style, this is a popular account of the Younghusband Expedition. Millington's real name was Mark Synge and he was an officer on the expedition.

179 **On the frontier and beyond: a record of thirty years' service.**
Frederick O'Connor. London: John Murray, 1931. 355p.

O'Connor was a member of the Younghusband Expedition and then served as British Trade Agent at Gyantse. His book also describes the visit of the Panchen Lama to India and his meeting with the Dalai Lama in Peking in 1908.

180 **With mounted infantry in Tibet.**
W. J. Ottley. London: Smith, Elder, 1906. 275p.

Ottley commanded the mounted infantry on the Younghusband Expedition. The appendices include the texts of Macdonald's order for assaulting Gyantse Dzong, the speech by Younghusband on the signing of the Lhasa Convention and Macdonald's last despatch from Tibet in which he reviewed the whole expedition.

181 **Papers relating to Tibet.**
London: HMSO, 1904. 314p. map. (Cd. 1920: British Parliamentary Papers, 1904, vol. LXVII, p. 779–1101).

The first of a series of British official documents which sought to justify the British government's decision to despatch the Younghusband Expedition and its overall policy towards Tibet, this volume contains documents covering the period 1889–1904. These documents are essential reading for anyone making a serious study of Anglo-Tibetan relations. At the time the selection of which documents were included was regarded (not least by Younghusband himself) as highly controversial, but eighty years on, with the present government's obsession with secrecy verging on the paranoid, it seems extraordinary that the government published so many key documents so close to the events with which they were concerned. See also *Further papers* (Cd. 2054, 2730, 5240) above.

182 The Thirteenth Dalai lama.
Lobsang Rapgay. *Bulletin of Tibetology* (1977), no. 2, p. 25–30.

The 13th Dalai Lama was the first to realize the importance of the economic and social development of the country. Amongst the reforms he introduced were the abolition of capital punishment (except for treason), and the establishment of the first primary schools, postage stamps and paper money, and some Tibetans were sent abroad to study for the first time. Perhaps most important, he was also responsible for upholding the country's independence.

183 General Huang Mu-sung at Lhasa, 1934.
Hugh E. Richardson. *Bulletin of Tibetology* (1977), no. 2, p. 31–5.

This article discusses a little-known incident in Tibetan history. Following the death of the 13th Dalai Lama, the Chinese government was quick to try to take advantage of the situation by attempting to persuade the Tibetans to declare a republic and join China as one of the '5 Races'. However, negotiations led nowhere and the end result was merely the establishment of a Chinese liaison office in Lhasa. The event is interesting in showing that at that time the Tibetans did not recognize even the nominal suzerainty of China.

184 The truth about Tibet.
A. Maccallum Scott. London: Simpkin, Marshall, Hamilton, Kent & Co., 1905. 75p. map.

This contemporary pamphlet puts the case against the Younghusband Expedition and the policies that lay behind it. The author castigates the 'deplorable slaughter' and the 'futility of the entire proceedings for any practical purpose'.

185 Tibet and the Tibetans.
Tsung-lien Shen, Shen-chi Liu. Stanford, California: Stanford University Press, 1953. 191p.

Shen and Liu were members of the Chinese mission to Lhasa in 1943. Their book provides an interesting description of the social conditions, political organization and foreign relations of Tibet in the period immediately prior to the Communist take-over.

186 Peking's "peaceful liberation" of Tibet in retrospect.
Shih Hung-lin. *Issues and Studies* vol. 21, no. 5 (May 1985), p. 106–25.

This article analyses the Chinese Communist Party's policies towards the national minorities from the 1920s onwards with the focus on both the political and the military measures taken by China in 1950–51. Using the bait of 'free federation' the Chinese were able to split the Tibetan leadership, but even so the 'liberation' was hardly peaceful and the increasing harshness of Chinese rule led directly to the 1959 uprising.

187   The Simla Convention 1914: a Chinese puzzle.
Nirmal C. Sinha.   *Bulletin of Tibetology* (1977), no. 1, p. 35–9.

This article addresses the problem of whether the Simla Convention was legal or not, being merely initialled, not signed, by only two of the parties concerned, Britain and Tibet and not by China. If it is legal it serves the cause of Tibet as indicating that Tibet was sufficiently independent to sign an international agreement; if it is not legal it serves the cause of China, yet the irony is that China approves many of its provisions and would not wish to give them up.

188   Le mendiant de l'Ambo. (The beggar of Ambo.)
Heather Stoddart.   Paris: Société d'Ethnographie, 1985. 395p. map. bibliog.

This is an important biography, drawing on many primary sources, of one of the most controversial figures in the history of 20th-century Tibet. Gedun Chompel (1905–51) was for some an eminent religious figure and historian (he was author of *The white annals* [q.v.]), but for others he was was nothing more than a political agitator and agent of the communists. Certainly he was in Tibetan terms a radical who wanted to modernize his country. Imprisoned for his beliefs, he ultimately failed in his attempts to introduce reforms which might have saved Tibet from its fate at the hands of the Chinese after his death.

189   Tibet from Buddhism to Communism.
Heather Stoddart.   *Government and Opposition* vol. 21, no. 1 (Winter 1986), p. 76–95.

This interesting article examines an aspect of Tibet's history which has received little coverage elsewhere: the nascent reform movement which grew up amongst Tibetan intellectuals and radicals in the years before 1951. The history of the Tibetan Progressist (or Improvement) Party which was formed in 1939 is covered, as are the careers of a number of the leading Tibetan radicals, including Gedun Chompel, the historian, dialectician and pan-Tibetan nationalist who was imprisoned for a time and was the author of *The white annals* (q.v.). It is interesting that Shakabpa's history (q.v.) has no mention of the radical movement, but it does receive coverage in the more recent work by Goldstein (q.v.).

190   The Thirteenth Dalai Lama.
Tokan Tada.   Tokyo: Centre for East Asian Cultural Studies, 1965. 115p. map. (East Asian Cultural Studies Series, no. 9).

The author studied Buddhism in Tibet and was personally acquainted with the 13th Dalai Lama. He outlines the Dalai Lama's relations with both Britain and Russia and his attempts to modernize his country.

191 **Daughter of Tibet.**
Rinchen Dolma Taring.   London: Wisdom, 1986. 324p. maps.
(A Wisdom Tibet Book. Yellow Series.)
This is a new edition of a book which was first published in 1970. The author was born
in 1910 and grew up in the closely knit world of the Tibetan nobility. Educated in
Darjeeling she was the first Tibetan woman to be able to speak and write English. She
first married Dasang Dadul Tsarong, the commander-in-chief of the Tibetan army, and
then Jigme Taring, a prince of Sikkim. Her memoirs give a lively impression of life in
the higher echelons of Tibetan society, and in this new edition she has added an
account of her work amongst the Tibetan refugee communities in India and her recent
reunion with some of her family still in Tibet.

192 **Travels of a consular officer in eastern Tibet, together with a history of
the relations between China, Tibet and India.**
Eric Teichman.   Cambridge, England: Cambridge University Press,
1922. 248p. maps.
This is a work of both travel and history since Sir Eric Teichman was sent as a
mediator in the frontier dispute between China and Tibet in 1918. His account of the
fighting on Tibet's eastern border and of Tibet's increasing rejection of its nominal
suzerain is of particular value. Teichman's attempts to find a solution to the problem
were ultimately unsuccessful as the Chinese eventually refused to settle the dispute.
Despite these more sombre undertones, however, his book can also be enjoyed as an
informative and well-illustrated travelogue.

193 **Lhasa and its mysteries, with a record of the expedition of 1903–04.**
L. A. Waddell.   London: John Murray, 1905. 530p. maps.
Waddell's book gives much useful background information on Tibet as well as a
detailed account of the Younghusband Expedition. Having already written a book on
The Buddhism of Tibet (q.v.) Waddell was well placed to write a well-informed work
of this nature.

194 **Memoirs of a political officer's wife in Tibet, Sikkim and Bhutan.**
Margaret Williamson, in collaboration with John Snelling.   London:
Wisdom, 1987. 240p. maps.
Margaret Williamson made two visits to Tibet in the 1930s when she accompanied her
husband on his tours of duty. Her memoirs include her impressions of Lhasa at that
time and an account of her meeting with the 13th Dalai Lama. A selection of her
photographs are reproduced to accompany the text.

195 **India and Tibet.**
Francis Younghusband.   Hong Kong: Oxford University Press, 1985.
maps. bibliog.
Younghusband's own account of his mission to Tibet in 1904–5 and its consequences
was first published in 1910. It is clearly written with the aim of showing that his and
Curzon's policy was the correct one and that the later repudiation of the mission by the
British government led to a series of lost opportunities culminating in the occupation of
Lhasa by the Chinese in 1910. This new edition contains a useful introduction and
bibliographical note by Alastair Lamb (q.v.).

1951–

196 From the land of lost content: the Dalai Lama's fight for Tibet.
Noel Barber. Boston, Masachusetts: Houghton Mifflin, 1970. 235p.
maps. bibliog.

The author gives a detailed account of the Tibetan revolt in 1959 based largely on interviews with participants who later fled abroad.

197 The Chinese occupation of Tibet: a lesson from history.
Gary Bullert. *Journal of Social, Political and Economic Studies*,
vol. 11, no. 1 (Spring 1986), p. 17–37. bibliog.

This article discusses the Chinese takeover of Tibet in the 1950s in the context of China's current attempts to 'readmit' Taiwan to China. The author argues that the fundamental causes of Tibet's failure to retain its independence were diplomatic isolation and, more importantly, its lack of a modernized well-equipped army. The result was that a country which had failed to modernize itself was then forcibly modernized by alien occupation forces.

198 Life in the Red Flag People's Commune.
Dhondup Choeden. Dharamsala, India: Information Office of
His Holiness the Dalai Lama, 1978. 70p.

This heartfelt indictment of Chinese policies is all the more effective because the author was a poor peasant who was initially prepared to support Communist policies because she disliked the inequalities of the old Tibet. She was a trusted and ranking cadre of the Chinese rulers and was for a time appointed political officer for her village. Her descriptions of the system of political education, the administrative structure of a People's Commune and the effects of the Cultural Revolution are thus of particular interest. Eventually she came to recognize Chinese rule as being in essence old-style colonialism with the Tibetans reduced to economic and political subservience, and in 1973 she fled to India.

199 Autonoom Tibet. (Autonomous Tibet.)
Simone Cloud. Amsterdam: Universiteit van Amsterdam,
Anthropologisch-Sociologisch Centrum, 1983. 18p. bibliog. (Working
paper no. 30).

In this analytical survey of Tibet under Chinese rule, Cloud argues that true autonomy or even significant participation by Tibetans in the political process has never been more than a sham; the Chinese central government has always retained real control. Even the recent changes have brought little real improvement, and the economic situation (the worst in China) is contrasted with Tibet's self-sufficiency before the Chinese invasion.

200 Concerning the question of Tibet.
Peking: Foreign Languages Press, 1959. 275p.

A propagandist publication put out by the Chinese shortly after the Tibetan revolt. It contains material published between 28 March and 30 April 1959, together with some background information and an article 'The revolution in Tibet and Nehru's philosophy' which appeared originally in *The People's Daily*.

201 In haste from Tibet.

Rinchen Dakpa, B. A. Brooke.   London: Robert Hale, 1971. 174p. map.

This is a fairly unsophisticated account of one young boy's recollections of life in Tibet in the years leading up to the 1959 uprising and of his escape from Tibet when he was twelve years old. Rinchen Dakpa's home was originally in west Tibet. He moved to Lhasa in 1954 and then to Kongpo in southeastern Tibet when his uncle was made governor of the province; from there they fled to Darjeeling in 1959. His recollections are of interest in providing a 'boy's eye view' of life in pre-1959 Tibet.

202 Tibet: mort ou vif. (Tibet: dead or alive.)

Pierre-Antoine Donnet.   Paris: Gallimard, 1990. 356p. maps. bibliog.

This well-researched and readable history covers the whole period since 1951, with one chapter providing a summary of earlier events; greatest emphasis is given to the 1980s and to the increasing signs of unrest which have manifested themselves in Tibet in recent years. The Chinese record in Tibet is exposed as cultural, linguistic and religious genocide, carried out against a background of indifference on the part of the rest of the world. This harsh judgement is all the more convincing because the author, having lived for many years in China himself, is far from being anti-Chinese in outlook. Appendices include the texts of the Seventeen Point Agreement in 1951, the Five Point Plan of the Dalai Lama, promulgated in Washington in 1987, and the address of the Dalai Lama to the European Parliament on 15 June 1988.

203 Tibet transformed.

Israel Epstein.   Beijing: New World Press, 1983. 566p. map.

Based on three journeys to Tibet in 1955, 1965 and 1976, during which he interviewed several hundred Tibetans, Epstein's account of Tibet's recent history emphasizes the material progress that has been made since 1951. He admits that errors occurred during the period of leftist dominance and the Cultural Revolution but argues that by 1980-82 all these defects were being corrected and that there had by then been a resumption of steady progress based on flexible policies suited to local conditions. Appendices give details of serf rebellions in the 'old' Tibet and the texts of important Chinese Communist Party policy statements.

204 Facts about Tibet, 1961–1965.

New Delhi: Bureau of His Holiness the Dalai Lama, 1965. 58p. maps.

Under the headings 'Continued violation of human rights', 'Colonization of Tibet' and 'Military build up in Tibet' this report seeks to show, from eye-witness reports, the domination and persecution of the Tibetan people by China and its army. There is an historical note setting out the case for an independent Tibet, and a summary of the main provisions of the Dalai Lama's proposed new constitution, promulgated in 1963. The conclusion of the report is that the people of Tibet have been deprived of their right to self-determination and denied the freedom they enjoyed prior to the Chinese invasion.

205 **Captured in Tibet.**
Robert Ford. London: George Harrap, 1957. 256p. maps.
Robert Ford was a radio operator employed by the Tibetan government in Chambo near the Chinese border. When the Chinese invaded in 1950 he was able for a time to continue broadcasting messages to Lhasa reporting on the situation. Eventually he attempted to escape but was captured and spent the following four years in a Chinese prison being interrogated and subjected to various forms of political re-education. His book is a valuable eye-witness account of a crucial period in Tibetan history.

206 **The timely rain: travels in new Tibet.**
Stuart Gelder, Roma Gelder. London: Hutchinson, 1964. 248p.
The Gelders travelled in Tibet in 1962 and, like so many Western visitors during that period, they lay great stress on the material and social progress that they perceived as having taken place in Tibet since 1959, claiming that there had been no political or social reform or improvement in living standards before the Chinese took over. Their dismissal of the accusations that the Chinese were oppressing the Tibetans and destroying their culture reads oddly now that even the Chinese authorities admit grave errors were made at that time.

207 **Communist China and Tibet: the first dozen years.**
George Ginsburgs, Michael Mathos. The Hague: Martinus Nijhoff, 1964. 218p. bibliog.
This is a scholarly investigation of the transitional period in Tibet's history between 1951 and 1959 and of the revolt of 1959 and its aftermath. The authors stress the effects of Chinese migration into Tibet and conclude that both Chinese control over Tibet and the adoption of communist policies are irreversible. They see the mass of the peasantry as being neutral – not quite convinced by the material improvements brought by the Chinese yet not overtly hostile to the new régime either, with many of the problems facing the authorities being the result of introducing reforms too quickly.

208 **The last Dalai Lama: a biography.**
Michael Harris Goodman. London: Sidgwick & Jackson, 1986. 364p. maps. bibliog.
Written with the co-operation of the Dalai Lama, and based in part on interviews with him, his family and his close associates, this is primarily a political rather than a religious biography. The emphasis is on the period before the Dalai Lama's flight to India, but the last part of the book covers the establishment of the Tibetan government-in-exile in Dharamsala and presents the Dalai Lama's views on the current situation in Tibet and his hopes for the future.

209 **Great ocean: an authorised biography of the Buddhist monk Tenzin Gyatso, His Holiness the Fourteenth Dalai Lama.**
Roger Hicks, Ngakpa Chogyam. Shaftesbury, England: Element Books, 1984. 207p. bibliog.
This is a sympathetic but fair-minded biography which addresses three main themes: the biography of the Buddhist monk Tenzin Gyatso, the biography of the thirteen previous incarnations of the Dalai Lama and the political biography of the 14th Dalai Lama as leader of his people. The religious significance of the Dalai Lama is given

greater prominence than in Goodman's biography (q.v.). The Chinese do not come well out of this book, but, as the authors state, they have attempted to express the truth as best they can.

210 **Tibet fights for freedom: the story of the March 1959 uprising as recorded in documents, despatches, eye-witness accounts and world-wide reactions: a white book.**
Edited by Raja Hutheesing.   Bombay, India: Orient Longmans, 1960. 243p. maps.

Using a broadly chronological arrangement, this book brings together a most valuable collection of contemporary source materials concerning the 1959 revolt in Tibet, including newspaper reports, statements in the Indian Parliament and official Chinese statements and broadcasts. The large number of Indian press reports and comments is particularly notable as many of these would be hard to obtain otherwise.

211 **Frontier callings.**
Prem Nath Kaul.   Delhi: Vikas, 1976. 148p. maps.

Kaul's book provides an important and necessary corrective to the laudatory accounts of the 'new Tibet' produced by Anna Louise Strong and other sympathizers with the Chinese. The author was Indian Consul-General in Lhasa for the first two years after the Dalai Lama's flight and the picture he paints of Tibet is a very different one from Ms Strong's (q.v.). He writes of food shortages, indiscriminate arrests and an increasingly repressive police state in which Tibetans were forced to inform on their friends, family and neighbours. He later worked for three-and-a-half years with the Tibetan refugees in India and includes an account of the refugee communities in India in his book.

212 **The Dalai Lama: a biography.**
Claude B. Levenson, translated by Stephen Cox.   London: Unwin Hyman, 1988. 291p.

This full-length biography of the Dalai Lama includes coverage of the 1988 riots in Lhasa and the Dalai Lama's new policy of the 'Middle Way' proposing limited autonomy rather than complete independence for Tibet. Based in part on interviews with the Dalai Lama, it is both a personal and a political biography which is well researched and readable.

213 **Betrayal of Tibet.**
Jyoti Prakesh Mitter.   Bombay, India; New York: Allied Publications, 1964. 192p. map. bibliog.

An attack on the policy of appeasement which Nehru adopted towards China forms the theme of this book. The author argues that no policy which allows China to be paramount in Tibet will ever be in the interest of India. India should recognize Tibet as an independent country and adopt a more realistic foreign policy to counter the military threat posed by Chinese activities in Tibet.

214 The revolt in Tibet.
Francis Robert Moraes. New York: Macmillan, 1960. 223p.

In this strongly anti-communist account of the 1959 uprising, Moraes argues that the Tibetan tragedy shows that there can be neither compromise nor co-existence with communism and that communist promises are not to be believed.

215 The tragedy of Tibet.
Eva M. Neterowicz. Washington, DC: Council for Social and Economic Studies, 1989. 96p. maps. (*Journal of Social, Political and Economic Studies*, Monograph series, vol. 19).

This is an unashamedly polemical account of Tibet's history since the Communist invasion. Its aim is to warn those who may still believe that the Chinese may be becoming more lenient in their plans for domination of Tibet. What is here chronicled, with ample documentation, is nothing less than the attempt to destroy an entire civilization and society through persecution, physical destruction and increasing Chinese migration to and settlement in Tibet. It is a book which, especially in the light of recent events, makes sobering reading.

216 The 1959 Tibetan rebellion: an interpretation.
Dawa Norbu. *China Quarterly*, no. 77 (March 1979), p. 74–93.

This scholarly article analyses Chinese policies in Tibet during the years 1951–59 and tries to establish the causes of the 1959 revolt. Norbu concludes that the fundamental cause of the revolt was the clash between two diametrically opposed value systems and that conflict was inevitable as soon as the Chinese started to interfere with the religious and social structures in Tibet.

217 Red star over Tibet.
Dawa Norbu. New Delhi: Sterling, 1987. 2nd ed. 303p.

First published in 1974, this study describes conditions in Tibet during the 1960s. The author uses the experiences of his own family to explore Tibetan reactions to the old and the new society and to the changes introduced by the Chinese. Unlike many other accounts of this period which deal primarily with what happened in and around Lhasa, this book is firmly focused on rural Tibet and how the changes affected the world of the average poor peasant. Dawa Norbu's condemnation of the Chinese tyranny in Tibet is all the more effective because he is willing to give them credit for some of the reforms they introduced. The second edition contains some additional material, primarily on the cultural destruction wrought during the worst years of the ultra-leftist Cultural Revolution in 1966–68.

218 Warriors of Tibet: the story of Aten and the Khampas' fight for the freedom of their country.
Jamyang Norbu. London: Wisdom, 1986. 152p. (First published Dharamsala, India: Information Office, Central Tibetan Secretariat, 1979).

Aten, a Khampa warrior, recounts the history of his people and their fighting spirit and describes his life in the old Tibet before the Chinese invasion. He gives a first-hand account of the occupation and its effects on his family and his people, and describes his involvement in the guerrilla resistance movement in the period immediately following the invasion. Eventually he was forced to flee to India in 1960.

219 Tibet is my country.
Thubten Jigme Norbu, as told to Heinrich Harrer, translated from the German by Edward Fitzgerald. London: Rupert Hart-Davis, 1960. 264p. map.

The author was born in 1922 and is the oldest brother of the Dalai Lama. His autobiography tells of his early life as a novice, his move to Lhasa after his brother was recognized as Dalai Lama and his time as Abbot of the important monastery of Kumbum. His life story during these years in some respects mirrors that of the country as a whole, moving from a period of stability to one of increasing hopelessness in the face of Chinese pressure, and in 1959 he was one of those who fled to India with the Dalai Lama. The book contains some remarkable colour photographs of the 'old' Tibet.

220 Panchen Erdeni: Vice-Chairman of the Standing Committee of the Fifth National People's Congress.
Issues and Studies, vol. 17, no. 4 (April 1981), p. 78–84.

A brief factual biography of the 10th Panchen Lama who was born in 1938, installed in 1949 by the Chinese National government and died in 1989. Always a controversial figure who was accused by some of collaborating with the communists, he had a delicate balancing act to perform to gain the best deal he could for his people without alienating the Chinese authorities. Even so, it is worth remembering that he was purged and out of favour from 1964 to 1978. The emphasis in this article is on his earlier career in the 1950s and 1960s.

221 Requiem for Tibet.
George N. Patterson. London: Aurum Press, 1990. 234p. map.

This new book by George Patterson represents an updating of his earlier history *Tibet in revolt* (q.v.) and contains a certain amount of new material. His account of Tibet in the 1950s, the 1959 revolt and the subsequent flight of the Dalai Lama to India gains in immediacy and emotional power from the fact that he was an eye-witness and participant in many of the events he describes.

222 Tibet in revolt.
George N. Patterson. London: Faber and Faber, 1960. 197p. map.

This book provides a straightforward narrative history of events in Tibet between the 'peaceful liberation' of 1951 and the popular uprising in 1959, closing with the flight of the Dalai Lama to India. Patterson is particularly good on the internal divisions within Tibet which helped make the country such an easy prey for the Chinese. He also shows that many of the more progressive forces in Tibet initially welcomed some of the reforms introduced by the Chinese, but swiftly became disillusioned when the real nature of Chinese rule was revealed.

223 **Cavaliers of Kham: the secret war in Tibet.**
Michel Peissel. London: Heinemann, 1972. 258p. maps. bibliog.
Provides an account of the Chinese invasion of Tibet and the guerrilla war in the province of Kham which followed. The author travelled through the Nepalese province of Mustang where many of the guerrilla groups were based and gives a first-hand description of their camps and organization.

224 **Inside story of Tibet.**
Ratne Deshapriya Senanayake. Colombo, Sri Lanka: Afro-Asian Writers' Bureau, 1967. 164p.
The tone of this pamphlet exemplifies the trap that left-wing intellectuals in the Third World, and indeed elsewhere, were liable to fall into when considering the question of Tibet: so keen were they to condemn Western imperialism that they failed to recognize that the Chinese could be held guilty of the same crime. To state that 'the U.S. imperialists and Indian reactionaries instigated the upper strata reactionary clique of Tibet to stage an armed rebellion in March 1959 . . . the rebellion was suppressed by the people of Tibet with the assistance of the People's Liberation Army' indicates that Senanayake shared this peculiar blindness, and his work is now of interest only as a period piece.

225 **Tibetan interviews.**
Anna Louise Strong. Peking: New World Press, 1959. 209p.
The author was in Peking during the first half of 1959, and this account of Tibet's progress from 1951 to 1959 and of the 1959 uprising is based on interviews she held with both Tibetans and Chinese in the capital. The interviewees included the Panchen Lama, Ngapo Ngawang-Jigme, and some of the runaway serfs who had studied in Peking and were planning to return to Tibet to assist in the process of reform. The abolition of serfdom and the manorial rights of the monasteries are commended and examples of torture and injustice inflicted by the nobility and the monasteries are given to justify the actions of the Chinese.

226 **When serfs stood up in Tibet: report.**
Anna Louise Strong. Peking: New World Press, 1960. 325p. map.
The author was one of the first foreigners to visit Tibet after the 1959 uprising. She presents an optimistic account of the effects of the reform movement, with emphasis on the abolition of serfdom and the curbing of the powers of the monasteries. Gruesome details of the exploitation of the feudal authorities are given and there are accounts of meetings at which lamas were accused by their former serfs and forced to confess to their crimes.

227 **Freedom in exile: the autobiography of His Holiness the Dalai Lama of Tibet.**
Tenzin Gyatso, Fourteenth Dalai Lama. London: Hodder & Stoughton, 1990. 272p.
This new autobiography of the Dalai Lama is characterized by the same combination of wisdom and good humour that is found in his other writings. He describes both his early life before the Chinese invasion of Tibet and his life in India, following his flight in 1959, during which time he has rebuilt the Tibetan community abroad and promoted

world peace through a policy of non-violence. Readers interested in the recent political history of Tibet and in the mysteries of Tibetan Buddhism will find much of value in this important book whose inspirational theme is the triumph of hope over despair.

228 **The silent war in Tibet.**
Lowell Jackson Thomas.   London: Secker & Warburg, 1960. 284p. map.
Thomas gives an anti-communist account of the Chinese invasion of 1959 which is preceded by a description of the 'old' Tibet visited in 1949 by the author with his father.

229 **Tibet and the Chinese People's Republic: a report to the International Commission of Jurists by its Legal Inquiry Committee on Tibet.**
Geneva, Switzerland: International Commission of Jurists, 1960. 345p.
This is an important and often-quoted report by a specially constituted committee whose brief was to examine the charges made against the Chinese of genocide and the intention of destroying Buddhism in Tibet in the years following 1951. The committee also examined the legal status of Tibet. Overall their findings and conclusions constitute a detailed condemnation of Chinese rule in Tibet even before the excesses of the Cultural Revolution, whilst on the question of Tibet's status in international law they concluded that Tibet was 'at the very least a *de facto* independent state' in 1951; from this it followed that, having surrendered sovereignty in 1951, the Tibetans were entitled to reclaim it again in 1959.

230 **The Tibet revolution and the free world.**
Taipei, Taiwan: Asian Peoples' Anti-Communist League, 1959. 42p. map.
Recounts the events of 1959 and the Chinese oppression which preceded it from a strongly anti-communist viewpoint. We now know that the appeals to the free world to render physical aid to the Tibetans and to the United Nations to implement sanctions against China were to go unanswered.

231 **Tibet under Chinese Communist rule: a compilation of refugee statements 1958–1975.**
Dharamsala, India: Information & Publicity Office of His Holiness the Dalai Lama, 1976. 207p. map.
Contains the statements of twenty-seven refugees from Chinese-controlled Tibet. As is to be expected, they are far from complimentary about the benefits of Chinese rule, the general impression given being one of economic, social and political oppression and the exploitation of all levels of Tibetan society by the authorities.

232 **T'ien Pao: Chairman of the People's Government of the Tibetan Autonomous Region.**
Issues and Studies, vol. 15, no. 12 (Dec. 1979), p. 99–105.
T'ien Pao was the first minorities cadre to hold the highest post in the provincial hierarchy, being appointed in 1979. He was born in 1917 and joined the Communist Party in 1936, thereafter climbing his way up the political ladder and managing to

weather the storm of the Cultural Revolution relatively unscathed. This article gives a brief factual biography of his career to 1979.

233 **The real Tibet.**
 Susan Warren. New York: Far East Reporter, 1960. 32p.

This is an interesting period piece which follows the Chinese point of view on Tibet. With the defeat of the reactionary forces in Tibet, the author believes that only now are the Tibetan people in a position to shake off the shackles of feudalism and achieve both democracy and socialism. Ironically, she views the Chinese 'liberation' as being equivalent to the national liberation and anti-colonial movements in Africa and the rest of Asia and she compares the Dalai Lama to Cardinal Mindszenty – a highly exploited symbol behind which lie the forces of clerical reaction.

Population

234 **The 1982 population census of China: major figures.**
Compiled by the Population Census Office under the State Council, the
Department of Population Statistics of the State Statistical Bureau.
Hong Kong: Economic Information and Agency, 1982. 64p.
Includes the latest population census figures for Tibet and also gives the results for the
1953 and 1964 censuses. Most of the tables give figures for the Tibet Autonomous
Region and Table 9 is particularly useful in breaking down the population figures by
nationality. It should be noted that many of the statistics produced by the People's
Republic of China have been disputed by Tibetans abroad, but most impartial
observers have accepted the 1982 census as being generally accurate.

235 **Tibetans: a dwindling population: a comparative study.**
Jan Andersson. *Tibetan Review*, vol. 16, no. 10 (Oct. 1981), p. 6–13.
Tibet's population trends from the earliest times are reviewed in this article.
Andersson argues that the figures are often so speculative and so wide-ranging that
much of the investigation into Tibetan demography has to be largely guesswork.
However, the general conclusion can be drawn that there has been a decline in Tibet's
population, but that this is the result of natural rather than social or political causes as
some Chinese authorities assert.

236 **Changing population characteristics in Tibet, 1959–1965.**
Michael Freeberne. *Population Studies*, vol. 19, no. 3 (March 1966),
p. 317–20.
Discusses the various officially produced figures on Tibet's population from 1953
through to 1965. These showed a decline in population during the period 1953–59
followed by a modest increase during 1959–65. The Chinese explanation for this
increase was the improved living standards and health-care facilities introduced
following the abolition of serfdom (which was itself blamed for the previous fall in
population). The author notes that none of the statistics include the number of Chinese

resident in Tibet and speculates that this figure might be anywhere between 60,000 and 300,000.

237 New perspectives on Tibetan fertility and population decline.
Melvyn C. Goldstein. *American Ethnologist*, vol. 8 no. 4 (Nov. 1981), p. 721–38. bibliog.

This paper challenges the belief that Tibet's population decline since the 7th century AD was caused by a decline in fertility rates, themselves the result of social and psychological factors. Instead Professor Goldstein argues that fertility levels were sufficiently high to produce population growth but were counteracted by high mortality.

238 A note on Tibet's population.
Leo A. Orleans. *China Quarterly*, no. 27 (July/Sept. 1966), p. 120–2.

This short note discusses the unreliability of the Chinese population figures for Tibet and the reasons for this: 'statistics must serve the state' and thus the figures themselves are secondary to the main purpose of demonstrating social and economic progress in the region.

239 The population atlas of China.
Compiled and edited by the Population Census Office of the State Council of the People's Republic of China and the Institute of Geography of the Chinese Academy of Science. Hong Kong: Oxford University Press, 1987. 216p. maps.

Although covering the whole of the People's Republic, this atlas is very useful for obtaining information specifically on Tibet. Based on the 1982 census figures, it provides data on population distribution, ethnicity, sex and age structure of the population, demographic changes and trends, employment, education and family structure.

240 Growth of China's minority population.
Zhang Tianlu. *Beijing Review*, vol. 27, no. 25 (18 June 1984), p. 22–6.

Based on the official figures given in the national census results for 1953, 1964 and 1982, this article analyses the development of the national minority populations, including the Tibetans, and discusses their geographical locations, age structure and educational attainment. It is worth remembering that some, if not all, Chinese statistics are disputed outside China.

241 Tibet's population develops.
Zhang Tianlu. *Beijing Review*, vol. 30, no. 33 (17 Aug. 1987), p. 20–3.

This short article gives recent figures for population growth and age structure, and also contains some information on the development of the health service, on education and on employment. Amongst other trends, these statistics show that the median age of Tibetans is as low as 20.5 years and that employment in the service industries expanded rapidly during the years 1982–85.

Extraterritorial population

242 In exile from the land of snows.
John F. Avedon. New York: Knopf, 1984. 383p.

Based on a series of interviews, this highly readable book tells the story of the 1959 uprising and the subsequent mass exile of Tibetans in India through the experiences of certain individuals: a young man involved in politics, a guerrilla fighter, who was trained by the CIA, the State Oracle, a doctor who practises traditional Tibetan medicine, and the Dalai Lama.

243 Traditional Tibetan organization in the Himalayas and the problem of integration.
Bharpur Singh Brar. *Guru Nanak Journal of Sociology*, vol. 1, nos 1–2 (April/Oct. 1980), p. 63–6.

An article which describes some of the cultural and social differences between Tibetan and Indian communities which have hindered integration between the Tibetan refugee communities and their Indian neighbours.

244 The Tibetan community in exile.
John S. Conway. *Pacific Affairs*, vol. 48, no. 1 (1975), p. 74–86.

This short survey of the first fifteen years of the Tibetan refugee communities in India emphasizes the role played by foreign aid organizations in assisting the Tibetans to adapt to their new environment.

245 The lama and the jumbo-jet: report on a Tibetan meditation group in Switzerland.
Claes Corlin. *Ethnos*, vol. 42, nos 3–4 (1977), p. 149–55.

Reports on a group of Tibetan refugees in Switzerland who belong to the Nyingma order of Tibetan Buddhism. This group constitutes a minority within the Tibetan people settled in Switzerland, and they have attempted to maintain their traditions by performing traditional rituals, mostly led by lamas from abroad – hence the reference to the jumbo jet in the title.

246 Ten years in exile: an appraisal of the resettlement of Tibetan refugees in India.
C. R. L. Gooch. *Community Development Journal*, vol. 4, no. 4 (Oct. 1969), p. 198–203.

Presents a brief summary of the experiences of the Tibetan refugee communities in India during the years 1959–69. Gooch concludes that about 15,000 Tibetans became permanently resettled during that period whilst a further 12,000 were in process of becoming self-supporting. Many of the refugees had learnt new skills and successfully adapted to life in India, but the Tibetans generally had maintained their separate identity and their traditional culture and this had led in some instances to friction with the local Indian community.

247 **The presence of Tibet.**
Lois Lang-Sims. London: Cresset Press, 1963. 241p.
This early account of life in the first Tibetan refugee camps in northern India is interesting in illustrating a sympathetic Westerner's response to the plight of the Tibetans after 1959. Her fear that the Dalai Lama might prove susceptible to communism and become a collaborationist can now be seen to be wholly unfounded.

248 **Tibetans in Bhutan: problem of repatriation.**
R. C. Misra. *China Report*, vol. 18, no. 5 (1982), p. 25–32.
In 1959, 4000 Tibetan refugees settled in Bhutan, but in 1979 they were asked to leave by the Bhutanese government which cited the Tibetans' maintenance of their own communities and refusal to change their nationality as the main reasons for the change of policy.

249 **Tibetan foothold.**
Dervla Murphy. London: John Murray, 1966. map.
Dervla Murphy is well known as a travel writer whose wanderings have now taken her to many of the world's remoter areas. This book is one of her earlier works and describes her experiences in the Tibetan refugee camps of northern India which were then still fairly new.

250 **Tibetan refugees: youth and the new generation of meaning.**
Margaret Nowak. New Brunswick, New Jersey: Rutgers University Press, 1984. 200p. map. bibliog.
Looks at youth today in the Tibetan refugee communities in India and attempts to define the cultural symbols which act as dynamic forces in their lives. Three such symbols are given particular emphasis: the figure of the Dalai Lama, the concept of Tibetan independence and 're-enactment' or the dramatized scenario of 10 March as an annual commemoration of the Tibetan uprising of 1959. The author examines how these symbols are being transmitted to the new generation by integrating the old values with modern studies and analyses the cultural problems and conflicts that confront young Tibetans being brought up in a very different environment from their parents. She also describes the various Tibetan organizations in India and shows how they all fall under the pre-eminence of the government-in-exile in Dharamsala.

251 **Tibetans in migration.**
B. C. Olschak. *International Migration*, vol. 5 (1967), p. 187–95.
Describes the experiences of around 600 Tibetans who, after 1959, migrated to Switzerland with some of the children being housed in the Pestalozzi village at Trogen. Switzerland seemed to be a suitable country for them to move to as its environment is similar to that of Tibet and, after seven years, the author maintains that the Tibetans have integrated into their new environment whilst at the same time remaining attached to their own traditions and beliefs.

252 **Tibetans in India: a case study of Mundgod Tibetans.**
T. C. Palakshappa. New Delhi: Sterling, 1978. 119p. map. bibliog.
Obtained by field observations and survey data collection techniques, this is an account of what is happening in one of the Tibetan refugee settlements in India. The author shows that although the Tibetan community has retained its cultural and religious identity, there have been changes as well, especially in the area of education. The younger generation has become more mobile, both geographically and occupationally, and is more receptive to new ideas. There has also been a gradual process of absorption into Indian society and it is now for the new generation to lay the foundations for the long-term future of the Tibetan communities in India on a different base from before.

253 **Refugee problems in Vietnam, India, and Hong Kong, British Colony.**
Washington, DC: U.S. Government Printing Office, 1966. 36p. (House report 1769, 89th Congress, 2nd session; Congressional Serial Set vol. 12715–2).
Although this Congressional report is primarily concerned with the problems of Vietnamese refugees, it does include a short report on the American aid programme to the Tibetan refugee communities in India. This programme supported projects which provided food, housing, medical care, technical training and agricultural assistance to the refugees, and by 1965 the US government had allocated $1.4 million for them.

254 **The uprooted Tibetans in India: a sociological study of continuity and change.**
Girija Saklani. New Delhi: Cosmo, 1984. 452p. maps. bibliog.
In this investigation of the problems of adaptation and adjustment faced by the Tibetan communities in India, Saklani finds that, despite a conscious effort to preserve the institutions, values and attitudes of the past, there have been many changes. Young people in particular have challenged many of the traditional structures of Tibetan society and there have been significant shifts in both the class and the family structure of the Tibetan communities, with much greater emphasis on individual achievement. Perhaps most significant of all, there is now a separation between the sacred and the secular spheres, something which would have been inconceivable in the old Tibet.

255 **Tibetan Homes Foundation report 1966–67.**
Mussorie, India: Hyratt Press, 1967. 18p.
The Tibetan Homes were founded in 1962 to care for the large number of Tibetan orphan children in India, and to ensure that they were not only brought up in a secure, healthy environment, but also were taught the Tibetan religion, culture and way of life. This report gives some idea of the work of these Homes.

256 **Tibetans in exile, 1959–1980.**
Dharamsala, India: Information Office of His Holiness the Dalai Lama, 1981. 306p. map.
Gives a detailed account of the Tibetan communities in India, Nepal and Bhutan. The emphasis is on the development of the Tibetan administration-in-exile but there are also sections dealing with education, industry and handicrafts and the establishment of

cultural and medical institutions. The general work of settlement and rehabilitation is also covered.

257 **Girl from Tibet.**
Tseten Dolkar, as told to John Windsor.   Chicago, Illinois: Loyola University Press, 1971. 164p.
This autobiography of a young Tibetan girl who was brought up in Lhasa but later lived in Kalimpong, Sikkim, and then went as a student to the United States is a straightforward and sometimes moving account of one Tibetan's experience of adjusting to life in the outside world. The earlier part of the book is interesting in suggesting that the Chinese occupation in 1951 was generally orderly and faced little opposition other than in the province of Kham.

Women

258 **Women of wisdom.**
Tsultrim Allione.   London; Boston, Massachusetts: Routledge & Kegan Paul, 1984. 282p. bibliog.
There are very few traditional Tibetan stories concerning women. This volume presents a translation of the biographies of six female mystics, the earliest of whom lived in the 11th century and the most recent in the mid-twentieth century. The individual biographies are preceded by a survey of the role of women in Tibetan society.

259 **Place of women in Tibetan society.**
A. V. Arakeri, K. G. Gurumurthy.   *Journal of the Karnatak University: Social Sciences*, vol. 15 (1979), p. 75–87. bibliog.
An interesting survey of the status of women in traditional Tibetan society which concludes that, although women had a lower status than men, there were a number of factors peculiar to Tibet – under-population, economic scarcity and polyandry – which made the position of women better than in India or China and in practice brought them an equal socio-economic position in society.

260 **Sky dancer: the secret life and songs of the Lady Yeshe Tsogyel.**
Keith Dowman.   London: Routledge & Kegan Paul, 1984. 379p. bibliog.
A translation of a text originally written in the 9th century and rediscovered in the 17th century which describes the spiritual practice and evolution of the famous woman saint Yeshe Tsogyel who was the consort of Padma Sambhava. It is of particular interest in being one of the few Tibetan texts that deal with woman on the tantric path or indeed mentions women at all. The commentary by the author elucidates the historical and religious background and women's place in the tradition.

261 **Tibetan women, then and now: a faithful and vivid account of the status and role of Tibetan women who lived in ancient Tibet as well as those who are living today in and outside Tibet.**
Indra Majupuria. Gwalior, India: M. Devi, 1990. 279p. maps. bibliog.
This is an important and pioneering study, based on extensive research and fieldwork of the cultural, economic and social conditions of women at all levels of society, both inside Tibet itself and amongst the Tibetan communities abroad. Topics covered include the role of women in religion, dresses, ornaments and jewellery, marriage both traditional and modern, divorce, rape, prostitution, family planning, the participation of women in the political process, and their role in the country's economy. Short biographies of thirty prominent Tibetan women, both past and present, are also provided. The book is profusely illustrated, both in colour and in black and white.

262 **Women and Tibet.**
Tibet Journal. Special issue, vol. 12, no. 4 (Winter 1987), 104p. bibliog.
The articles in this useful compilation address not just the role of women in Tibet but also the wider questions regarding Tibetan ideas about women, the female and the feminine. Barabara Aziz's study of the social world of women in Tibet, which details Tibetan women's work in a modern hotel in Lhasa, thus both complements and forms a contrast with articles on the female yogi Yeshe Tsogyel and on nuns and nunneries in Tibet.

Anthropology and Ethnology

263 **Tibetan frontier families: recollections of three generations from Ding-ri.**
Barabara Nimri Aziz.   Durham, North Carolina: Carolina Academic
Press, 1978. 292p. maps. bibliog.
Based on interviews, this study presents a portrait of the lives of three generations of
Tibetans, covering the period 1885–1960, in Ding-ri on the Tibet–Nepal border. The
picture which emerges is not of a static feudal society but of a socially mobile
prospering community with its fair share of opportunists and vagabonds. The author
stresses the secular rather than the religious forces which influenced the community
and discusses the patterns of kinship and marriage, the social structure of the village
community and the various forms of social organization to be found there.

264 **Anthropologie Tibétaine.** (Tibetan anthropology.)
E. C. Buchi, A. Guibaut, G. Olivier.   Paris: École française
d'extrême-orient, 1965. 164p. bibliog. (Publications hors-série de
l'École française d'extrême-orient).
Contains two papers, 'Anthropologie des Tibétains' by G. Buchi and 'Anthropologie
des Tibétains orientaux' by A. Guibaut and G. Olivier. Both are based on extensive
field-work and conclude that the Tibetans are to be classed within the Mongoloid
population group and are closest to the north Chinese. Eastern Tibetans generally
differ from those in the rest of Tibet by being taller and having a darker skin and a
greater robustness.

265 **Customs and superstitions of Tibetans.**
Marion H. Duncan.   London: Mitre Press, 1964. 265p.
A fascinating anthology of people's beliefs and the rituals which marked the stages of
their lives: birth, marriage, religious festivals and death. The role of animals and birds
in Tibetan life and beliefs is also recounted, as is the general structure of traditional
law and government. Duncan lived for many years on the eastern border of Tibet and
this book is the result of his observations of the people he lived amongst.

266 **Fields on the hoof: nexus of Tibetan nomadic pastoralism.**
Robert B. Ekvall. New York: Holt, Rinehart & Winston, 1968. 100p.
map. bibliog. (Case Studies in Cultural Anthropology).

The author lived for eight years with the nomadic pastoralists and this is an authentic survey of the society and culture of the aBrog Pa as they were in the period before 1950. This culture represented a complex interweaving of many different factors, many of them special to a high-altitude environment.

267 **Peace and war among the Tibetan nomads.**
Robert B. Ekvall. *American Anthropologist*, vol. 66, no. 5 (Oct. 1966), p. 1119–48. bibliog.

Based largely on Ekvall's observations during the eight years he spent amongst the nomadic pastoralists, this article examines the causes of wars, the nomadic pattern of life as a training for war, weapons and weapon taboos, military tactics, and the role of mediators and the peacemaking process.

268 **Some aspects of divination in Tibetan society.**
Robert B. Ekvall. *Ethnology*, vol. 2, no. 1 (Jan. 1963), p. 31–9. bibliog.

Divination is deeply rooted in Tibetan society and its occurrence is ubiquitous in Tibetan behaviour patterns. It forms part of the pre-Buddhist culture of Tibet, but has also achieved a certain legitimacy within Buddhist theory and practice. In this article Ekvall shows that divination is both mechanical (as in the throwing of dice) and subjective (as in prophecy) and that the diviners employ quasi-magical techniques but also act as individual repositories of information which can be collated and then reformed in giving answers and guidance.

269 **Tibetan nomadic pastoralists: environments, personality and ethos.**
Robert B. Ekvall. *Proceedings of the American Philosophical Society*, vol. 118, no. 6 (Dec. 1974), p. 519–37.

In this article Ekvall describes both the physical environment and the values and beliefs of the high-altitude nomadic pastoralists. As is the case with many groups of nomads who inhabit a harsh environment they tend to look down on the settled farmers who inhabit the more fertile valleys; courage, hospitality and freedom are the qualities that are most highly prized.

270 **Toward a people's anthropology.**
Fei Hsiao Tung. Beijing: New World Press, 1981. 121p. map. (China Studies Series).

A collection of essays by a leading Chinese social anthropologist. The essay 'Ethnic identification in China' deals with the composition of China's family of nations, their differentiation and identification. 'Modernization and national minorities in China' analyses the socio-economic and cultural gap between the Hans and the other nationalities, including Tibetans, of a rapidly industrializing China.

271 **Himalayan anthropology: the Indo-Tibetan interface.**
Edited by James B. Fisher.   The Hague: Mouton, 1978. 567p.
bibliogs. (World Anthropology).
Many of the papers in this volume were originally submitted to the IXth International
Congress of Anthropological and Ethnological Sciences held in Chicago in 1973. Under
the general theme of the Indo-Tibetan interface the contributors examine topics such
as Tibetan oracles, Bon rituals and resource competition amongst the Tibetan refugees
in south India.

272 **Nomads of western Tibet: the survival of a way of life.**
Melvyn C. Goldstein, Cynthia M. Beall.   London: Serindia, 1990.
192p.
Melvyn Goldstein and Cynthia Beall spent 16 months living on the remote Changtang
Plateau amongst the nomadic pastoralists, and the result is this superbly illustrated
book. In the text they give a detailed and fascinating account of all aspects of the
nomads' life-style and describe how their entire culture was threatened with total
extinction during the period of the Cultural Revolution. The economic reforms of the
1980s have resulted in the re-establishment of much of the old culture and the return of
the nomads to their old ways, but, as the authors make clear, this is still a society
which is struggling for cultural survival.

273 **Use of human skulls and bones in Tibet.**
Berthold Laufer.   Chicago, Illinois: Field Museum of Natural History,
1923. 24p. bibliog. (Field Museum of Natural History leaflet no. 10).
Human skulls and other bones have been traditionally used in Tibet both for practical
purposes and for religious ceremonies. There are, for example, richly ornamented
drinking bowls made out of skulls and musical instruments such as trumpets made out
of human thigh bones. Laufer describes these and other examples, and relates the
custom of using human bones for these purposes in Tibet to similar customs of other
ancient societies such as the Scythians.

274 **The dynamics of polyandry: kinship, domesticity and population on the
Tibetan border.**
Nancy E. Levine.   Chicago, Illinois: University of Chicago Press,
1988. 309p. bibliog.
Polyandry has always played an important role in Tibetan society. This book presents a
systematic account of fraternal polyandry amongst the Nyinba, an ethnically Tibetan
group living in Nepal. Unlike some other writers on the subject, Professor Levine
argues that polyandry cannot be explained solely by economic or demographic reasons.
Beliefs about kinship, heredity and social obligation also play a part. Thus polyandry,
as well as affecting personal relationships, forms an integral part of the complex
economic, social and political structure of the community, and assists in perpetuating a
social order that divides the community into two groups, the landholders and their
former serfs.

275 **Das tibetische Staatsorakel.** (The Tibetan state oracle.)
René de Nebesky-Wojkowitz. *Archiv für Völkerkunde*, III Bd. (1948),
p. 136–55. bibliog.
Describes the role of prophecy in Tibetan society, some of the leading oracles of the
country, including the Lhasa oracle, and the ceremonies associated with them.

276 **A study of polyandry.**
Prince Peter of Greece and Denmark. The Hague: Mouton, 1963.
601p. maps. bibliog.
Included in this general anthropological account of polyandry are detailed descriptions,
based on extensive fieldwork, of the polyandry of both Tibet proper and western Tibet
(Ladakh). Prince Peter found that demographic, economic, sociological and personal
factors all played a part in the emergence of polyandry, but that, in Tibet at least, it
was the economic factors – the prevention of the division of property for example –
that were the most important.

277 **Phallic symbols in Tibet.**
Hugh E. Richardson. *Bulletin of Tibetology* vol. 9, no. 2 (July 1972),
p. 25–7.
Phallic symbols in Tibet are not connected with a religious cult as in India, but are
magical 'navel stones' or 'earth pegs' which were erected to ward off evil from their
vicinity. Hugh Richardson also suggests that the strange wooden figures, nine feet tall
and usually in pairs, which are also to be found in Tibet are manifestations of the same
kind.

278 **Old age in the Tibetan context.**
Elliot Sperling. *Saeculum* vol. 30 no. 4 (1979), p. 434–42.
Demonstrates that the idea of age producing wisdom has few roots in Tibetan
civilization. Tibetan Buddhism sees old age as just one segment of a much longer cycle
of births and rebirths, and although old people are treated with respect they receive no
special treatment.

Language

Dictionaries

279 New English–Tibetan dictionary.
Norbu Chophel. Dharamsala, India: Tibetan Library, 1985. 206p.
This basic dictionary, intended primarily for use by Tibetans, contains a vocabulary of about 8000 words, with brief definitions of each.

280 A dictionary of Tibetan and English.
Alexander Csoma de Kőrös, assisted by Songs-Rgyas Phun-Tshogs.
New Delhi: Cosmo, 1978. 351p.
This is a reprint of the original 1834 edition of the first dictionary of Tibetan and English, compiled by the Hungarian scholar and explorer Alexander Csoma de Kőrös, which has since become a classic. It contains entries from Tibetan to English only.

281 Tibetan–English dictionary of modern Tibetan.
Melvyn C. Goldstein. Kathmandu: Ratna Pustak Bhander, 1983.
3rd ed. 1234p. (Bibliotheca Himalayica. Series 2, vol. 7).
This extensive dictionary contains between 35,000 and 40,000 entries and is compiled mainly from textual materials rather from than other dictionaries.

282 Tibetan–English dictionary of Buddhist terminology.
Tsepak Rigzin. Dharamsala, India: Library of Tibetan Works and Archives, 1986. 479p. bibliog.
Four hundred main entries and over 6000 sub-entries are included in this dictionary. The English definitions are largely derived from the pattern of oral translation evolved in the Buddhist philosophy classes held at the Library of Tibetan Works and Archives.

Grammars and phrasebooks

283 **Textbook of colloquial Tibetan language.**
Sherab Gyaltsen Amipa. Zurich, Switzerland: The author, 1974. 97p.
Designed for the English-speaking student, this textbook contains an introductory
grammar, but consists mainly of useful phrases in English and Tibetan.

284 **Tibetan phrasebook** (with two 90-minute audio cassette tapes).
Andrew Bloomfield, Yanki Tshering. Ithaca, New York: Snow Lion,
1987. 144p.
This very useful teaching aid provides an introduction to the phonetic system of
Tibetan and a simple grammar. As well as containing phrases and dialogues, each
chapter is preceded by a vocabulary and useful information on Tibetan customs.
Appendices give information on dates, days and time and there is a specialized
religious and monastic vocabulary as well as a general vocabulary.

285 **Say it in Tibetan: conversation in colloquial Tibetan** (with audio cassette
tape).
Norbu Chophel. Dharamsala, India: The author, 1989. 129p.
The layout of this introduction to Tibetan, specifically designed for tourists, is
reminiscent of that found in the Berlitz guides, with conversations grouped according
to subject: 'Shopping', 'Travel directions' and 'Visiting a dentist' are typical examples.

286 **An introduction to the grammar of the Tibetan language.**
Sarat Chandra Das. Delhi: Motilal Banarsidass, 1983. [various
pagings].
First published in 1915, this extensive grammar is designed to help both the general
reader in understanding the grammatical structure of Tibetan and also the Buddhist
scholar seeking access to the original texts. The principal grammatical rules are
presented in a logical if somewhat daunting fashion.

287 **Modern spoken Tibetan: Lhasa dialect.**
Melvyn C. Goldstein, Nawang Nornang. Kathmandu: Ratna Pustak
Bhander, 1984. 3rd ed. 409p. (Bibliotheca Himalayica. Series 2,
vol. 14).
This manual was prepared for use in an introductory course to the Lhasa dialect (used
by government officials and generally understood by all Tibetans). It contains three
parts: the first consists of twenty lessons which comprise the basic patterns of spoken
Tibetan and a working vocabulary of around 700 words; the second consists of a
selection of folk tales and conversations; and the third has Tibetan–English and
English–Tibetan glossaries, both of which give the written Tibetan forms, and various
lists of, for example, the numbers and days of the month.

288 **Tibetan for beginners and travellers.**
Melvyn C. Goldstein. Kathmandu: Ratna Pustak Bhander, 1982. 62p.
This short work provides a simple introduction, suitable for the first-time traveller,
which does not use Tibetan written forms.

289   A grammar of the Tibetan language, literary and colloquial.
    Herbert Bruce Hannah.   Delhi: Motilal Banarsidass, 1985. 399p.
This grammar was originally published in 1912. It covers both literary and colloquial
Tibetan, using the Lhasa dialect in the latter case.

290   Tibetan language: three study tools.
    Nawang Thondup Narkyid.   Dharamsala, India: Library of Tibetan
    Works and Archives, 1974. 327p.
A practical guide which aims to provide understanding of the essentials of Tibetan
writing, spelling and pronunciation.

291   Textbook of colloquial Tibetan: dialect of central Tibet.
    George N. Roerich, Lobsang Phuntshok Lhalungpa.   New Delhi:
    Manjusri Publishing House, 1972. 280p. bibliog. (Bibliotheca
    Himalayica. Series 2, vol. 3).
This textbook comprises three parts: grammar, conversational exercises and
vocabulary. The conversational exercises are given both in transcription and in the
Tibetan script, and similarly the vocabulary gives both the modern pronunciation and
the literary form. There is a helpful list of useful phrases and Tibetan proverbs, and a
record is available as a study aid either separately or with the book.

292   Tibetan newspaper reader.
    Kamil Sedlacek.   Leipzig, Germany: Veb Verlag Enzyklopädie, 1972.
    2 vols.
These volumes are intended for the student who has completed a basic course of
spoken or literary Tibetan and has a good idea of the structure of the language, but
beginners might find them useful too. Volume 1 contains a selection of sixty-three
articles from the Tibetan text of the pictorial magazine *Ren-Min Hua-Bao* (Chinese
Pictorial) which is published in Beijing for Tibetan-speaking nationals of China.
Transliterated and translated texts are provided, together with grammatical notes.
Volume 2 contains a Tibetan–English glossary of about 1500 terms and phrases
obtained from the articles in volume 1.

293   Modern Tibetan language.
    Lobsang Thonden. Dharamsala, India: Library of Tibetan Works and
    Archives, 1984–86. 2 vols.
This is a comprehensive and up-to-date textbook for teaching Tibetan through the
medium of English. A standard grammar section comes first and other features include
word-by-word translations, phonetics and complete sentence translations. The Tibetan
script is used, but also accompanied by a romanized script. The books include practical
exercises.

Phonology

294 **Tibetan phonology.**
Willa Dawson. PhD thesis, University of Washington, Seattle, 1980.
143p. bibliog. (Available from University Microfilms, Ann Arbor,
Michigan, order no. AAC 8109722).
Based on the spoken Tibetan of Lhasa, this thesis analyses some major phonological
processes which affect the vowels and tones.

295 **Aspects of the phonology of Amdo Tibetan: Ndzorge saeme xora dialect.**
Jackson T.-S. Sun. Tokyo: Institute for the Study of Languages and
Cultures of Asia and Africa, 1986. 267p. bibliog. (Monumenta
Serindica, no. 16).
Sun analyses in detail the synchronic and diachronic phonology of a Tibetan dialect
which has previously received little attention.

Tibetan script

296 **L'écriture cursive tibétaine.** (The Tibetan cursive script.)
Jacques Bacot. Paris: Imprimerie Nationale, 1912. 78p.
Describes, with many examples, the regular and ornamental scripts in common use at
the time.

297 **Origin of Tibetan writing.**
Berthold Laufer. *Journal of the American Oriental Society*, vol. 38
(1918), p. 34–46.
Western scholars in the late 19th and early 20th centuries were divided as to whether
the Tibetan script originated in India or Turkestan. In this article Laufer vigorously
attacked the idea that Khotan was the source and put the case for India very strongly;
this is the accepted theory today.

298 **The Tibetan system of writing.**
Roy Andrew Miller. Washington, DC: American Council of Learned
Societies, 1956. 30p. (American Council of Learned Societies. Program
in Oriental Languages. Publication series B, Aids no. 6).
This pamphlet provides a useful introduction to writing the Tibetan script as it operates
in present-day usage, with notes on the basic principles of spelling. Many examples,
together with an introductory text and translation, are included.

299   A short history of Tibetan script.
Ribur Ngawang Gyatso.   *Tibet Journal*, vol. 9, no. 2 (Summer 1984),
p. 28–30.

This brief introduction to the subject indicates that the unique Tibetan script dates
from the 7th century AD and was created by Thanmi Sambhota.

Religion

General

300 Religious observances in Tibet: patterns and functions.
Robert B. Ekvall.   Chicago, Illinois: Chicago University Press, 1964.
313p. bibliog.
This is an important book which examines religious practice from an anthropologica
viewpoint. Thus the religious practices of Tibet are seen as a series of behavioura
patterns which make sense in the context of the Tibetans' world view. Environmental
cultural and social factors are all taken into account in the analysis of such practices a
offering, circumambulation and divination which are all prevalent in Tibet. Althougl
primarily concerned with Buddhist practice, the book also contains a brief section o
the pre-Buddhist religions of Tibet.

301 The religions of Tibet.
Helmut Hoffmann, translated by Edward Fitzgerald.   London: George
Allen & Unwin, 1961. 199p. bibliog.
Mainly historical in character, this book emphasizes the Bon religion, the developmen
of Buddhism in India and its arrival in Tibet and the religious struggles of the 8th an
9th centuries. Later chapters describe the rise of the Lamaist sects and th
establishment of the theocratic state of the Dalai Lamas.

**302 Oracles and demons of Tibet: the cult and iconography of the Tibetan
protective deities.**
René de Nebesky-Wojkowitz.   The Hague: Mouton, 1956. 666p.
bibliog.
Based on fieldwork and a study of the relevant Tibetan texts, this is a key work for th
study of Tibet's protective deities and oracles. It includes some notes on Tibeta
shamanism and a detailed description of the methods used in divination by the oracles

303 **Tibetan religious dances: Tibetan text and annotated translation of the**
     'chams yig.
     René de Nebesky-Wojkowitz, edited by Christoph von Fürer-
     Haimendorf, appendix by Walter Graf.   The Hague: Mouton, 1976.
     319p. bibliog. map. (Religion and Society, 2).
Written before the flight of the Dalai Lama in 1959 and left uncompleted at the
author's death, this is a detailed description and analysis of Tibetan ritual dances from
the Bon period onwards, based on both textual evidence and fieldwork. Of particular
interest is the translation of the texts which include detailed choreographic instructions
for the performance of the dances. The appendix by Walter Graf is concerned with the
performance of Tibetan music and its notation.

304 **Tibet's terrifying deities: sex and aggression in religious acculturation.**
     F. Sierksma.   The Hague: Mouton, 1966. 284p. bibliog.
Sierksma's study provides a fascinating and readable analysis of Tibet's demonic gods
and goddesses. The author argues that in the time of the great kings the aggressive and
feudal cultural pattern of Tibet clashed with the pacific qualties of Buddhism. The
resulting social contrasts intensified the aggressive characteristics of which these deities
are a significant symptom. The task of the gods was to frighten away the adversaries of
Tibet and its Buddhism but they were most feared by the Tibetans themselves. The
drastic magic and mysticism associated with these fighting and copulating deities were
clearly connected with the material and social reality of Tibet. The book is finely
illustrated, partly in colour.

305 **The religions of Tibet.**
     Giuseppe Tucci, translated from the German and Italian by Geoffrey
     Samuel.   London: Routledge & Kegan Paul, 1980. 340p. bibliog.
This book was originally published in German but has been updated for the English
edition. It is a comprehensive yet readable work by one of the foremost authorities on
the subject. He describes the general history of Buddhism in Tibet, describes the
principal characteristics of Lamaism and writes about life in the monasteries, religious
festivals, the folk religion and the doctrines of the most important schools of Buddhist
thought in Tibet. A final chapter describes the earlier native Bon religion.

Bonism

306 **The treasury of good sayings: a Tibetan history of Bon.**
     Edited and translated by Samten G. Karmay.   London: Oxford
     University Press, 1972. 365p. map. (London Oriental Series. vol. 26).
A partial translation of the Tibetan text *Legs-bshad-mdzod*, a history of the Bon
religion as conceived by the Bonpos themselves. The material is arranged in roughly
chronological order, with each section dealing with a different stage in the
development of the Bon religion.

307 **The highest deities of the Tibetan Bon religion.**
B. I. Kuznetsov. *Tibet Journal*, vol. 6, no. 2 (Summer 1981),
p. 47–52.
The names of the three most important divinities of Tibetan Bonism are identified in this article which also relates them to Iranian deities.

308 **Tibet Bon religion: a death ritual of the Tibetan Bonpos.**
Per Kvaerne. Leiden, The Netherlands: E. J. Brill, 1985. 34p.
bibliog. (Iconography of Religions. Section XII. East and Central Asia.
Fascicule 13).
Provides a detailed description of one particular ritual of the Bonpos, accompanied by 48 plates. The introductory chapters place Bonism and the Bonpo death rituals in historical perspective.

309 **Die tibetische Bon-Religion.** (The Tibetan Bon religion.)
René de Nebesky-Wojkowitz. *Archiv für Völkerkunde*, II Bd. (1947),
p. 26–68. bibliog.
This important academic study by a leading Tibetologist gives a general introduction to the Bon religion, with notes on the pantheon of Bon deities, Bon doctrines and rites and the healing powers of its priests.

Buddhism

310 **Open secrets: a western guide to Tibetan Buddhism.**
Walt Anderson. New York: Viking, 1979. 230p.
Written by a non-Buddhist, this is an introductory book whose stated aim is to make Buddhism a little more intelligible to Westerners. To do this the author admits in the preface that he has 'deliberately Americanized it a bit, drawn out its similarities to themes that run through our own culture'. He sees Tibetan Buddhism less as a religion than as a psychology – a tool to help readers see the world and their own lives more clearly.

311 **A lamp for the path and Commentary.**
Atisa, translated and edited by Richard Sherburne. London: George
Allen & Unwin, 1983. 226p. bibliog.
Atisa lived in the 11th century and spent much of the latter part of his life in Tibet where he initiated many reforms in the practices of Tibetan Buddhism. *A lamp for the path* is his major work and it is in essence a guidebook for spritual endeavour. The *Commentary* provides practical explanations for further reflection and study. Some of the major themes throughout Atisa's works, as in many other Buddhist texts, are compassion, insight, emptiness and bliss.

312 **The jewel in the lotus: a guide to the Buddhist traditions of Tibet.**
Edited and with an introduction by Stephen Batchelor.   London:
Wisdom, 1987. 280p. bibliog. (A Wisdom Basic Book. Orange Series).
A useful introductory book which brings together a clear account of Tibetan Buddhism
and selections of teachings from the four major traditions that have flourished in Tibet.
Included are teachings of the present Dalai Lama, Longchen Rabjampa, Tsong-ka-pa,
and songs and stories of Milarepa, the famous Tibetan yogi and poet.

313 **Cult of Tara: magic and ritual in Tibet.**
Stephen V. Beyer.   Berkeley, California: University of California
Press, 1978. 542p. bibliog.
This is a difficult but important book which attempts to formulate the processes and
presuppositions of Buddhist ritual through the analysis of one particular cult, that of
the goddess Tara. This includes a consideration of both the philosophical basis and the
practice of the Tara tantra and a demonstration of its ramifications in monastic
ceremony, folklore, literature and magic.

314 **L'église jaune.** (The yellow church.)
Robert Bleicksteiner.   Paris: Payot, 1950. 292p. bibliog.
This work was first published in German (Vienna: Josef Belf, 1934) and, although
dated, is still useful in describing the religious practices of Tibetan Buddhism. Some
critics have rated it more highly than Waddell's classic *The Buddhism of Tibet* (q.v.).

315 **The history of Buddhism in India and Tibet.**
Bu-ston, translated from the Tibetan by E. Obermiller.   Delhi: Sri
Satguru, 1986. 231p. (Bibliotheca Indo-Buddhica, no. 26).
This is a translation of the second part of a classic Tibetan history of Buddhism. It
begins with the life of Buddha and ends in the 13th century. The section dealing with
the history of Buddhism in Tibet begins with the genealogies of the royal kings and
contains a detailed account of the spread of Buddhism, its persecution and re-
establishment, and lists all the principal teachers of Buddhism active in Tibet during
the period covered.

316 **Buddhist iconography.**
Lokesh Chandra.   New Delhi: Aditya Prakashan, 1988. 3rd rev. ed.
2 vols.
These two volumes of line drawings provide a monumental presentation of the entire
Buddhist pantheon.

317 **Atisa and Tibet: life and works of Dipamkara Srijnana in relation to the
history and religion of Tibet.**
Alaka Chattopadhyaya, with Tibetan sources translated under Lama
Chimpa.   Delhi: Motilal Banarsidass, 1981. 593p. bibliog.
An account of the life of the great Bengali pandit Atisa who lived in the 11th century
and spent the last years of his life in Tibet where he initiated many reforms in Tibetan
Buddhism. Some Tibetan source materials relating to Atisa are given in English
translation and there are also translations of some of his more important works. This

book also discusses the early history of Tibet and Indo-Tibetan contact during this period, and provides a history of Buddhism in Tibet during the 7th to the 11th centuries.

318 **Journey into vastness: a handbook of Tibetan meditation techniques.**
Ngakpa Chogyam. Shaftesbury, England: Element Books, 1988. 269p.

This book presents a practical guide to techniques of meditation and exercises that are suitable for both the beginner and the more advanced student. It is illustrated with photographs of a variety of meditation postures, calligraphies and line drawings.

319 **The rise of esoteric Buddhism in Tibet.**
Eva M. Dargyay. Delhi: Motilal Banarsidass, 1977. 272p. bibliog.

A scholarly study of the history of the 'old school' of Tibetan Buddhism, which includes biographies of some of the famous Tibetan sages.

320 **An introduction to Tantric Buddhism.**
Shahsi Bushan Dasgupta. Berkeley, California: Shambhala, 1974. 211p. bibliog.

Tantra has always played a key role in Tibetan Buddhism. This book provides a useful introduction to the different schools of tantric Buddhism and their philosophical basis, and also describes some tantric practices.

321 **The divine madman: the sublime life and songs of Drukpa Kunley.**
Translated by Keith Dowman, Sonam Paljor. London: Rider, 1980. 176p. map.

Drupka Kunley, who lived in the 16th century, is one of the most popular of the Tibetan saints and *The divine madman* is a biography in the form of an anthology of anecdotes and songs. It is a remarkable document as it combines compassion and sublime mysticism with the earthiness of the people and a total lack of inhibition; many of its passages are definitely not for the puritanical and it is no doubt this element of it which has contributed to its continuing popularity. It can be read for its revelation of a mind liberated from all preoccupations, preferences or bias, but, for the social historian, it can be equally revealing in its description of 16th-century Tibet and Bhutan.

322 **Matrix of mystery: scientific and humanistic aspects of rDzogs-chen thought.**
Herbert V. Guenther. London; Boulder, Colorado: Shambhala, 1984. 317p. bibliog.

Guenther provides a scholarly and comprehensive study of the rDzogs-chen tradition in Tibetan Buddhism which is aimed at the more advanced student. He relates Tibetan Buddhist teachings to modern scientific and humanistic perspectives and shows how traditional religious and modern secular perspectives on the nature of reality interface.

323 **Meditation on emptiness.**
Jeffrey Hopkins, assistant editor Elizabeth Napper. London:
Wisdom, 1983. 1017p. bibliog. (A Wisdom Advanced Book. Blue
Series).
The major work of Professor Hopkins, a leading Western scholar of Buddhism, this
book describes the meditational practices by which emptiness can be realized.
Translations of a number of important Buddhist texts are included and there is also a
brief survey of the history of different Buddhist schools of thought.

324 **The Tantric distinction: an introduction to Tibetan Buddhism.**
Jeffrey Hopkins, edited by Anne C. Klein. London: Wisdom, 1984.
176p. bibliog. (A Wisdom Intermediate Book. White Series).
Unlike Professor Hopkins's other works this is not primarily a translation of Buddhist
texts but a personal account of Mahayana Buddhism. He explains the function of the
guru, the concept of emptiness, meditation and the ideal of the bodhisattva, and
describes the whole Buddhist approach to life. This book is especially useful to the
student who already has some knowledge of the basics of Buddhism but wants to know
more.

325 **The history of the sixteen Karmapas of Tibet.**
Karma Thinley. Boulder, Colorado: Prajna Press, 1980. 150p.
bibliog.
The Karmapas are the spritual leaders of the Karma Kagyu sect of Tibetan Buddhism.
The present Karmapa is the sixteenth in a line which began in the 12th century.
Biographies of all sixteen are included in this book; like all traditional Tibetan
biographies they are intended not only to present the history of their lives and
teachings, but also to act as inspirational texts which can be used to cultivate devotion
in the reader. The biographies contain the customary descriptions of magical or semi-
magical powers such as divination, the ability to change the weather and healing
powers which one finds in many other works of this kind.

326 **Buddhism in the Tibetan tradition: a guide.**
Geshe Kelsang Gyatso, translated by Tenzin P. Phunrabpa, edited by
R. F. Lister, M. R. Lister. London: Routledge & Kegan Paul, 1984.
132p.
Intended as an introduction to the basic teachings of the Buddha, this book outlines
the ways in which the student can develop a 'good heart' and examines key concepts
such as reincarnation, emptiness, liberation and enlightenment.

327 **Knowledge and liberation: Tibetan Buddhist epistemology in support of
transformative religious experience.**
Anne C. Klein. Ithaca, New York: Snow Lion, 1986. 283p. bibliog.
From the beginning Buddhist philosophy has been concerned with defining and
overcoming the limitations of ordinary perception. Thus conceptual thought is able to
lead to a liberated understanding and a transformative religious experience. This book,
which draws on a selection of Indian and Tibetan texts, explores the workings of both
direct and conceptual cognition, and is a useful text for the reader seeking a more than
superficial understanding of the fundamental issues of Buddhist philosophy.

328 **Early Ch'an in China and Tibet.**
Edited by Whalen Lai, Lewis R. Lancaster. Berkeley, California:
Asian Humanities Press, 1983. 450p. bibliog. (Berkeley Buddhist
Studies Series, 5).
The papers published in this volume were originally presented at a conference in San
Francisco. They represent an attempt to place the history of Zen Buddhism on a firm
basis especially as regards the contact between Chinese and Tibetan Buddhism. The
second section of the book deals specifically with Tibet and has papers on 'The study of
Tibetan Ch'an manuscripts recovered from Tun-Huang' and 'Meditation trends in early
Tibet'.

329 **Death, intermediate state and rebirth in Tibetan Buddhism.**
Lati Rinbochay, Jeffrey Hopkins. London: Rider, 1979. 86p. bibliog.
Presents the text, with commentary, of an 18th-century treatise on death and rebirth.
This discusses in detail the processes and stages of dying, entry into the intermediate
stage between this life and the next and the process of rebirth; it concludes with an
exposition of the supreme form of yoga which leads not to the cycle of death and
rebirth but to the transformation into Buddhahood.

330 **Mind in Tibetan Buddhism: oral commentary on Ge-shay Jam-bel-sam-
pel's 'Presentation and awareness of knowledge. composite of all the
important points; Opener of the new intelligence'.**
Lati Rinbochay, translated, edited and introduced by Elizabeth
Napper. London: Rider, 1980. 181p. bibliog.
This important text is used by Tibetan monks for the formal enquiry into mind and
consciousness. Using the text as a basis, Lati Rinbochay provides an extensive
commentary, drawing on oral tradition, which illustrates the methods used by Tibetan
Buddhists in their search for right knowledge. Elizabeth Napper's introduction places
the work in the context of Indian and Tibetan Buddhism and describes the main
divisions of consciousness and mind which are found in that tradition.

331 **Secret doctrines of the *Tibetan Book of the Dead*.**
Detlef Ingo Lauf. Boulder, Colorado; London: Shambhala, 1977.
254p. bibliog.
A detailed account of the doctrines and iconography which make up the Tibetan
understanding of death. It also provides a psychological commentary on the *Tibetan
Book of the Dead*, and makes useful comparisons between Tibetan beliefs and those of
other cultures and civilizations.

332 **The hundred thousand songs of Milarepa.**
Translated and annotated by Garma C. C. Chung. New Hyde Park,
New York: University Books, 1962. 2 vols.
Part literature, part biography, part religious classic, this famous work by the great
11th-century Tibetan yogi Milarepa is a difficult book to classify. The first part contains
stories of Milarepa's subjugation and conversion of demons, the second has stories of
his relations with and instructions to his human disciples, and the third contains a
miscellaneous selection of stories. In all sections, each story shows Milarepa's personal

experience in a specific situation; and overall the stories also provide much information about the religious life and practices of the period.

333 **Death and dying in the Tibetan tradition.**
Glenn H. Mullin. London; Boston, Massachusetts: Arkana, 1986. 251p. bibliog.

In the West death has become a taboo subject, but this is not the case in Tibet where it is seen as just one stage on the long process of attaining Buddhahood. Drawing on nine Tibetan texts, including the *Tibetan Book of the Dead*, this book provides a good introduction to the Tibetan view of death and dying, covering such topics as meditation techniques to prepare for death, inspirational accounts of the deaths of saints, methods of achieving longevity and divining the time of death, and ways of easing the transition to other forms of consciousness at death.

334 **Path of the Bodhisattva warrior: the life and teachings of the Thirteenth Dalai Lama.**
Compiled and edited by Glenn H. Mullin, biography by Glen H. Mullin. Ithaca, New York: Snow Lion, 1988. 387p. bibliog.

The first third of this book contains a biography of the 13th Dalai Lama (1876–1933), a ruler who combined great spirituality with a bold approach to temporal affairs. Mullin stresses his spiritual leadership but also shows that he was successful politically in maintaining Tibet's independence. The remainder of the book contains a selection of some of his more important writings and talks including his 'Heart of the enlightenment teachings', 'Sermons at the great prayer festival' and 'Guide to the Buddhist Tantras'.

335 **Dzog Chen and Zen.**
Namkhai Norbu, edited with a preface and notes by Kennard Lipman. Oakland, California: Zhang Zhung Editions, 1984. 40p.

Discusses the relationship between Zen Buddhism and Zogpen in the context of the encounter in the 7th to the 9th centuries between the Chinese Zen Buddhists and the various currents of esoteric Buddhism then developing in Tibet. There is also a brief summary of the origins of Tibetan Buddhism and the role of Padma Sambhava in bringing Buddhism to Tibet.

336 **Women in Buddhism: images of the feminine in the Mahayana tradition.**
Diana Y. Paul. Berkeley, California: University of California Press, 1985. 2nd ed. 333p. bibliog.

Paul examines the various roles and sexual stereotypes played by women in the Buddhist tradition (for example the roles of mother, nun, friend or bodhisattva), and describes the positions taken by different groups of Buddhists towards the positive and negative attributes of women.

337 **Mahayana texts translated into western languages: a bibliographical guide.**
Compiled by Peter Pfandt. Cologne, Germany: E. J. Brill, 1983. 167p.

For readers who do not know oriental languages this listing of Buddhist texts which have been translated into Western languages will be particularly useful. Arrangement is alphabetical by title and there are also title indexes in Sanskrit, Tibetan, Chinese and Japanese.

338 **Tibetan meditation: theory and practice.**
S. K. Ramachandra Rao. New Delhi: Arnold-Heinemann, 1979. 112p.

This is a useful short introduction to both the theory and practice of Tibetan meditation which includes a number of practical exercises. Brief biographies of seven of the most important practitioners of Tibetan meditative techniques, all of whom lived in the 11th and 12th centuries, are also provided.

339 **Secret visions of the Fifth Dalai Lama: the Gold Manuscript in the Fournier Collection.**
Samtan Gyaltsen Karmay. London: Serindia, 1988. 246p. bibliog.

This is one of the most remarkable books in this bibliography. Discovered only recently, this manuscript is perhaps the only illustrated secret autobiography in the world. Begun in 1674, executed by the 5th Dalai Lama's personal calligrapher, and completed 11 years after the Dalai Lama's death, it provides a detailed narrative in words and pictures of his visionary experiences from the age of 6 to the age of 65, one year before his death. It thus portrays the inner mystical life of a remarkable man, but illustrates not just his spiritual development but also his thinking on the conduct of his government and the welfare of Tibet in general. The 67 illustrations in the original manuscript are here reproduced in colour, and the whole book can fairly be described as sumptuous.

340 **Selected works of the Dalai Lama I: bridging the sutras and tantras.**
Compiled, edited and translated by Glenn H. Mullin. Ithaca, New York: Snow Lion, 1985. 2nd ed. 258p. bibliog.

This collection brings together sixteen texts by the 1st Dalai Lama (1391-1474) including discourses on the Tara tantra and emptiness, and is accompanied by a traditional biography.

341 **Selected works of the Dalai Lama II: the tantric yogas of Sister Niguma.**
Compiled, edited and translated by Glenn H. Mullin. Ithaca, New York: Snow Lion, 1985. 239p. bibliog.

The 2nd Dalai Lama (1476-1542) chose as sources for his considerable literary output practices from some of the lesser-known sects and lineages of Tibetan Buddhism. The sixteen texts collected here include detailed instructions for the making and empowering of 'flower essence pills' which free the practitioner from the need for ordinary food, and the explicit tantric yogas of Sister Niguma. There is also a traditional biography of the 2nd Dalai Lama.

342   **Selected works of the Dalai Lama III: essence of refined gold.**
       Commentary by HH the Dalai Lama XIV, compiled, edited and
       translated by Glenn H. Mullin.   Ithaca, New York: Snow Lion, 1985.
       2nd ed. 270p. bibliog.

This selection includes an exposition by the 3rd Dalai Lama (1543–88) of Atisha's *A
lamp for the path to enlightenment*, which is the basis of the Lam-rim teachings,
accompanied by a number of other shorter works and a traditional biography.

343   **Selected works of the Dalai Lama VII: songs of spiritual change.**
       Compiled, edited and translated by Glenn H. Mullin.   Ithaca, New
       York: Snow Lion, 1985. 2nd ed. 205p. bibliog.

The 7th Dalai Lama wrote extensive commentaries on the tantras and over 1000
mystical poems and prayers. This volume contains a selection of his tantric songs and
poems of spiritual instruction for developing the mind. It is accompanied by a
traditional biography.

344   **Buddhism in Tibet.**
       Emil Schlagintweit.   Leipzig, Germany: Brockhaus, 1863. 403p.
       bibliog.

A general history of Buddhism, an historical account of Buddhism in Tibet and a
description of its organization, its deities, its buildings and its monuments are all
provided in this classic work of early European scholarship in the subject. It is worth
remembering, however, that few Europeans had visited Tibet proper at the time it was
written, and that it is therefore based on literary sources and on what was known of
Tibetan Buddhism as it was practised in the Himalayan border lands such as Sikkim
and Ladakh.

345   **Buddhist Himalaya: travels and studies in quest of the origins and
       nature of Tibetan religion.**
       David L. Snellgrove.   Oxford, England: Bruno Cassirer, 1957. 324p.
       maps. bibliog.

This is a major study of Tibetan religion and society which relates Tibetan Buddhism
to its origins in Nepal and India. It is a good book for someone coming new to the
subject.

346   **Indo-Tibetan Buddhism: Indian Buddhists and their Tibetan successors.**
       David L. Snellgrove.   London: Serindia; Boston, Massachusetts:
       Shambhala, 1987. 640p. maps. bibliog.

This highly illustrated study provides a comprehensive survey of Indian Buddhism and
its subsequent establishment in Tibet. The author concentrates on the Tantric period of
Buddhist theory and practice from the 8th to the 13th centuries, and emphasizes the
role played by the central Asian kingdoms along the Silk Road in the gradual process
of Tibetan conversion. He also describes the cultural changes that occurred in Tibet as
a result of its rule over an extensive empire in the 7th to the 9th centuries.

347 **Practice and theory of Tibetan Buddhism.**
Geshe Lhundup Sopa, Jeffrey Hopkins. London: Rider, 1976. 164p. bibliog.

Useful to students interested in tantric practice, this book contains translations of some key texts. The first part concerns the daily practice of Tibetan monks and comprises the text of a meditation manual written by the 4th Panchen Lama (1781–1852), whilst the second part, an annotated translation of the 'Precious garland of the tenets', written in the 18th century, is concerned with the theory behind the practice and with Buddhist philosophy.

348 **On two Tibetan pictures representing some of the spiritual ancestors of the Dalai Lama and the Panchen Lama.**
A. von Stael-Holstein. Peking: Lazarist Press, 1932. 24p.

The first of the two pictures dates from the time of the 8th Dalai Lama (circa 1758) and represents him surrounded by twenty-five of his spiritual ancestors. The second also dates from the 18th century and depicts the Panchen Lama Blo bzan dpal ldan ye ces and twelve of his spiritual ancestors. Brief biographical notes are provided on each of them.

349 **Buddhism of Tibet.**
Tenzin Gyatso, Fourteenth Dalai Lama, translated and edited by Jeffrey Hopkins. Ithaca, New York: Snow Lion, 1987. 219p.

Comprises four texts which the Dalai Lama wrote or chose with Western readers particularly in mind. The first two are by the present Dalai Lama: 'The Buddhism of Tibet' explains the main principles and practices of Buddhism, and 'The key to the middle way' is a treatise on the key concept of emptiness. 'The precious garland' is renowned for its description of the bodhisattva path of compassion; and 'The song of the four mindfulnesses' is a short poem by the 7th Dalai Lama which is intended to be used as a basis for meditation on mindfulness for the guru, altruism, deity yoga and emptiness.

350 **Kindness, Clarity and Insight.**
Tenzin Gyatso, Fourteenth Dalai Lama, translated and edited by Jeffrey Hopkins, co-edited by Elizabeth Napper. Ithaca, New York: Snow Lion, 1984. 232p.

Twenty lectures, elucidating basic doctrines of Tibetan Buddhism and given by the Dalai Lama during his tours of North America in 1979, 1980 and 1981, are collected in this volume. At these lectures the Dalai Lama generally began by speaking in English on the general themes of kindness and compassion, and then moved on to discuss a variety of subjects using a more complex vocabulary in Tibetan; these pasages have been translated into English for this book.

351 **Opening the eye of new awareness.**
Tenzin Gyatso, Fourteenth Dalai Lama, translated by Donald S. Lopez
Jr. with Jeffrey Hopkins. London: Wisdom, 1985. 143p. bibliog. (A
Wisdom Intermediate Book. White Series).
The text of this book was written by the Dalai Lama in 1963, four years after his flight
from Tibet. It is a concise and straightforward account of the main features of Tibetan
Buddhism, covering such topics as ultimate truth, the trainings in ethics, meditation
and the qualities of Buddhahood. His history of Buddhism in Tibet is designed to
relate it to Indian Mahayana Buddhism and thus to refute the idea that Lamaism is
unrelated to the central currents of Buddhist thought. Also included in this volume are
the texts of lectures given by the Dalai Lama in 1979 and 1980 which are on the same
theme and complement the main text.

352 **The opening of the wisdom-eye and the history of the advancement of**
Buddhadharma in Tibet.
Tenzin Gyatso, Fourteenth Dalai Lama. Wheaton, Illinois:
Theosophical Publishing House, 1972. 178p. (A Quest Book).
First written in the 1960s, this treatise by the Dalai Lama presents a brief history of
Buddhism in Tibet followed by an exposition of the basic teachings of Buddha. Special
emphasis is placed on the 'threefold training': supreme virtue, supreme collectedness
and supreme wisdom. Practice is as important as belief in Buddhism, and the Dalai
Lama describes some of the paths the disciple can take to train and develop both mind
and heart in the quest for enlightenment.

353 **Buddha mind: an anthology of Longchen Rabjam's writings on Dzogpa**
chenpo.
Tulku Thondup Rinpoche, edited by Harold Talbott. Ithaca, New
York: Snow Lion, 1989. 466p. bibliog.
An anthology of writings on Dzogchen by an acknowledged master, Longchen Rabjam
who lived in the 14th century. Dzogchen is the innermost esoteric philosophy and
meditation training which awakens the essential nature of the mind, and the aim of this
collection is to make this philosophy accessible to both the specialist and the non-
specialist alike.

354 **The life and teachings of Tsong Khapa.**
Edited by Robert A. F. Thurman. Dharamsala, India: Library of
Tibetan Works and Archives, 1982. 258p.
Tsong-ka-pa (1357–1419) was one of the most significant Buddhist teachers. This book
brings together both a biography of him, based on a traditional one, and a selection of
his writings including mystic conversations with bodhisattvas and spiritual songs.

355 **The Tibetan Book of the Dead, or the after-death experiences on the Bardo plane, according to Lama Kazi Dawa-Samdup's English rendering.**
Compiled and edited by W. Y. Evans-Wentz. London: Oxford University Press, 1957. 3rd ed. 249p.

According to tradition, this key text for an understanding of Tibetan Buddhism dates back to the time of Padma Sambhava himself and was later hidden until the time was ripe for it to be revealed. It describes the processes of death, of existence after death and of rebirth which are fundamental to Tibetan Buddhist belief and which are of almost equal interest to Western psychologists and theologians. The text can be used as a breviary and read on the occasion of death, but it was also intended to serve as a guide to the living as well as the dying. The introduction by Evans-Wentz is itself an important commentary on both the text itself and the doctrines it embodies.

356 **The Tibetan Book of the Great Liberation, or the method of realizing nirvana through knowing the mind.**
Introduction, annotations and editing by W. Y. Evans-Wentz.
London: Oxford University Press, 1954. 261p.

Like the *Tibetan Book of the Dead*, this key text for the understanding of Tibetan Buddhism dates back to the time of Padma Sambhava, who may himself have been its author. It sets forth the essence of Mahayana Buddhism, and in this edition is accompanied by the biography of Padma Sambhava. The lengthy and scholarly introduction by Evans-Wentz is again an important commentary on the text itself and the doctrine it contains.

357 **The Tibetan Dhammapada: sayings of the Buddha: a translation of the Tibetan version of the Udanavarga.**
Compiled by Dhamatrata, translated and introduced by Gareth Sparham, edited by Beth Lee Simon. London: Wisdom, 1986. 235p.
(A Wisdom Basic Book. Orange Series).

This compilation of the Buddha's sayings is more usually associated with south Asia, but is known in Tibet as well. It consists of a series of verses with titles such as Impermanence, Desire, Beauty and Actions. Overall, it gives a good impression of the down-to-earth and practical nature of the Buddha's wisdom.

358 **Tibet's great yogi Milarepa: a biography from the Tibetan, being the Jetsun-Kahbum or biographical history of Jetsun Milarepa, according to the late Lama Kazi Dawa-Sandup's English rendering.**
Edited with an introduction by W. Y. Evans-Wentz. London: Oxford University Press, 1951. 2nd ed. 315p.

Milarepa is one of the greatest religious and literary figures of Tibet. He lived in the 11th to the 12th centuries and his biography is intended to demonstrate that right knowledge is obtained not by good deeds and professions of faith but by self-discipline of the mind and making it immune to worldly influences. Incidentally the biography contains much fascinating information on the social conditions of the time, and also describes some of Milarepa's yogic powers, such as the power of bodily flight, a phenomenon which has been observed in Tibet even in the present century. Milarepa was also a considerable poet and many of his poems and songs are included in this volume.

359 **Compassion in Tibetan Buddhism.**
Tsong-ka-pa, with Kensur Lekden's 'Meditations of a Tantric abbot', edited and translated by Jeffrey Hopkins. London: Rider, 1980. 254p. bibliog.

Describes ways of generating compassion according to oral and written Tibetan traditions. The first part comprises a series of meditations by Kensur Lekden describing how to reflect on personal relations so that compassion is generated. The second part consists of a work by the 14th-century writer Tsong-ka-pa explaining the importance of compassion and describing the deeds motivated by it. Taken as a whole, therefore, this book presents a combination of a contemporary lama's meditations and the explanations of an earlier master on the general theme of compassionate commitment to the well-being of others.

360 **Tantra in Tibet: the Great Exposition of Secret Mantra.**
Tsong-ka-pa, introduced by Tenzin Gyatso, Fourteenth Dalai Lama, translated and edited by Jeffrey Hopkins. London: George Allen & Unwin, 1977. 252p. bibliog. (The Wisdom of Tibet Series, 3).

The Great Exposition of Secret Mantra by Tsong-ka-pa (1357–1419) presents the principal characteristics of all the Buddhist tantra systems and explains the difference between sutra and mantra. The translation of the original text is preceded by an introduction and commentary by the Dalai Lama and followed by a supplement intended to clarify the key concepts of emptiness, transformation and the purposes of the four tantras.

361 **The yoga of Tibet: the Great Exposition of Secret Mantra: 2 and 3.**
Tsong-ka-pa, introduced by Tenzin Gyatso, Fourteenth Dalai Lama, translated and edited by Jeffrey Hopkins. London: George Allen & Unwin, 1981. 274p. bibliog. (The Wisdom of Tibet Series, 4).

A sequel to the same author's *Tantra in Tibet* (q.v.) which presents the process of meditation in action and performance tantra. The text is preceded by an introduction by the Dalai Lama which explains the meditation rites of deity yoga, the tantric process by which a yogi cultivates appearance in a Buddha's divine body.

362 **The Buddhism of Tibet, or Lamaism with its mystic cults, symbolism and mythology, and its relation to Indian Buddhism.**
L. Austine Waddell. London: W. H. Allen, 1895. 598p. bibliog.

In its day this was a pioneering work, and although Waddell was in some way an unsympathetic student of Tibetan Buddhism and his book needs to be read with care, it remains an important source.

363 **Mahayana Buddhism: the doctrinal foundations.**
Paul Williams. London: Routledge, 1989. 317p. bibliog.
Provides an accessible introduction to the principles and philosophy of Mahayana Buddhism, as well as placing it in its historical and cultural context. This is a good book for someone coming new to the subject.

364 **In praise of Tara: songs of the saviouress.**
Martin Willson. London: Wisdom, 1986. 487p. bibliog. (A Wisdom Intermediate Book. White Series).
Tara is one of the most popular Buddhist deities, and she has inspired some of the finest Buddhist literature. This book contains a selection of this literature, including a history of the origin of the Tantra of Tara and songs in praise of her from Indian and Tibetan devotees, accompanied by notes and commentaries by the compiler.

365 **Introduction to Tantra: a vision of totality.**
Lama Thubten Yeshe, compiled and edited by Jonathon Landaw.
London: Wisdom, 1987. 173p. bibliog. (A Wisdom Basic Book. Orange Series).
In this introductory book, Lama Yeshe presents a clear summary of the essence of tantra which explains the various meditation methods and shows how tantra fits into the framework of conventional Buddhist practices such as karma, renunciation and compassion.

366 **The life and liberation of Padmasambhava: Padma bKa'i Thang.**
Recorded by Yeshe Tsogyal, rediscovered by Terchen Urgyan Lingpa. Emeryville, California: Dharma, 1978. 2 vols.
This is a traditional Tibetan biography, attributed to his consort Yeshe Tsogyal, of Padma Sambhava, the founder of Buddhism in Tibet who was also responsible for the spread of Buddhism in other neighbouring Himalayan regions in the 8th century.

Christian missions

367 **Tibetan tales.**
Geoffrey T. Bull. London: Hodder & Stoughton, 1966. 124p.
These stories and sketches of the author's life on the Tibetan–Chinese border in the period immediately preceding the Chinese invasion are written in a lively and humorous style, and this book gives a good impression of a missionary's life and work in the field.

368 **Trente ans aux portes du Thibet interdit 1908–1938.** (Thirty years at the gates of forbidden Tibet, 1908–38.)
Francis Gore. Hong Kong: Sociétés des Missions-Étrangères de Paris, Maison de Nazareth, 1939. 388p. map.

This detailed history of the Catholic missions in Tibet during the first part of the 20th century also includes much useful material on the politics, religion and economy of Tibet during that period. Part 2 contains one of the few descriptions of the fighting between Chinese and Tibetan troops around the time of the First World War.

369 **Histoire de la mission du Thibet.** (History of the Tibetan mission.)
A. Launay. Paris: Desclée de Brouwer, 1903. 2 vols.

Launay gives a detailed account of attempts made by French missionaries to enter Tibet and establish mission stations there. Most of his book covers the period 1846–1901, but the early chapters contain some information on the earlier Roman Catholic missions to Tibet.

370 **Martyr in Tibet: the heroic life and death of Father Maurice Tornay, St. Bernard missionary to Tibet.**
Robert Loup, translated from the French by Charles Davenport. New York: David McKay, 1956. 238p. bibliog.

A biography of the Swiss missionary Father Tornay who was based at Yerkalo on the eastern marches of Tibet and was murdered in mysterious circumstances when his caravan was ambushed in 1949.

371 **The origin of the Tibetan Pioneer Mission, together with some facts about Tibet.**
London: Morgan & Scott, 1894. 21p.

This short contemporary pamphlet gives some details about the formation of the mission, based at Yatung in the east of Tibet, and the work of Annie Taylor whose own diary of her journey of 1892 has been published in W. Carey's *Travel and adventure in Tibet* (q.v.).

372 **Shelton of Tibet.**
Flora Beal Shelton. New York: G. H. Doran, 1923. 319p.

This is a biography (by his widow who lived on until 1966) of the American missionary Albert Leroy Shelton who was based on the eastern border of Tibet from 1904 until his death in 1922. It includes an account of the fighting between Chinese and Tibetan troops around the time of the First World War.

373 **La prima missione cattólica nel Tibet.** (The first Catholic missions in
Tibet.)
Giuseppe M. Toscano.   Parma, Italy: Istituto Missioni Estere, 1951.
320p. maps.

It is now well known that the first Westerners to visit Tibet were the Catholic
missionaries, mostly Jesuits. Toscano gives a detailed history of the early Catholic
missions to Tibet with the emphasis on the 17th- and early 18th-century missions.
Amongst the journeys covered are those of Antonio de Andrade (1624) who reached
Tsaparang, and Cacella and Cabral (1627–28) who travelled from Bhutan to Shigatse.

Social Conditions

374 **The people of Tibet.**
   Sir Charles Bell.   Oxford, England: Clarendon Press, 1928. 319p.
   maps. bibliog.
This is a classic work which no student of Tibet's social history can afford to ignore. It is based on the author's twenty years' experience of Tibet and presents a portrait of the whole spectrum of society ranging from the nobility at the top down through traders, herdsmen and peasants to beggars and robbers at the bottom. The life of women and children is also described and there are chapters on Tibetan food, drinking and smoking, etiquette and Tibetan games and amusements.

375 **Tibetan village communities: structure and change.**
   Eva K. Dargyay.   Warminster, England: Aris & Phillips, 1982. 110p.
   maps. bibliog.
Based on interviews with Tibetan refugees, this study attempts to reconstruct the village structure of pre-1959 Tibet. Detailed information is given on such topics as land tenure, crops, family and social organization in a rural community and the economic structure of the community, and a final chapter presents a summary of changes made in the traditional social structures by the Chinese authorities.

376 **Serfdom and mobility: an examination of the institution of "human lease" in traditional Tibetan society.**
   Melvyn C. Goldstein.   *Journal of Asian Studies*, vol. 30, no. 3 (May 1971), p. 521-34.
An interesting article on social structure and stratification in traditional Tibet. Professor Goldstein argues that although serfdom was prevalent in Tibet, this did not mean that it was an entirely static society. There were several types of serf sub-status of which one of the most important was the 'human lease' which enabled a serf to acquire a degree of personal freedom. This was because it offered an alternative in which, despite retaining the concept of lordship, the serfs were not bound to a landed estate.

377 Tibet leaps forward.

Hsi Chang-hao, Kao Yuan-mei. Peking: Foreign Languages Press, 1977. 116p.

The flavour of this book is easily ascertained from some of the paragraph headings: 'No return to the old system', 'Blood sucking exploitation', 'Advancing along the socialist road' and 'Tibetans and Hans are members of one family' are typical examples. It therefore offers only a partial view of conditions in Tibet today.

378 Games of the Tibetans.

Siegbert Hummel, Paul G. Brewster. Helsinki: Suomalainen Tiedeakatemia, 1963. 33p. bibliog. (F. F. Communications, vol. 77/2, no. 187).

Describes an aspect of Tibetan life that has received little attention. It does not cover sports such as archery or wrestling, but rather traditional dice and board games, complete with diagrams. Mention is also made of traditional pursuits such as swinging (which formed part of the New Year customs), riddle games (popular at marriage ceremonies) and children's games, shuttlecock, hopscotch and 'wolf and sheep' being amongst the most common of these.

379 Tibet no longer mediaeval.

Edited by Jin Zhou, text by Zhu Li. Beijing: Foreign Languages Press, 1981. 176p. maps.

This book aims to show how Tibet has developed during the last thirty years of Chinese rule. Topics covered include farming, industry and transport, art, education and health. Overall, it gives a somewhat superficial account which emphasizes the material progress that has been made but has nothing to say of the political and cultural oppression which many would say has accompanied it.

380 Report from Tibet.

Beijing: *China Reconstructs*, 1983. 40p. (What's New in China, 3).

A short pamphlet which outlines the current situation in Tibet after the implementation, following 1980, of the new policies designed to correct the abuses of the Cultural Revolution. It includes a report on the first visit to Tibet by the Panchen Lama for 18 years.

381 We Tibetans: an intimate picture, by a woman of Tibet, of an interesting and distinctive people, in which it is shown how they live, their beliefs, their outlook, their work & play, & how they regard themselves and others.

Rin-chen Lha-mo (Mrs Louis King), with a historical introduction by Louis King. London: Seeley, Service, 1926. 228p.

Born and brought up in the eastern province of Kham, the author was the first Tibetan woman to marry a European and settle in the West. Her book is a classic, and also enjoyable, account of life in the old Tibet, with a plethora of details on all aspects of daily life from folk tales to children's games. Her husband's introduction provides a useful historical background.

382 **Tibet today.**
Peking: Foreign Languages Press, 1974. 117p.
This collection of 'socialist realist' photographs of modern-day Tibet is of a frankly propagandist nature.

383 **Tibetan social philosophy.**
Tibet Journal. Special issue, vol. 11, no. 4 (Winter 1986), 113p. bibliog.
This collection of articles covers aspects of how Tibetan society was organized as well as how Tibetans reflected on that organization. The article by Melvyn Goldstein is especially important because it challenges some of the traditional views of Tibetan serfdom. He thinks previous writers on Tibet have been too squeamish in tackling this subject and he uses the opportunity to develop his ideas on the system of 'human lease' which provided some social mobility for the serfs. The article by Franz Michael is also of interest in arguing that traditional Tibetan society was capable of modernizing itself and could have done so had the Chinese not invaded and brought about more violent change.

384 **Legal aspects of land tenure in Tibetan society.**
Thomas W. Wiley. *Tibet Journal*, vol. 9, no. 1 (Spring 1984), p. 3–19.
Wiley demonstrates that the principal features of the Tibetan system of land tenure were rigidity, flexibility and security. The system was rigid in that it was allied to the tax estate, but flexible in that at intervals the tax structure was reviewed and amended. There was security for most peasant farmers because they enjoyed life tenure. Nobles on the other hand had less security but a higher standard of living.

Tibetan Medicine

385   **Tibetan Buddhist medicine and psychiatry: the diamond healing.**
Terry Clifford.   Wellingborough, England: Aquarian Press, 1984.
268p. bibliog.
This book provides a comprehensive introduction to the Tibetan art of healing. Using straightforward language the author discusses the components of Tibetan Buddhist medicine: its religious, psychological and philosophical foundations, its history, traditions and rituals and its methods of diagnosis and cure. The second half of the book deals particularly with Tibetan medical psychiatry and includes a translation of the psychiatric chapters of the 'Four tantras' or 'Gyu-zhi' in which the author attempts to correlate the Tibetan expressions with modern psychiatric disturbances.

386   **Formulary of Tibetan medicine.**
Vaidya Bhagwan Dash.   Delhi: Classics India Publications, 1988.
453p. (Indo-Tibetan Medicine Series, no. 2)
One hundred and sixty-four popularly used and therapeutically effective recipes are described with reference to their ingredients, parts of these ingredients used, the weight in which each ingredient is to be added, special methods of preparation, therapeutic indications and dosage. Tibetan terms are given alongside romanized forms and the weights and measures are given in traditional measures and metric equivalents. The text is accompanied by a large number of illustrations and diagrams.

387   **Materia medica of Indo-Tibetan medicine.**
Vaidya Bhagwan Dash.   Delhi: Classics India Publications, 1989.
2nd ed. 647p. (Indo-Tibetan Medicine Series, no. 1)
This study of a traditional text gives information on the therapeutic utility of medicinal plants, metals, minerals, gems, jewellery, animal products and the ingredients of food and drink, and adds details of natural and herbal remedies.

388   **An introduction to Tibetan folk medicine.**
Dorsh Marie Devoe.   *Curare*, vol. 4, no. 1 (1981), p. 57–63.
Based on interviews with a number of elderly Tibetans, this article outlines some of the
basic folk medical practices. These often involve the use of materials or practices which
would normally be regarded as harmful, but, as with folk medicine in other cultures,
they are often believed to have surprisingly beneficial results.

389   **Health through balance: an introduction to Tibetan medicine.**
Yeshi Donden, edited and translated by Jeffrey Hopkins.   Ithaca, New
York: Snow Lion, 1986. 252p.
Based on the author's lectures presented at the University of Virginia in 1980, this is a
good introduction to the subject. Its basic theme is how the Tibetan medical system
restores and maintains the balance of the body through a variety of treatments which
include diet and behaviour modification as well as the use of medicines. The author
considers factors of personality, age, diet, behavioural patterns and physical
surroundings and describes a wide variety of curative techniques.

390   **Foundations of Tibetan medicine.**
Elizabeth Finckh, translated by Fredericka M. Houser.   Dulverton,
England: Watkins, 1978. 2 vols. bibliog.
This is a detailed academic study by a specialist in internal medicine who trained also
in neurology and psychiatry. She wrote these books in close consultation with the Dalai
Lama's personal physician. Their theme is an analysis of two chapters of the 'Gyu-zhi'
from which the system of Tibetan medicine and the first two sections of Tibetan
medical science, the healthy and the diseased organisms with their terminology, can be
expounded.

391   **Lectures on Tibetan medicine.**
Lobsang Dolma Khangkar, compiled and edited by K. Dhondup.
Dharamsala, India: Library of Tibetan Works and Archives, 1986.
218p.
The author gave these lectures on Tibetan medicine in Australia and Holland and they
thus form a useful introduction for Western readers. They cover the fundamental
concepts of Tibetan medicine, its history and the various cures and concepts
propounded in its general and secret medical tantras. The methods used in training a
Tibetan doctor are described; and there are sections dealing with conception and the
Tibetan medical concept of insanity.

392   **Tibetan therapeutic massage.**
Lobsang Rapgay.   Dharamsala, India: The author, [1985?]. 58p.
(Tibetan Medical Sciences Series).
Massage forms an integral part of Tibetan medical theory and practice and can work as
an external therapy. In this short introduction there are descriptions of practical
massage techniques (with diagrams) and a list of the massage treatments appropriate to
different disorders.

393 **Handbook of traditional Tibetan drugs: their nomenclature,**
composition, use and dosage.
T. J. Tsarong. Kalimpong, India: Tibetan Medical Publication, 1986.
101p. bibliog.

Lists the composition and use of 175 popular Tibetan natural drugs. Although the book
is intended for the increasing number oᶠ patients resorting to alternative medicine, it
might also be useful to scholars and researchers looking for alternatives to toxic
modern synthetic drugs. The compiler claims that all the drugs listed here are available
from practitioners and manufacturers of Tibetan medicine in south Asia.

Politics and
Government

394 **Tibet today: current conditions and prospects.**
John F. Avedon.   London: Wisdom, 1988. 32p. bibliog.
This pamphlet, drawn mainly from Avedon's submission to the US Congress, offers a
brief assessment of the social and political conditions in present-day Tibet including a
report on the anti-Chinese demonstrations in Lhasa in 1987 and 1988. Chinese
immigration into Tibet, unemployment, health care, education and the role of the
military in Tibet are amongst the topics touched on.

395 **Land and polity in Tibet.**
Pedro Carrasco.   Seattle, Washington: University of Washington
Press, 1959. 307p. maps. bibliog.
An important contribution to the study of the Tibetan political system. The subject of
this book is the system of land tenure as related to political organization, with
particular emphasis being placed on the peasant level of organization as demonstrated
in the management of family holdings and the nature and structure of the village
communities. The author stresses the importance of land revenue as the foundation of
the state structure and discusses the means by which it was raised. He also examines
the characteristics and roles of the bureaucracy, the ruling class and the church, and
concludes that the Tibetan system, based on a status economy rather than a market
economy, can in some senses be compared to European feudalism.

396 **A Tibetan principality: the political system of Sa sKya.**
C. W. Cassinelli, Robert B. Ekvall.   Ithaca, New York: Cornell
University Press, 1969. 425p.
Based on extensive interviews with members of the royal family of Sa sKya and the
official who was their tutor, this book describes in detail the structure of both the
central and the local government of the principality, the role of the hereditary nobility
and the monasteries, the sources of government revenue and the land and property
structure of the region. The authors are careful to point out that the functions and
concern of Tibetan government were very different from those in the West. They were
not interested in solving problems or drawing up policies to improve society, nor were

they expected to. Their concerns were the maintenance of peace, the protection of property, the collection of revenue and the promotion of religious observance. Thus, without ideological divisions, power struggles tended to degenerate into manoeuvrings for position or prestige.

397 Communist China's difficulties in ruling Tibet.
Ya-chun Chang. *Issues and Studies*, vol. 25, no. 1 (Jan. 1989), p. 110–27.

Chang argues that the Chinese communists are fundamentally opposed to Tibetan independence, not only because it would violate, as they see it, China's territorial integrity, but also because Tibet is vital to China's security and strategic interests on its southwestern border. Thus, even the 'Middle Way' proposed by the Dalai Lama would be unacceptable to them, and yet a continuation of absolute rule from Beijing is equally unacceptable to most Tibetans.

398 Tibet: past and present.
Hungdah Chiu, June Teufel Dreyer. Baltimore, Maryland: University of Maryland School of Law, 1989. 25p. (Occasional papers/Reprint series in Contemporary Asian Studies no. 4–1989, 93).

Hungdah Chiu's paper examines Tibet's political history and status, whilst June Teufel Dreyer discusses the recent unrest in Tibet. she outlines the course of the anti-Chinese demonstrations in Tibet and the negotiations which took place between the Chinese government and the Dalai Lama. These were stalled in 1988 and the conclusion of this paper is that unless they are restarted a situation similar to that in Northern Ireland may arise. It is argued that a type of internal self-government similar to that proposed for Hong Kong might be the best solution, but this depends on movement on the part of the Chinese and on the Dalai Lama being able to restrain his own more extremist followers.

399 Constitution of Tibet; promulgated by His Holiness the Dalai Lama, March 10, 1963.
New Delhi: Bureau of the Dalai Lama, 1963. 90, 33p. (In Tibetan and English).

Designed by the Dalai Lama and his advisers with the aim of bringing greater democracy into the Tibetan political system, this constitution represents a fusion of Buddhist philosophy, the spiritual and temporal heritage of Tibet, and the ideas of the modern world. It is intended to secure a democratic system based on justice and equality before the law. The American influence is strong, with the executive and legislative arms of government separated from each other. The Dalai Lama retains executive power, but legislative power is vested in the National Assembly, 75% of whose members are directly elected (the remaining 25% being representatives of local councils, monasteries and the Dalai Lama). Elections are to take place every five years. Needless to say this liberal constitution has never been in force in Tibet itself.

400 **A dialogue on Tibet (I). Our differences with the Dalai Lama.**
Beijing Review, vol. 30, no. 42 (19 Oct. 1987), p. 14–15.

This is a short report of a question-and-answer session with senior officials of the Chinese State Nationalities Commission. Their replies could not make the Chinese position on Tibet clearer: they would like the Dalai Lama to return, but any form of separatism or self-government is totally ruled out.

401 **China's forty millions: minority nationalities and national integration in the People's Republic of China.**
June Teufel Dreyer. Cambridge, Massachusetts: Harvard University Press, 1976. 333p. map. bibliog. (Harvard East Asian Series, 87).

The minorities problem has occupied an important place in Chinese policy-making since 1949, with the Chinese themselves viewing the problem as essentially one of integration. For reasons of defence, economics and national pride the Han Chinese find it impossible to conceive of relinquishing control over the minorities, yet at the same time they wish to obtain their loyalty to the state. As this book makes clear, this classic dilemma has resulted in numerous shifts of policy, yet it remains unresolved today. Indeed, recent events, both in Tibet and in China itself, have made the problem even more acute than when this book was written.

402 **The Chinese presence in Tibet: a thirty year assessment.**
June Teufel Dreyer. *Tibetan Review*, vol. 16, no. 12 (Dec. 1981), p. 8–14.

This article gives a brief review of the changing Chinese policies towards Tibet since 1951. The conclusion is that despite several periods of repression and much destruction the forces of Tibetan Buddhism and nationalism remain strong inside Tibet, and that the situation there continues to be unstable despite recent Chinese attempts to be more accommodating.

403 **From liberation to liberalisation: views on 'liberated' Tibet.**
Dharamsala, India: Information Office of His Holiness the Dalai Lama, 1982. 216p.

A compilation of articles which presents varying perspectives on the trend of liberalization apparent in Tibet in recent years. They include articles by Western journalists, Tibetans who were members of the second and third fact-finding missions sent by the Dalai Lama to Tibet, individual Tibetans who visited the country privately, and Western tourists. The views of the Westerners are generally more favourable than those of the returning Tibetan exiles, but all agree that Tibet has suffered under Chinese rule and that the Chinese show little understanding of or sympathy for the Tibetan population.

404 **The balance between centralization and decentralization in the traditional Tibetan political system.**
Melvyn C. Goldstein. *Central Asiatic Journal*, vol. 15 (1971), p. 170–82.

Goldstein argues that the Tibetan political system was a theo-aristocratic polity, characterized by an overlap of personnel between the central government and various religious and aristocratic sub-units. This centralization co-existed with hereditary decentralization in a mixture unique to Tibet. In many of his detailed arguments he explicitly criticizes the conclusions of Cassinelli and Ekvall in their *A Tibetan principality* (q.v.).

405 **Lhasa street songs: political and social satire in traditional Tibet.**
Melvyn C. Goldstein. *Tibet Journal*, vol. 7, nos 1 & 2
(Spring/Summer 1982), p. 56–66.

Tibetan street songs perform the same function as political cartoons do in the West. It is not known when they originated but around 200 such songs exist from the 18th century onwards. This article gives some examples and provides the political background and significance of each of them.

406 **The minorities and the military in China.**
William R. Heaton. *Armed Forces and Society*, vol. 3, no. 2 (Winter 1977), p. 325–42.

This article demonstrates that the People's Liberation Army (PLA) has been used by the Chinese authorities since their occupation of Tibet to assist in carrying out the policy of national integration with China. The army has maintained order, prevented secessionist movments gaining power and provided facilities for construction work. At the same time it has carried out an active policy of political education and thus attempted to transfer the Tibetans' loyalties. Heaton concludes that these policies have reduced the possibilities for minority separatism becoming an active force in Tibet, a conclusion that appears more questionable in the light of recent events both in Tibet and in China itself.

407 **China and its national minorities: autonomy or assimilation?**
Thomas Herber. London: M. E. Sharpe, 1989. 164p. bibliog.
(An East Gate Book).

Herber's book includes a useful chapter on 'The Tibet question' which attempts to be fair-minded to all sides, something which is becoming increasingly rare as the debate over Tibet's status and future becomes more polemical following recent events in both China and Tibet itself. He argues that a hard line by the party leadership in Beijing may ultimately be counter-productive and prevent the very unity of China's dominions it is intended to achieve. The Dalai Lama's 'Middle Way' is commended as a good starting point for negotiations on Tibet's political future, but Herber also makes the important point that a democratic solution to the problem is not possible without major changes in China itself.

408 **On negotiations with the Dalai Lama.**
Hua Zi. *Beijing Review*, vol. 32, no. 11 (13–19 March 1989), p. 24–6.

This short article makes the Chinese position on Tibet very clear. The author accuses the Dalai Lama of being behind the riots in Lhasa in 1987 and 1988 and states that any form of separatism is totally unacceptable.

409 **The function and status of the Dalai Lama in Tibet.**
Lois Lang-Sims. London: Tibet Society, [1959?]. 3p. (Tibet Society
paper, no. 1).

Both the temporal and the religious functions of the Dalai Lama are outlined in this
pamphlet, which stresses that to a Tibetan the two functions are indivisible; the ruler
rules through virtue of being the vehicle of the divine compassion operating in human
affairs.

410 **Communist China's policy toward Tibet.**
Hollis S. Liao. *Issues and Studies*, vol. 17, no. 2 (Feb. 1981),
p. 23–35.

Liao analyses China's policies towards Tibet in the years immediately following the fall
of the Gang of Four. This period was one of relative relaxation, but Liao indicates
that, despite attempts by the present leadership to blame the Gang of Four for
everything that has gone wrong, they are themselves responsible for Tibet's present
poverty and backwardness, whilst the ideological indoctrination first introduced in the
1950s remains largely intact.

411 **How the Chinese rule Tibet.**
J. Michael Luhan. *Dissent*, vol. 36, no. 1 (Winter 1989), p. 21–3.

Based on personal observations made on a recent visit to Tibet, the author presents
evidence of the Chinese colonization of Tibet. He points out that almost all the shops
and restaurants in Lhasa are Chinese and that little of the Western tourist money
which is spent in Tibet reaches the Tibetans themselves. He includes an eye-witness
account of the massacre in the Jokhang on 5 March 1988, and concludes that what the
Chinese term autonomy is merely a euphemism for 'colonialism wedded to trickle
down economics'.

412 **Rule by incarnation: Tibetan Buddhism and its role in society and state.**
Franz Michael. Boulder, Colorado: Westview Press, 1982. 227p.
bibliog. (A Westview Special Study).

Using Max Weber's framework of the interrelationship between religion and the
emergence of social and political systems, Michael analyses the central concepts of
Tibetan Buddhism and applies them to the social and political order of Tibet. He
surveys the ecclesiastical and secular arms of government, the various government
bodies and their procedures, the system of provincial and local government, and the
general social order. The result is an important study, not only of the structure of
Tibetan society and politics but also of the broader general issue of the modernization
of traditional societies.

413 **Tibet after Mao Ze Dong.**
Eva M. Neterowicz. *Journal of Social, Political and Economic
Studies*, vol. 13, no. 4 (Winter 1988), p. 405–27. bibliog.

This review of Chinese policy in Tibet since the Cultural Revolution suggests that,
although an attempt has been made to improve the Tibetan economy and although a
few monasteries have been rebuilt, conditions have only marginally improved and the
long-term aim of the Chinese remains the destruction of Tibetan culture and religion.
The popular demonstrations of 1987 and 1988 showed that the Tibetan people were

still seeking political freedom amd the preservation of their religion, but the harsh repression that followed demonstrated the Chinese response only too clearly. Like other recent accounts, this article stresses the effects which massive Chinese immigration into traditional Tibetan areas has had, so that the Tibetans are now a minority race in many districts of their own country and even Lhasa has the appearance of a Chinese city.

414 **Aristocracy and government in Tibet 1728–1959.**
Luciano Petech.   Rome: Istituto Italiano per il Medio ed Estremo Oriente, 1973. 274p. bibliog. (Serie Orientale Roma, Vol. XLV)

This book examines the role the prominent families of the Tibetan aristocracy played in the Tibetan political system. Professor Petech argues that real power was limited to a small number of families and that there was no substantial difference in the power and wealth they held in 1950 from what it had been in 1750. Throughout that period the administrative machinery of government functioned as a partnership between the clergy and the nobility with no commoner admitted to any middle- or high-ranking office. He gives details of the histories of a number of noble houses to prove this contention and makes the illuminating comparison between the Tibetan political system and that of the Papal States in their last stages.

415 **Present policies for Tibet.**
China Reconstructs, vol. 29, no. 10 (Oct. 1980), p. 16–20.

This interview with a member of the State Nationalities Commission reveals the Chinese government's policies towards Tibet in the period immediately after the fall of the Gang of Four: relaxation of economic policies, greater encouragement of agriculture, abolition of many compulsory services and a general liberalization; any problems or mistakes can conveniently be blamed on the ultra-leftists in power during the Cultural Revolution.

416 **Questions and answers on the Lhasa riots.**
Beijing Review, vol. 31, no. 47 (21–27 Nov. 1988), p. 15–19.

These interviews with officials of the Chinese Ministry of Public Security, the Supreme People's Court and the Ministry of Foreign Affairs are useful in giving the official Chinese line on the riots which took place in Lhasa in the autumn of 1987 and spring of 1988.

417 **The government and politics of Tibet.**
Ram Rahul.   Delhi: Vikas, 1969. 160p. bibliog.

Rahul's book was a pioneering study in the theory and practice of Tibetan government from the time of the First Dalai Lama up to the flight of the Fourteenth Dalai Lama in 1959. A full description is given of the roles of the different officers of state, political institutions and officers at all levels of government all set within a chronological framework.

418 **Tibet as a stateless society and some Islamic parallels.**
Geoffrey Samuel. *Journal of Asian Studies*, vol. 41, no. 2 (Feb. 1982), p. 215–29. bibliog.

Samuel argues that there are structural differences between Tibet and other Buddhist states in Asia. In Tibet there was traditionally a great degree of local autonomy and right up until the 20th century the concept of a centralized state can hardly be said to have existed; neither the religious nor the political authorities were able to gain complete supremacy over the other. Parallels with Morocco and the North West Frontier Province are drawn to show that Buddhism in Tibetan society had many similarities with structurally similar Islamic societies.

419 **What is it behind the Dalai Lama's 'plan'?**
Sha Zhou. *Beijing Review*, vol. 33, no. 8 (19–25 Feb. 1990), p. 21–3.

This article presents a succinct summary of the Chinese government's response to the Dalai Lama's proposals (announced when he received the Nobel Peace Prize in December 1989) for establishing Tibet as a 'peace zone' or buffer state. The following extracts reflect the tone of both the Chinese official response and this article: 'Tibet is an inalienable part of China. On this question of such major importance to the future of the Chinese nation, there is no room for bargaining'; 'Independence, semi-independence or independence in disguised form is unacceptable'.

420 **Tibet, 10th March 1959.**
London: Tibetan Community in Britain, [1984?]. 12p.

This short pamphlet, published to mark the 25th anniversary of the Tibetan uprising, is less concerned with the events of 1959 than with posing the Tibetan question as it stands today. It puts forward the case in history and international law for Tibet's independence and includes a short article by the Dalai Lama in which he states that the free will of the Tibetan people is the only basis for determining their destiny and future relationship with China.

421 **Tibet: myth vs. reality.**
Beijing: *Beijing Review* Publications, 1988. 177p. (China in Focus).

A collection of articles, documents and carefully selected excerpts from books whose stated purpose is 'to counter the false charges against China concerning Tibet'. The customary historical arguments are deployed to demonstrate that Tibet is an integral part of China, whilst the picture painted of improving social and political conditions is very different from that of less partial outside observers.

422 **The PRC occupation of Tibet.**
Julian Weiss. *Journal of Social, Political and Economic Studies*, vol. 12, no. 4 (Winter 1987), p. 385–99. bibliog.

The author argues that since the fall of the Gang of Four and the supposed liberalization which followed, there have been only cosmetic changes to China's policy towards Tibet. The suppression of the peaceful protests by Tibetans in 1987 indicates that, for all China's show of liberalization, its policies towards Tibet are still a mixture of brutalization and colonialism.

Human Rights

423 **Chinese human rights abuses in Tibet, 1959–1982.**
[n.p.]: Committee to Voice the Aspirations of the Tibetan People,
[198–?]. 32p.

A report which claims that, despite efforts by the Chinese government to convince the
outside world to the contrary, Tibetans are still denied both political self-government
and fundamental human rights such as freedom of expression or the right of assembly.
Not only humans are said to have suffered – the catalogue of Chinese abuses even
includes the elimination of colonies of hares and marmots and the reduction in Tibet's
bird population.

424 **A dialogue on Tibet (II). Religion, crime and citizen's rights.**
Beijing Review, vol. 30, no. 43 (26 Oct. – 1 Nov. 1987), p. 21–2.

This short report of a question-and-answer session with senior officials of the Chinese
State Nationalities Commission attempts to show, not wholly successfully, that there is
now freedom of religious belief in Tibet and that all the mistakes made during the
Cultural Revolution have now been rectified.

425 **Tibet in China: a report for International Alert.**
Lord Ennals, Frederick R. Hyde-Chambers. London: International
Alert, 1988. 66p.

This pamphlet is the result of a fact-finding mission to Tibet undertaken in the spring
of 1988. The authors conclude: 'we are absolutely convinced that the depth of feeling
in Tibet will ensure that the issue of democratic and civil rights will grow in intensity
unless positive moves are made by the Chinese authorities to meet some of the Tibetan
demands.'

426 **Human Rights in Tibet: Hearing before the Subcommittees on Human Rights and International Organizations, and on Asian and Pacific Affairs of the Committee on Foreign Affairs, House of Representatives, 100th Congress, First Session, October 14, 1987.**
Washington, DC: US Government Printing Office, 1988. 160p.
These hearings were called to assess the state of human rights in Tibet following the anti-Chinese demonstrations in Lhasa in 1987 and to consider their implications for American foreign policy. Discussion ranged over such topics as the extent of religious freedom in Tibet, the effects of Chinese immigration and the Dalai Lama's proposals aimed at resolving the political conflict between Tibet and China; an appendix includes the text of his five-point peace plan.

427 **Merciless repression: human rights abuses in Tibet.**
New York: *Human Rights Watch*, Asia Watch Committee. 1990. 100p.
This report details the recent alleged abuses by the Chinese security forces against the Tibetans, and places them in the wider context of China's political and cultural repression of Tibet.

428 **The Chinese and human rights in Tibet: a report to the Parliamentary Human Rights Group.**
W. P. Ledger.   London: Parliamentary Human Rights Group, [1987?].
43p. bibliog.
This report covers the 1987 riots in Tibet as well as earlier events. The conclusion is that mistrust of China remains very strong amongst Tibetans, but that recent liberalization has led to improvements. Nevertheless Tibetans remain discriminated against in their own country and are increasingly outnumbered by Chinese immigrants in most towns. This last development poses the greatest threat to Tibet, but Tibetans also remain deprived of many fundamental human rights as defined by the UN declaration. The author believes that worldwide publicity and pressure can help reverse some of the Chinese policies.

429 **The Tibetans.**
Chris Mullin.   London: Minority Rights Group, 1981. 16p. maps.
bibliog. (Minority Rights Group report, no. 49)
Provides a summary of China's minorities policies in Tibet in theory and in practice, with the conclusion that, despite lip-service to the contrary, the object of Chinese policy has been sinocization with little regard to local feelings or wishes. The report was nevertheless considered by many critics to be too favourable to the Chinese, and the revised edition, published in 1983, is noticeably harsher in its judgement.

430 **The quest for universal responsibility: human rights violations in Tibet.**
Howard C. Sacks.   Dharamsala, India: Information Office, Central
Tibetan Secretariat, 1983. 53p.
The author argues the case for Tibetan self-determination, based on the will of the people rather than on legal claims or past legal ties, and gives a brief summary of Chinese human rights violations in Tibet since 1959. Appendices include a number of the key documents necessary to an understanding of Tibet's international status and the texts of the 1959 and 1961 UN resolutions on Tibet.

431 **Tibet: the facts: a report prepared by the Scientific Buddhist Association for the United Nations Commission on Human Rights.**
London: Scientific Buddhist Association, 1984. 22p. bibliog.

This sobering report concludes that about one million Tibetans have perished at the hands of the Chinese since 1950. It also accuses the Chinese of criminal mismanagement of Tibet's natural resources and of continuing cultural and religious oppression.

432 **Tibet to Tiananmen: Chinese human rights and United States foreign policy.**
W. Gary Vause. Baltimore, Maryland: University of Maryland School of Law, 1989. 47p. (Occasional papers/Reprints series in Contemporary Asian Studies no. 6–1989, 95).

This study analyses China's record on human rights in the light of both recent events in Tibet and the Tiananmen Square massacre in Beijing itself in 1989, and attempts to suggest an appropriate response on the part of the US government. Vause argues that whereas the human rights question is a matter of legitimate concern to the US involvement in the separatist movement and the Dalai Lama's political programmes is not, and that these issues should be dealt with entirely separately.

433 **Tibetan deputies on "human rights".**
Wang Peng, Yang Xiaobing. *Beijing Review*, vol. 32, no. 17 (24–30 April 1989), p. 23–5.

Most of the other entries in this section are all highly critical of the situation regarding human rights in Tibet; this article is included to show the other side of the coin. It consists of a number of interviews with highly placed members of the Tibetan 'establishment' who, naturally enough, find little fault with the existing situation and contrast it favourably with the conditions in the country before 1959.

Foreign Relations

434 China and Tibet, 1708–1959: a résumé of facts.
Zahiruddin Ahmad.   Oxford, England: Oxford University Press, 1960.
31p. maps. bibliog. (Chatham House Memoranda).
Tibet's international status and its relationship with China have never been easy matters on which to reach a satisfactory conclusion. This is a useful introduction for the non-specialist to the history of China's presence in Tibet from the 18th century onwards, with some coverage of Tibet's relations with Britain and Russia as well.

435 The boundary question between China and Tibet: a valuable record of the Tripartite Conference between China, Britain and Tibet held in India, 1913–1914.
Peking: [n.p.], 1940. 150p.
Reproduces the texts of some of the papers from the Tripartite Simla Conference, including the statements of each of the three parties on the boundaries of Tibet.

436 The evolution of India's northern borders.
P. C. Chakravarti.   New York: Asia Publishing House, 1971. 179p.
Tibet plays a subsidiary role in this account, the primary purpose of which is to produce arguments in favour of India's position in the boundary dispute with China.

437 Convention between the United Kingdom and China respecting Tibet, signed at Peking, April 27, 1906; to which is annexed the Convention between the United Kingdom and Tibet signed at Lhasa, September 7, 1904.
London: HMSO, 1906. 8p. (Cd. 3088: British Parliamentary Papers 1906, vol. CXXXVI, p. 119–26).
The official texts of the two conventions concerning Tibet which were negotiated by Britain as a result of the Younghusband Expedition reveal the British desire both to open up Tibet for trade and to prevent any foreign power interfering in the country.

438 Russia in Central Asia in 1889 and the Anglo-Russian question.

George Nathaniel Curzon. London: Longmans Green, 1889. 477p.

The importance of this work to a study of Tibet is that it represents the thinking of the man who, fifteen years later, as Viceroy of India, was to launch the Younghusband Expedition into Tibet. Curzon's book represents a classic exposition of the 'forward' policy of the British in Asia, a policy designed solely to protect their position in India by pre-empting Russian expansionism in Central Asia. In view of later events, it is therefore interesting that even at this date Curzon was warning of the dangers of Tibet falling into the Russian sphere of influence.

439 A brief study of the Bhutan–Tibet relations.

Srikant Dutt. *Tibetan Review*, vol. 13, no. 11 (Nov. 1978), p. 12–15.

Following the Chinese occupation of Tibet many Tibetans fled to Bhutan. However, relations between the Tibetans and the Bhutanese, never very good, deteriorated when Tibetan refugees were accused of plotting against the king of Bhutan in 1974. Written in the light of these events, this article attempts to analyse the poor relations between the two countries.

440 India–China–Tibet triangle.

Ram Gopal. Lucknow, India: Pustak Kendra, 1964. 225p.

Summarizes the claims and counter-claims over the disputed border between India and China and examines Tibet's international status. A selection of the relevant documentary sources is reproduced in the appendices. Tibet plays a somewhat secondary role to the main theme of Indo-Chinese relations in this book.

441 The Tibetan frontiers question from Curzon to the Colombo Conference: an unresolved factor in Indo-Sinic relations.

Frederic A. Greenhut II. New Delhi: S. Chand, 1982. 178p. maps. bibliog.

Many of the studies of the Indo-Chinese border dispute pay little attention to Tibet's own history and disputed international status. This book attempts to relate the dispute to its historical origins. Greenhut stresses the complexity of the dispute and the multiplicity of factors involved, and argues that the highly individualistic nature of Tibetan society and political organization were a major factor in causing the dispute to remain unresolved for so long.

442 A study of the treaties and agreements relating to Tibet: a documentary history of international relations of Tibet.

Hengtse Tu. Taichung, Taiwan: Tunghai University, 1971. 218p. bibliog.

Presents the text of over thirty documentary records relating to Tibet's international relations and status, ranging in time from the record of Tibetan conquests in western China in 763 AD, recorded on a stone pillar below the Potala, up to the United Nations General Assembly resolution on the question of Tibet in 1961. Materials selected for inclusion range from formal treaties and trade regulations to official statements on Tibet's status from a variety of sources.

443   **Tibet and imperial China: a survey of Sino-Tibetan relations up to the end of the Manchu dynasty in 1912.**
Josef Kolmas.   Canberra: Centre of Oriental Studies, Australian National University, 1967. 81p. (Australian National University, Centre of Oriental Studies. Occasional paper no. 7)
This brief introduction to the subject also includes some information on British relations with Tibet.

444   **Tibet, China and India, 1914–1950: a history of imperial diplomacy.**
Alastair Lamb.   Hertingfordury, England: Roxford Books, 1989. 594p. bibliog.
Alastair Lamb has written extensively on the history of Tibet and its part in the relations between British India and China and this book can be seen as a sequel to his *British India and Tibet, 1766–1910* (q.v.). It gives an elegant and well-researched introduction to the still unresolved border dispute between India and China, in which the southern borders of Tibet play a key part, and provides a sound basis for an understanding of the establishment of the McMahon Line and the events which have followed.

445   **The history of early relations between China and Tibet: from Chiu tang-shu: a documentary survey.**
Don Y. Lee.   Bloomington, Indiana: Eastern Press, 1981. 267p. bibliog.
Gives the English and Chinese text of an important documentary source covering the period of the T'ang dynasty up to 849 AD.

446   **The Sino-Indian border dispute: a legal study.**
Chih H. Lu.   Westport, Connecticut: Greenwood Press, 1986. 143p. bibliog. (Contributions in Political Science, no. 139).
Lu discusses the Sino-Indian border dispute in the context of international law and in the process reviews the problems surrounding Tibet's southern and western boundaries during the 20th century.

447   **The north-eastern frontier: a documentary study of the internecine rivalry between India, Tibet and China.**
Parshotam Mehra.   Delhi: Oxford University Press, 1979–80. 2 vols. bibliog.
This collection of documents grew up as an adjunct to the author's *The McMahon Line and after* (Macmillan, 1974). It gives the texts of most of the key documents covering the relations between Britain (and later India), Tibet and China, and includes formal treaties, government memoranda and exchange of notes, and the reports of agents on the spot, all essential source material for a study of India's north-east frontier region. There are also useful biographical sketches of all the major players in this particular version of 'the Great Game'.

448 **Tibet and her neighbours: a presentation of the historic facts of Tibet's relations with neighbouring states.**
Hugh E. Richardson.   London: Tibet Society, [1960?]. 5p. map.
A short papmhlet such as this cannot explore all the complexities of Tibet's relationship to China and international status over the centuries. Rather it should be seen as a polemical tract in the debate over Tibet's status sparked off by the events of 1959. Richardson argues that the historic relationship between China and Tibet never extended to full sovereignty, and that since the 1951 agreement was extorted under duress it should not be regarded as valid.

449 **Tibet at the United Nations.**
Hugh E. Richardson.   London: Tibet Society, [1960?]. 6p. map.
(Tibet Society paper, no. 3).
Gives a brief report of the debate on Tibet at the United Nations following the Chinese invasion of 1959. The indecisiveness and irresolution of both the British and the Indian delegates is highlighted.

450 **Mongols of the twentieth century.**
R. A. Rupen.   Bloomington, Indiana: Indiana University Press, 1964.
2 vols. bibliog. (Indiana University Publications. Uralic and Altaic Series, vol. 37)
This work is useful in giving information on Russia's relations with Tibet in the early 20th century. The Russian government was able to use Buryats such as Dorjieff as their agents in Tibet and there is some evidence that the Tibetans, faced with increasing pressure from both the British and the Chinese, occasionally considered employing Russian influence as a counterweight.

451 **Tibet: self-determination in politics among nations.**
Swarn Lata Sharma.   New Delhi: Criterion, 1988. 229p.
Sharma begins his book by stating the case for Tibetan self-determination. He then goes on to use Tibet as a case-study in an examination of the contrast between the 'pompous rhetorics' and actual behaviour of nations towards the norms of international law and morality, and suggests that as both the United States and the USSR have improved their relations with China, so their interest in the Tibet question has declined. India's need to maintain relations with her powerful neighbour has similarly coloured her approach to the problem.

452 **Tibet in the United Nations, 1950–1961.**
New Delhi: Bureau of His Holiness the Dalai Lama, [1975?]. 311p.
This is a useful compilation of proceedings in the United Nations on the occasions when Tibet was discussed during the period 1950–61. The texts of all the relevant UN documents, debates in the General Assembly and UN resolutions are included.

453 **Himalayan frontiers: a political review of British, Chinese, Indian and Russian rivalries.**
D. Woodman.   London: Barrie & Rockliff, 1969. 423p. maps.
Woodman's book gives a general history of the Himalayan frontier disputes. The texts of some of the relevant treaties and other documents are included in the appendices. The account of the Simla Conference is particularly useful.

Economy

454 **Almanac of China's economy 1981, with economic statistics for 1949–1980.**
Compiled by the Economic Research Centre, the State Council of the People's Republic of China and the State Statistical Bureau.
Hong Kong: Modern Cultural Company, 1982.
Contains a section on 'Economic development in Tibet Autonomous Region' by the General Office of the People's Government, Tibet Autonomous Region. It includes some statistics as well as a general survey of economic conditions in the region.

455 **Poudre d'or et monnaies d'argent au Tibet (principalement au XVIIIe siècle).** (Gold dust and silver money in Tibet, principally in the 18th century.)
Lucette Boulnois. Paris: Centre National de la Recherche Scientifique, 1982. 248p. maps. bibliog. (Cahiers népalais).
A well-researched and thorough history of gold in Tibet, covering its extraction, circulation and uses through all periods of history up to the present time, accompanied by a more detailed examination of Tibet's silver coinage in the 17th and 18th centuries, when Nepal minted Tibet's coins from silver provided by the Tibetans themselves.

456 **On trade between Calcutta, Darjeeling, Bhootan and Tibet (and between Assam, Tibet and west China).**
A. Campbell, H. Hopkinson. *Journal of the Royal Society of Arts*, vol. 17 (1869), p. 558–73.
The interest of this article today is that it provides a contemporary viewpoint on how the British saw trade with Tibet developing in the mid-19th century.

457 **First railway to the "Roof of the World".**
Chen Rinong. *China Reconstructs*, vol. 31, no. 1 (Jan. 1982),
p. 29–33. map.
This article was published to mark the completion of the railway line from Xining to
Golmud, a project which was started in the 1960s, abandoned during the Cultural
Revolution and restarted only in 1975. Eventually it is intended to take the line right
through to Lhasa, but already the line has brought economic benefits to Tibet as a
whole and Golmud, which has become the transport and communications hub linking
Tibet to the rest of China, in particular.

458 **China's reforms of Tibet and their effects on pastoralism.**
G. E. Clarke. Brighton, England: Institute of Development Studies,
1987. 60p. bibliog. (Institute of Development Studies, Discussion paper
237).
Based on fieldwork amongst the pastoral communities of southwestern and central
Tibet, this study concludes that whilst the changes that have taken place since 1978
have allowed a fuller economic use to be made of the existing infrastructure simple
analogies with the rest of China are inappropriate to Tibet. Large-scale investment by
the state in such things as roads, the growth of a private cash economy and the
development of an open market pricing system are all seen as positive developments,
but many problems of urban–rural linkage remain.

459 **Cooch Behar and Bhutan in the context of Tibetan trade.**
Arabinda Deb. *Kailash*, vol. 1, no. 1 (1973), p. 80–8.
In this article Deb examines the trade between Tibet and Bhutan in the late 18th and
early 19th centuries and discusses the attempts of the British in India to increase trade
with China via the land route through Tibet.

460 **Tibet and Bengal: a study in trade policy and trade pattern, 1775–1875.**
Arabinda Deb. *Bulletin of Tibetology* (1984), no. 1, p. 17–32.
Deb describes the trade patterns between Tibet and Bengal from the time of George
Bogle's mission to the end of the 19th century, relating their fluctuations to the various
wars of the period.

461 **Government, monastic and private taxation in Tibet.**
Surkhang Wangchen Gelek. *Tibet Journal*, vol. 11, no. 1 (Spring
1986), p. 21–40.
This article gives details of all the taxes payable both to the clerical and the lay
authorities in the old Tibet.

462 **The impact of China's reform policy on the nomads of western Tibet.**
Melvyn C. Goldstein, Cynthia M. Beall. *Asian Survey*, vol. 29, no. 6
(June 1989), p. 619–41.
This article, which is based on extensive fieldwork, concludes that the new Chinese
economic policies, implemented after 1980, have produced a considerable improvement in living standards amongst the nomadic pastoralists. Following decollectiviza-
tion, the nomads reverted to their traditional household system of production which

led to an increasing involvement in a market economy. Equally importantly, they were able to regain a measure of control over their culture and lifestyle.

463 Taxation and the structure of a Tibetan village.
Melvyn C. Goldstein. *Central Asiatic Journal*, vol. 15 (1971), p. 1–27.
In this article Goldstein examined the complex system of local and central taxation of one Tibetan village and county, Samada, which is situated near to Gyantse. The more general system of local government administration is also discussed.

464 Some dynamics of Indo-Tibetan trade through Uttarkhnada (Kumaon-Garhwal), India.
Maheshwar P. Joshi, C. W. Brown. *Journal of the Economic and Social History of the Orient*, vol. 30, no. 3 (Oct. 1987), p. 303–17.
This article gives a short historical survey of the trade between India and Tibet through the Kumaon-Garhwal region of Uttar Pradesh from the 17th century to the 19th century. The principal products to be exported from Tibet were gold, borax, horses and dogs and in return came pearls, corals, glass beads and cloth; during the period of British rule in India a trade in salt and grain was also built up.

465 Interest rates in Tibet.
Jampel Kaldhen. *Tibet Journal*, vol. 1, no. 1 (July/Sept. 1975), p. 109–12.
This note on the various rates of interest prevailing in the pre-1959 Tibetan economy also includes a useful table of Tibetan money. The credit practices and accompanying terminology have largely disappeared amongst the Tibetan community abroad and of course no longer exist in Tibet itself.

466 Buddhist monastic economy: the jisa mechanism.
Robert J. Miller. *Comparative Studies in Society and History*, vol. 3, no. 4 (1961), p. 427–38.
Jisa is a Tibetan word which means 'community property'. In practice, it describes the methods of using money or material goods which are given to the Buddhist monasteries to purchase religious services for the donor. This was a major element of the economic activities of the monasteries and Miller castigates as 'parasitic' in the sense that the system required economic growth in order to operate and yet there was no growth in the general economy; thus the monasteries fed off the lay community to the latter's disadvantage. It remains open to doubt, however, whether the Tibetan people themselves would have viewed their economy in this materialistic way.

467 India's trade with central Asia via Nepal.
Jahar Sen. *Bulletin of Tibetology*, vol. 8, no. 2 (July 1971), p. 21–40.
India's trade with Tibet and other areas of central Asia from the 16th century to the end of the 19th century is the subject of this article. The author finds that, despite the lure of central Asia, most official reports indicated that the possibilities for trade with Tibet were limited, and that the physical and political difficulties which prevented further development of trade were often underestimated.

468 **Tibet's economic reforms: an analysis.**
Liao Shu-hsing. *Issues and Studies*, vol. 22, no. 9 (Sept. 1986),
p. 69–85.

Liao Shu-hsing's analysis of the economic reforms introduced in the early 1980s indicates that the reforms had four main aims: to ameliorate anti-communist feelings by improving living standards, to reflect China's general 'open door' policy, to facilitate modernization, and to persuade the Dalai Lama and the other exiles to accept China's rule over Tibet. The reforms provided for greater individual responsibility, greater freedom in production, a more diversified economy with less emphasis on grain-growing and more on animal husbandry, and greater subsidies from the central government in Beijing. However, all this has not been enough and the author concludes that a weak infrastructure and lack of trained personnel mean that the immediate outlook is not good.

469 **Articles of Tibet trade, 1784.**
Nirmal C. Sinha. *Bulletin of Tibetology* (1984), no. 1, p. 21–5.

Despite the reputation of Tibet as physically and politically unsympathetic to trade, the authorities in India did make several attempts to build it up in the late 18th century. This article describes the report of Samuel Turner to the Bengal government and suggests that at that time the level of trade was actually quite high.

470 **Macro exchanges: Tibetan economics and the role of politics and religion.**
Thomas W. Wiley. *Tibet Journal*, vol. 11, no. 1 (Spring 1986),
p. 3–20.

The general structure of the Tibetan economy as it was before 1950 is surveyed in this wide-ranging article. Wiley divides the population into two basic groups: food producers and non-food producers. The former paid taxes and provided labour and other services to the latter who in return provided governmental and religious services to the country as a whole. He stresses that the nominally religious exchanges of this society were also economic in character: celibacy, for instance, also prevented excessive population growth.

Education

471 Cadre education in Tibet.
Roy Beena Burman. *China Report*, vol. 13, no. 1 (1977), p. 11–15.

Burman describes the way the Chinese set about changing the educational system after the 1951 takeover. Whereas previously education had been primarily religious and in the hands of the monasteries, the Chinese gradually introduced local schools with communist teachers. To begin with, some religious instruction was still provided, but by the 1960s this had been phased out.

472 The system of monastic education in Tibet.
Lama Chimpa. *Indian Studies, Past and Present*, vol. 6, no. 1 (Oct.-Dec. 1964), p. 99–105.

The author was himself a student at Drepung Monastery during 1943–49, and he provides a first-hand account of the system of education that existed in Tibet prior to the communist takeover. He describes the course of study that was followed in the learning of philosophy (the complete course took 19 years), and chronicles a typical day of a student. Special colleges were established for the study of specialized disciplines such as medicine and astronomy, but it is interesting to note that in old Tibet education was (with the exception of a few elementary schools in the towns) confined to the monasteries, and that there was no provision for the education of children of the common people or of women at all.

473 Education in Tibet.
Tashi Dorjee. *Tibet Journal*, vol. 2, no. 4 (Winter 1977), p. 31–7.

This article describes the various systems of education which existed in Tibet before the changes introduced by the communists. There were schools for monk cadres and for lay officials planning to enter the government administration, special schools for the study of medicine and astrology, and private schools primarily for the children of the nobility. Some details of the curricula are included.

474 **Language planning for China's ethnic minorities.**
June Teufel Dreyer. *Pacific Affairs*, vol. 51, no. 3 (Fall 1978),
p. 369–83.
Although dealing with the Communist Party's attitude towards minority languages
throughout the People's Republic of China, this article is of obvious importance to a
study of language policies in Tibet since 1951. It charts the relationship between the
changing policies and the main political trends of the period such as the Great Leap
Forward and the Cultural Revolution, but finds that whether the official policy was one
of tolerance or repression, the minorities showed a marked reluctance to learn Han,
whilst the Han Chinese living in the minority areas showed an equal reluctance to learn
the local language.

475 **National-minority education in the People's Republic of China.**
John N. Hawkins. *Comparative Education* (1978), no. 1, p. 147–62.
This article provides an overview of Chinese educational policies towards the national
minorities from 1949 up to the mid-1970s. Hawkins argues that that Han–minority
educational relations have not been a simple matter of sinocization; rather, there has
been disagreement and conflict between the Chinese and minority leaders as they have
attempted to follow policies designed to satisfy the divergent interests of both groups,
with the struggle between conflict and integration remaining finely balanced.

476 **The education of national minorities in communist China.**
C. T. Hu. Washington, DC: US Government Printing Office, 1970.
30p. (Office of Education report OE-14146).
Hu describes the education of China's fifty-four national minorities against the
background of the country's internal politics, and shows how the government's attempt
to integrate minorities into the mainstream of China's national life has affected its
educational policies in minority areas. Some statistics are contained in the appendices.

477 **Education among minority peoples.**
Li Yongzeng. *Beijing Review*, vol. 26, no. 42 (1983), p. 16–23.
In this article, which deals with the education of all China's minority nationalities, the
author admits that it will be some time before universal education can be achieved in
the minority areas, but blames the slow progress on feudalism and the poor economic
conditions which the Chinese inherited from the past. There is also a brief account of
the work of the Central Institute for Nationalities in Beijing.

478 **Research guide to education in China after Mao, 1977–1981.**
Compiled by Billie L. C. Lo. Hong Kong: University of Hong Kong
Centre of Asian Studies, 1983. 221p. bibliog. (Centre of Asian Studies
Bibliographies and Research Guides, no. 21).
This compilation contains three kinds of information: statistics, information about
conferences and a lengthy bibliography. There are sections on education for the
national minorities under each of these headings. The information was collected from
both primary and secondary sources, drawing on more than twenty periodicals,
newspapers and yearbooks covering the period 1977–81.

Education

479 **Debate in Tibetan Buddhist education.**
Daniel Perdue. Dharamsala, India: Library of Tibetan Works and
Archives, 1976. 111p. bibliog.

Debate has always formed a major part of Tibetan Buddhist education. This book
provides an introduction to monastic debate through reproducing, with a commentary,
the first chapter of a Tibetan debating manual. This illustrates the general features of
this system of education and more generally of Buddhist logic and epistemology.

480 **Educational development in the PRC: regional and ethnic disparities.**
Liao Shu-hsing. *Issues and Studies*, vol. 22, no. 9 (Sept. 1986),
p. 73–94.

Drawing on the official 1982 census figures, this article argues that the level of illiteracy
is higher amongst the national minorities in China than amongst the Han population.
Tibet emerges as one of the worst areas with 75 per cent of the indigenous population
illiterate or semi-literate.

481 **Random notes from Tibet University.**
Yang Xin, Duo Fen. *Beijing Review*, vol. 31, no. 47 (21–27 Nov.
1988), p. 20–2.

This brief description of Tibet University, which was founded in 1985, reveals that it
has 778 students and that of its eight departments three concentrate solely on Tibetan
subjects: Tibetan language, Tibetan medicine and Tibetan arts. As one would expect
from an article in this journal, the overall picture that is given of the university is
entirely favourable.

Literature

General

482 Materials for a history of Tibetan literature.
Edited by Lokesh Chandra.   New Delhi: International Academy of
Indian Culture, 1963. 3 vols. bibliog.
Contains a selection of important texts in Tibetan, with introductions to each volume
in English.

483 Matériaux pour l'étude de la littérature populaire tibétaine. (Materials
for the study of Tibetan popular literature.)
A. W. Macdonald.   Paris: Presses Universitaires de France, Librairie
C. Klincksieck, 1967–72. 2 vols.
These two volumes contain twenty-one Tibetan stories, both in Tibetan and in French
translation, by Nagarjuna. Their subjects are the classic ones of religion, magic and the
supernatural.

484 Tibetan literature of the eighteenth century.
L. S. Savitsky, translated from the Russian by Stanley Frye.   *Tibet
Journal*, vol. 1, no. 2 (April/June 1976), p. 43–6.
This brief introduction to the subject gives a description of the general nature of
Tibetan literature followed by an analysis of the lyric poetry of the 6th Dalai Lama.

485 Recherches sur l'épopée et le barde au Tibet. (Researches into the epic
and the bard in Tibet.)
Rolf A. Stein.   Paris: Imprimerie Nationale, 1959. 639p. map. bibliog.
The subject of this massive and scholarly book is the Tibetan epic. It contains an
extensive bibliography of Tibetan, Mongol and Chinese sources.

Poetry

486 Songs of the Sixth Dalai Lama.
Translated from the Tibetan by K. Dhondup.   Dharamsala, India:
Library of Tibetan Works and Archives, 1981. 172p. bibliog.

Contains both Tibetan texts and English translations of the poems of the 6th Dalai
Lama. There is a very useful introduction which gives a brief history of the
controversial 6th Dalai Lama and an analysis of the poems and some of the problems
encountered in translating them, not least because some of them contain hidden tantric
meanings.

487 Love songs and proverbs of Tibet.
Marion Herbert Duncan.   London: Mitre Press, 1961. 239p.

Most of the poems and proverbs contained in this volume were collected by the author
during his stay in eastern Tibet during 1921–36 and were translated by him. The
majority of them are traditional, having been handed down orally over many
generations, but a few of them are of more recent date. A brief introduction to Tibetan
poetry points out that the majority of the love songs were composed for singing back
and forth between Tibetan men and women.

**488 The hundred thousand songs: selections from Milarepa, poet-saint of
Tibet.**
Translated from the Tibetan by Antoinette K. Gordon, with an
introduction by Peter Fingestein.   Tokyo; Rutland, Vermont: C. E.
Tuttle, 1961. 122p. bibliog.

Milarepa was born in 1039 and died in 1122. The songs, twenty-four of which are
translated in this selection, describe his life in the solitude of the mountains, his yogi
achievements in self-discipline and his attainment of freedom and enlightenment. Two
of them are here presented in musical transcription. Before his time the literature of
Tibet consisted mainly of historical or religious works; his songs and poems have
attained something of the status of classics, mainly because of their universal appeal,
equally comprehensible to scholars and villagers alike.

**489 Miraculous journey: further stories and songs of Milarepa, yogin, poet
and teacher of Tibet: thirty-seven selections from the rare collection**
Stories and songs from the oral tradition of Jetsun Milarepa.
Translated by Lama Kunga Rimpoche, Brian Cutillo.   Novato,
California: Lotsawa, 1986. 232p. bibliog.

This collection of previously untranslated narratives and songs of Milarepa differs from
The hundred thousand songs (q.v.) in both the range of material and the directness of
style. They range from advice given to villagers and nomads to the more profound
insights he vouchsafed to his closest disciples and, taken as a whole, give a more
intimate picture of his character and personality.

490 **Chants from Shangri-la.**
Original translation from the Tibetan by Flora Beal Shelton, revised and edited by Doris Shelton Still. Palm Springs, California: [n.p.], 1939. 93p.

Contains eighteen chants translated from handwritten books held by a lamasery in eastern Tibet. Most of them are reputed to have been written by Milarepa or his disciples.

491 **Wings of the white crane.**
Poems of Tshangs dbyangs rgya mtsho (1683–1706), translated by G. W. Houston. Delhi: Motilal Banarsidass, 1982. 53p.

Gives the English and Tibetan texts of poems by the 6th Dalai Lama. These poems often have two or even three levels of meaning; whilst expressing religious concepts they may also have an erotic second meaning. The language of the poems also contains this duality for it uses vocabulary fom both the classical literary language and the colloquial language of the period.

Drama

492 **Harvest festival dramas of Tibet.**
Marion Herbert Duncan. Hong Kong: Orient Publishing, 1955. 275p. map.

Presents the English text of three indigenous harvest festival dramas: the religious emancipation of the fairy Drowazangmo, the historical drama of Songtsan Gampo, and the emancipation of the noble-born fairy sprite Nangsa Ohbum. Between the sections are photographs of performances witnessed by the author in 1925, 1929, 1930 and 1931 at Batang. There is a useful introductory chapter on Tibetan mystery plays and the harvest festival which explains that all the plays in essence portray the triumph of Buddhism over the previous spirit worship of the Bon religion.

493 **More harvest festival dramas of Tibet.**
Marion H. Duncan. London: Mitre Press, 1967. 123p.

The two plays in this volume, *Drimeh Kundan* and *Donyoh Dondruh*, are translations of Indian dramas into the Tibetan language and adapted to be acted according to Tibetan theatrical practice for performance at the harvest festival dances. The general themes of the plays are the same as those presented in Duncan's earlier work and there are again photographs of performances.

494 **Notes sur le théâtre tibétain.** (Notes on Tibetan theatre.)
André Migot. *Revue d'Histoire du Théâtre* (1958), no. 1, p. 9–20.

This article gives a brief introduction to both the religious and the secular drama, mime and dance of Tibet. Migot points out that the repertoire is quite small, and he gives synopses of some of the more well-known dramas.

495 **Tales from Tibetan opera.**
Edited and narrated by Wang Yao. Beijing: New World Press, 1986.
214p.

A collection of eight Tibetan stories frequently performed in Tibet. This book gives only the synopsis of each opera, not the complete text. There is a useful short introduction to Tibetan opera as a whole which explains that it is a comprehensive performing art which presents the stories through the medium of singing and dancing. The texts, dances, melodies, masks and costumes took shape by assimilating religious rites and Tibetan folklore.

496 **Three Tibetan mysteries: Tchrimekunden, Nansal, Djronzanmo, as performed in Tibetan monasteries.**
Translated from the French version of Jacques Bacot, with an introduction, notes and index, by H. I. Woolf. London: Routledge, 1924. 268p. (Broadway Translations).

These three dramas are representative of Tibetan theatre as a whole. The first, one of the most frequently performed, tells the story of the Buddha-to-be who passes a life of remarkable trials, all of which he has brought onto himself through his passion for charity and superhuman virtue. The second is the story of two children and their struggles against a wicked queen; it is thus an allegory of the general struggle of good against evil and the ultimate triumph of the former. The final drama is a much later work and is more secular in tone; it presents a portrait of Tibetan manners through a study of characters where everything is normal and controlled, with few of the marvels that characterize the other works.

497 **The younger brother Don Yod . . . being the secret biography from the words of the Glorious Lama the Holy Reverend Blo bZang Ye SHes.**
Translated by Thubten Jigme Norbu, Robert B. Ekvall.
Bloomington, Indiana: Indiana University Press, 1969. 148p. bibliog.

The title of this work is misleading as it is not the biography of the 2nd Panchen Lama, but a fanciful allegory, narrated by the Panchen Lama, with a clear political purpose. Despite being narrated in the third person, the story is essentially drama and was played all over Tibet especially in autumn and at the New Year festivals. The story contains two distinct themes: one is political in character and concerns intrigues and power struggles, the other is a folk theme of the love between two half-brothers. The original text dates from the 17th century and was intended to show the primacy of the Panchen Lama over the Dalai. This edition contains the text in both Tibetan and English.

Prose

498 Lama: a novel of Tibet.
Frederick R. Hyde-Chambers.   London: Souvenir Press, 1984. 476p.
maps.

Set in the period 1956–59, this is a sweeping saga of the destruction of the old Tibet, written by a Westerner strongly sympathetic to Tibetan culture.

499 The superhuman life of Gesar of Ling.
Alexandra David-Neel, Lama Yongden, translated with the
collaboration of Violet Sydney.   London: Rider, 1959. 271p.

The epic of Gesar of Ling has been described as the *Iliad* of central Asia. The hero is a deified warrior king who, with his magic weapons and riding on his winged horse, triumphs over the forces of evil and injustice. Many of the stories and poems involve demons, spells and magic creations, but, like many of the Greek myths, it is thought that they have some basis in historical fact. Originally orally transmitted, later some of the stories were written down and grouped in a subject order.

500 Tibetan tales derived from Indian sources.
Translated from the Tibetan of the Kangyur by F. Anton von
Schiefner, and from the German into English by W. R. S. Ralston.
London: Routledge, 1926. 368p. (Broadway Translations).

The fifty stories and tales presented in this volume are drawn from the Kanjur. Most of them contain little that is specifically Tibetan, having their roots in far older versions in India.

501 Mipam: the lama of five wisdoms: a Tibetan novel.
Lama Yongden, English version by Percy Lloyd.   Albany, New York:
State University of New York Press, 1987. 340p.

First published in 1938, this is the first novel written by a Tibetan lama especially for Western readers. The author was the adopted son of Alexandra David-Neel. The characters are very two-dimensional but they have clearly been drawn with affection, and the work is of interest for the portrait it paints of the old Tibet.

Art

General

502 **Les arts du Népal et du Tibet.** (The arts of Nepal and Tibet.)
Gilles Beguin. Paris: Desclée de Brouwer, 1987. 158p. map. bibliog.
This is an excellent introduction to the art of Tibet which covers architecture, painting and sculpture. The general approach is chronological and the book is well illustrated throughout. A glossary of Tibetan divinities and a topographical index increase its usefulness as a reference work.

503 **The art of Burma, Korea, Tibet.**
Alexander B. Griswold, Chewon Kim, Peter H. Pott. New York: Greystone Press, 1968. rev. ed. 273p. maps. bibliog. (Art of the World).
This useful introduction to the subject emphasizes that the paramount influence on Tibetan art was religion. Thus the artist created works to meet ritualistic needs rather than as a response to unhampered creative impulses. There are thirty colour plates of wooden and bronze sculptures, scroll paintings and decorated ritual objects such as priests' helmets and reliquary caskets.

504 **Early Sino-Tibetan art.**
Heather Karmay. Warminster, England: Aris & Phillips, 1975. 128p. bibliog.
Whereas most studies of Tibetan art emphasize its connections with Indian art, this book deals with its relationship to the art of China and central Asia. Paintings, woodcuts and bronzes all receive detailed examination with the aim of mapping the stylistic development of pre-17th-century Tibetan art.

505 **Tibetan art.**
John Lowry. London: HMSO, 1973. 111p. bibliog.
Describes fifty items from the collections of the Victoria & Albert Museum, London. These include thangkas, textiles, ivory prayer wheels and bronzes. Regrettably, none of the illustrations are in colour.

506 **Essais sur l'art du Tibet.** (Essays on Tibetan art.)
Ariane Macdonald, Yoshiro Imaeda (et al.). Paris: Librairie d'Amérique et d'Orient, 1977. 188p. map. bibliog.
A general introduction to different aspects of Tibetan art, partly in English and partly in French. Contributions include a detailed description of the Jokhang by Hugh Richardson and an article on Tibetan costume by Heather Karmay.

507 **Catalogue of the Tibetan collection and other Lamaist articles in the Newark Museum.**
Newark, New Jersey: Newark Museum Association, 1950–71. 5 vols.
The Newark Museum's Tibetan collection is one of the finest in the world and this illustrated catalogue forms an excellent introduction to it. Every kind of object is included, ranging from textiles, paintings, musical instruments and jewellery to fire-making and tobacco utensils, coins and stamps.

508 **Mystic art of ancient Tibet.**
Blanche Christine Olschak in collaboration with Geshe Thupten Wangyal. London: Allen & Unwin, 1973. 224p. bibliog.
This classic presentation of Tibetan art covers painted scrolls, frescos, book illustrations, bronzes, miniatures and sculptures in wood and stone. Among the 372 black-and-white illustrations is a series of 300 Tibetan icons, a chronological presentation of the saints and gurus of Tibetan Buddhism. There are also 142 colour plates.

509 **The art of Tibet.**
Pratapaditya Pal, with an essay by Eleanor Olsen. New York: Asia Society, 1969. 163p. bibliog.
The catalogue of an exhibition shown in the Asia House Gallery in 1969 which contains over 120 black-and-white illustrations and 4 colour plates. It is interesting that the exhibition included several everyday objects such as tea cups, beer jugs and saddles to illustrate that aesthetic sensibility was as present in the non-religious as in the religious context of Tibetan life.

510 **Lamaist art: the aesthetics of harmony.**
Pratapaditya Pal, Hsien-Ch'i Tseng. Boston, Massachusetts: Museum of Fine Arts, 1975. 56p.
A catalogue of the exhibits of the 'Hidden Treasures' exhibition held by the Boston Museum of Fine Art. Seventy-six examples of Tibetan art are described in detail and most are accompanied by illustrations. In the introduction the author describes the historical background, Lamaist imagery and the aesthetics of harmony, the three features which he sees as the keys to Buddhist art.

511 **Chine . . . Japon . . . Corée . . . Tibet . . .: catalogue des collections de la Bibliothèque Forney.** (China . . . Japan . . . Korea . . . Tibet . . .: catalogue of the collections of the Bibliothèque Forney.)
Joelle Pineau. Paris: Bibliothèque Forney, 1989. 234p.

Contains a bibliography of about fifty books and articles, in European languages, on all aspects of Tibetan art.

512 **Gyantse and its monasteries.**
Giuseppe Tucci, edited by Lokesh Chandra, from a first draft translation by Uma Marina Vesci. New Delhi: Aditya Prakashan, 1989. 3 vols. map.

This major study of the artistic treasures of the Gyantse area first appeared in Italian in 1941. The first part describes the art monuments (seventy-three major temples) around Gyantse and places them in the general context of Tibetan political, cultural and artistic history, with some emphasis on the influence of Indian Buddhist iconography. Part two contains a transcription and translation of the more significant inscriptions to be found in the temples, and part three includes approximately 400 black-and-white illustrations.

513 **Early temples of central Tibet.**
Roberto Vitali. London: Serindia, 1990. 150p. maps. bibliog.

This is a major visual and scholarly study of the monuments and styles of Tibetan art and architecture of the 8th to the 15th centuries. Amongst the temples which are studied in detail are the Jokhang in Lhasa, Kachu, Shalu, Yemar and Drathang. The book is profusely illustrated, mainly in colour, and there are also plans and elevations of the principal buildings which are described.

514 **Heritage of Tibet.**
W. Zwalf. London: British Museum Publications, 1981. 144p. map. bibliog.

Published in conjunction with a major British Museum exhibition of the same title, this book provides a concise and readable introduction to the civilization of Tibet, with particular emphasis on painting, sculpture, costumes and jewellery. Chapters on the history and religion of Tibet place the arts and crafts of the country in context. Well illustrated with twelve colour and eighty-five black-and-white photographs.

Painting

515 **Tibetan thangka painting: methods and materials.**
David P. Jackson, Janice A. Jackson, with appendix by Robert Beer. London: Serindia, 1984. 186p.

This book provides a detailed description of the techniques and principles of thangka painting and is designed for use by artists and others seeking to produce their own thangkas. The theories underlying the painting methods are explained and different chapters present the basic principles of composition and proportion; the book also contains a step-by-step guide to the making of a thangka from the preparation of the canvas through to the final application of the sacred symbols behind each figure. In order to help artists in the West, where the traditional pigments may not be available, Robert Beer's appendix discusses in depth how to use modern techniques and commercially available materials to produce a satisfactory thangka.

516 **Tibetan paintings: a study of Tibetan thangkas eleventh to nineteenth centuries.**
Pratapaditya Pal.   London: Ravi Kumar, Sotheby Publications, 1984. 225p. bibliog.
This is a lucid history of the various styles of thangkas, with particular emphasis placed on the earlier styles which flourished between the 11th and 15th centuries. Profusely illustrated with 115 colour plates and a number of black-and-white illustrations.

517 **Tibetan painted scrolls.**
Giuseppe Tucci, translated from the Italian by Virginia Vocca.   Rome: Libreria dello Stato, 1949. 2 vols.
Giuseppe Tucci's book remains the classic work on the subject which no serious scholar can afford to ignore. It is illustrated by 257 plates, some of them in colour.

Architecture

518 **The Potala of Tibet.**
Edited by Anthony Guise.   London: Stacey International, 1988. map. bibliog.
This is a revised edition of the 1982 book on the Potala listed below (q.v.). Like that, it is primarily a collection of sumptuous colour photographs, but the introductory article by Richard Kemp attempts to place the Potala in the context of Tibetan history.

519 **The Potala Palace of Tibet; hsi-tsang pu-ta-la kung.**
Shanghai: People's Art Publishing House; Hong Kong: Joint Publishing Co., 1982. 121p. map.
The Potala Palace in Lhasa, residence of the Dalai Lamas, is undoubtedly the greatest building in Tibet and arguably one of the greatest buildings in the world. This high-quality illustrated book provides the perfect introduction to it. Some of the illustrations of the interior are particularly noteworthy, whilst the introduction places the palace in its historical context.

520 **The architecture of Tibet: an introductory bibliography.**
Edward H. Teague.   Monticello, Illinois: Vance Bibliographies, 1985. 7p. (Architecture Series: Bibliography, A 1382).
This short survey of the subject provides a number of leads for further reading.

Crafts

521 **The Tibetan carpet.**
Philip Denwood.   Warminster, England: Aris and Phillips, 1974. 101p. maps. bibliog.
A detailed description of the materials and methods used in making traditional Tibetan carpets, with some notes on the origins of the craft and on some of the traditional design patterns. The book's value is enhanced by 24 colour plates and 83 black-and-white illustrations.

522 **Tibetan rugs.**
Hallavard Kare Kuloy.   Bangkok: White Orchid Press, 1982. 236p. bibliog.
A general introduction to the wide range of Tibetan rug designs, qualities and uses. The book describes the materials used and the methods of production, and attempts to identify the most commonly used symbols and design elements of Tibetan rugs. It is profusely illustrated.

523 **The tiger rugs of Tibet.**
Edited with an introduction by Mimi Lipton.   London: Hayward Gallery, 1988. 190p. bibliog.
This book was published to accompany the exhibition of the same name at the Hayward Gallery in 1988 and it includes colour plates of 108 tiger rugs. These rugs are extremely rare, the first example to reach the West being purchased by the Newark Gallery as recently as 1979. They were used in Tibetan New Year dances. The tiger was a symbol of power in Tibet and a tiger skin was considered a suitable seat for tantric practitioners, protecting them from environmental disturbances.

524 **Tibetan porcelain.**
Rinchen T. Sandhutsang.   *Tibet Journal*, vol. 8, nos 1/2 (Spring/Summer 1982), p. 81–2.
Porcelain was produced in Tibet only from the 8th to the 14th centuries AD. The technique was learnt from China and the finest wares, known as Thang-ker, were made at Yarlung Thangpoche during the 9th to 12th centuries. This article provides an interesting introduction to an almost forgotten Tibetan craft.

525 **Tibetan amulets.**
Tadeusz Skorupski.   Bangkok: White Orchid Press, 1983. 122p.
After placing the use of charms and amulets in the general context of Tibetan beliefs, this book gives a detailed description of 109 examples of Tibetan amulets and reproduces their design in line drawings.

526 **Tibetan and Himalayan woodblock prints.**
Introduction and captions by Douglas Weiner.   New York: Dover Publications, 1974. 66p.
Reproduces sixty-five woodblock prints collected by the compiler in India and Nepal. Like most Himalayan art, they are largely inspired by religious devotion.

Printing and book production

527 **The books of Tibet.**
Prince Peter of Greece and Denmark. *Libri: international library review*, vol. 5, no. 1 (1954), p. 20–8.

Contains a short history of printing in Tibet and a description of the physical composition of Tibetan books, which generally consist of loose leaves of bark or paper between two boards of wood. The article also includes short descriptions of some of the principal Tibetan texts, both religious and secular, and a note on the library holdings of Tibetan books in the West.

Music

528 **The ritual music of Tibet.**
Peter Crossley-Holland. *Tibet Journal*, vol. 1, nos 3 and 4 (Autumn 1976), p. 45–54. bibliog.
The author argues that Buddhist, Tantric and Bonist influences are all present in Tibetan ritual music which is not concerned with aesthetics or the pleasure of the senses, but is entirely symbolic and aimed at guiding humanity towards the truth.

529 **The state of research in Tibetan folk music.**
Peter Crossley-Holland. *Ethnomusicology*, vol. 11, no. 2 (May 1967), p. 170–87. bibliog.
Published and oral sources on Tibetan folk music are very scanty; this article reviews those sources that are available including records. It is interesting to note that the first recordings of Tibetan music were not made until 1944, and that recordings of folk music were not made until after the Chinese occupation, and then mainly amongst refugee communities abroad.

530 **Indian influences in Tibetan music.**
Ter Ellingson. *World Music*, vol. 24, no. 3 (1982). p. 85–93.
Shows that some of the features of Tibetan music that have been considered wholly indigenous do in fact have Indian origins; many of these features have now wholly disappeared from Indian culture so that their study will lead to a better understanding of both cultures.

531 **The mandala of sound: concepts and sound structures in Tibetan ritual music.**
Terry Jay Ellingson.   PhD thesis, University of Wisconsin, Madison, 1979. 831p. bibliog. (Available from University Microfilms, Ann Arbor, Michigan, order no. AAC 8001136).
The author describes this thesis as a systematic, although incomplete, descriptive and explanatory outline of Tibetan music; in fact it is a major study of all aspects of the subject, including a history of music in the Tibetan kingdom and in Indian and Tibetan Buddhism, an examination of the role of musicians in the monastic community, and sections describing musical concepts and theory, vocal music and melody, instrumental music and musical performance in the ritual context. The role of performers and composers and of music lessons and training are also discussed.

532 **La musique du bouddhisme tibétain.** (The music of Tibetan Buddhism.)
Ivan Vandor.   Paris: Buchet/Chastel, 1976. 138p. discography. (Les traditions musicales, VII).
Very little has been written on Tibetan music so this book is welcome as an introduction suitable for the layman and specialist alike. The first chapters cover the more general topics of Tibetan musical history and ritual, the composition of a Tibetan orchestra and Tibetan instruments leading on to the more specialized topics such as vocal music and Tibetan musical notation. The research for the book was carried out in Nepal and India in 1972–73.

Folklore

533 Folk culture of Tibet.
Norbu Chophel.   Dharamsala, India: Library of Tibetan Works and
Archives, 1983. 105p.

This is a useful and readable introduction to the popular omens, superstitions and beliefs of Tibet. Superstitions are described relating to the birth of a child, to man and his clothes, foods and animals, including a section on the significance of the language of ravens which reveals many messages and portents. The traditional interpretations of many Tibetan dreams are also explained.

534 Folk tales of Tibet.
Norbu Chophel.   Dharamsala, India: Library of Tibetan Works and
Archives, 1984. 186p.

Comprises a collection of twenty-eight stories from Tibet's oral folk tradition.

535 Tibetan folk tales.
Frederick Hyde-Chambers, Audrey Hyde-Chambers.   Boulder,
Colorado; London: Shambhala, 1981. 186p.

Contains a selection of over thirty legends and folk tales. They include a part of the epic of the warrior-king Gesar of Ling, some myths of creation, tales of the origins of some important deities and parables of men and animals.

536 **The life story of Drowa Sangmo.**
Translated by Cynthia Bridgeman Josayma with Losang Norbu
Tsonawa.   Dharamsala, India: Library of Tibetan Works and
Archives, 1983. 75p.
This traditional opera is one of the most popular folk tales of Tibet. Like all such tales
it is full of kings, queens, fairies and demons and is rich in religious symbolism.
Through prayer and fortitude, a young prince and princess overcome a series of
hardships and inherit a kingdom sworn to Buddhism.

537 **Folk tales of Tibet.**
Flora Beal Shelton.   Dallas, Texas: Story Book Press, 1951. 38p.
Contains ten short tales, collected from oral tradition. Each one is headed by an
apposite Tibetan proverb.

538 **Stories from beyond the clouds: an anthology of Tibetan folk tales.**
Clifford Thurlow.   Dharamsala, India: Library of Tibetan Works and
Archives, 1975. 188p.
Contains eleven short stories typical of Tibetan folklore.

539 **Tibetan folk songs from Gyantse and western Tibet.**
Collected and translated by Giuseppe Tucci, with two appendices by
Namkhai Norbu.   Ascona, Switzerland: Artibus Asiae, 1966.
2nd rev. ed. 200p. bibliog. (*Artibus Asiae. Supplementum* 22).
Contains the texts in both Tibetan and English of folk songs from Gyantse and
marriage songs from western Tibet, with some notes on nuptial rituals in Spiti. There
are no musical transcriptions.

Philately

540 The postal history of Tibet.
Arnold C. Waterfall.   London: Robson Lowe, 1965. 174p. bibliog.

Based on the author's own collection, which incorporated that of H. R. Holmes, and many of the stamps amassed by Colonel F. M. Bailey, this is a detailed description of all the stamps issued in Tibet, by the British, the Chinese and the Tibetans themslves, up to 1960. The first stamps appear to have been issued by the field post offices attached to the British Mission of 1903. The Chinese established post offices in 1909 and the first issue of Tibet's own stamps occurred in 1912. As well as a description of each issue, there are also sections dealing with handstamps and cancellations, with forgeries, and with the special issues of the various Everest expeditions.

Astronomy and Astrology

541   **An introduction to Tibetan astronomy and astrology.**
       Alexander Berzin.   *Tibet Journal*, vol. 12, no. 1 (Spring 1987),
       p. 17–28.
An interesting article which demonstrates that the Tibetan astronomical and astrological systems are derived from both classical Hindu and Chinese sources. The Tibetan system of astronomy is self-contained and was never intended for accurate navigation; to the Tibetans, therefore, it is immaterial that it does not correspond with Western observations. Astrology also differs from its Western counterpart in that it is perceived not in terms of influence from the planets but rather as the reflection of the results of the individual's previous behaviour.

Food

542 **Food in Tibetan life.**
Rinjing Dorje.   London: Prospect Books, 1985. 120p.
This is the most easily accessible book in English to describe Tibetan foods, their preparation and cooking, and their relation to Tibetan culture. The introductory chapters place Tibetan food in their appropriate cultural and social contexts, but the greater part of the book is devoted to Tibetan recipes. These are given in their true Tibetan form, but helpful alternative suggestions are made where an ingredient is not readily obtainable in Western countries.

543 **Tibetan cooking: a pioneer book on the food and cookery of the well known mysterious and one time forbidden land.**
Indra Majupuria.   Gwalior, India: S. Devi, 1981. 103p. bibliog.
An interesting and readable introduction to Tibet's food and cooking, written by a well-known student of Tibetan society.

Periodicals

544 **Bulletin of Tibetology.**
Gangtok, Sikkim: Sikkim Research Institute of Tibetology, 1964– .
3 issues per year.
Each issue generally contains a number of general-interest articles on Tibetan culture, religion and history.

545 **Central Asiatic Journal.**
Wiesbaden, Germany: Otto Harrassowitz, 1955– . semi-annual.
This scholarly journal has articles on the language, literature, history and archaeology of all the central Asian countries and territories including Tibet. Book reviews are included.

546 **Journal of the Tibet Society.**
Bloomington, Indiana: Tibet Society, 1981– . annual.
A scholarly journal containing substantial articles on a wide range of subjects relating to Tibet. Major book reviews are included.

547 **Tibet Journal.**
Dharamsala, India: Library of Tibetan Works and Archives, 1975– .
quarterly.
Under the direction of the Library of Tibetan Works and Archives, this journal contains both scholarly and general-interest articles on Tibetan culture and civilization. Each issue normally contains a number of book reviews. Several special thematic issues have also been produced.

Periodicals

548   **Tibet News Review.**
London: Tibetan Community in Britain, 1980– . irregular.

Contains notes and news of events in Tibet and amongst the Tibetan community abroad, mainly in Britain; generally insubstantial.

Bibliographies

549 **A guide to source materials in the India Office Library and Records for the history of Tibet, Sikkim and Bhutan 1765–1950.**
Amar Kaur Jasbir Singh.   London: British Library, 1988. 187p.
The principal section of this guide details the archives, both public and private, held in the India Office records which document the development of British India's relations with the Himalayan region. Also included are maps, official publications, prints and drawings, printed books in European languages and some Tibetan-language material.

550 **Bibliography of Asian Studies.**
Ann Arbor, Michigan: Association for Asian Studies, 1941– . annual.
This annual compilation of new Western-language publications, both books and journal articles, invariably includes a large number of titles concerning Tibet. Arrangement is by broad subject grouping, based on the Library of Congress subject headings. Unfortunately each annual volume tends to appear some four years after the year whose publications it covers; thus the latest volume at the time of writing is that for 1985.

551 **Bibliography of architecture, planning and landscape in China, including materials on Hong Kong, Manchuria, Mongolia and Tibet.**
Michael Hugo Brunt.   Monticello, Illinois: Council of Planning Librarians, 1976. 68p. (Exchange bibliography, no. 535).
The scope of this bibliography is considerably wider than the title suggests as it also covers political and foreign affairs, religion, history, social conditions, art, maps and directories. Approximately ninety titles concerned with Tibet are listed, mainly in European languages but also including some Chinese-language material.

552 **Light from Tibet.**
Richard Brook Cathcart. Monticello, Illinois: Vance Bibliographies, 1980. 7p. (Public Administration Series: Bibliography, p-482).
This is a brief bibliographical essay which focuses on the natural conditions of the Tibetan plateau and the development of water resources to provide electric power.

553 **Tibet: past and present: a select bibliography with chronology of historical events 1660–1981.**
Attar Chand. New Delhi: Sterling, 1982. 257p.
This unannotated bibliography contains 2311 entries. It covers only works published in English, but includes books, periodical articles, book reviews and doctoral dissertations. The arrangement is by subject and there is a comprehensive index.

554 **Bibliography of Tibetan studies, being a record of printed publications mainly in European languages.**
Sibadas Chaudhuri. Calcutta, India: Asiatic Society, 1971. 232p.
This unannotated bibliography contains 2032 entries, arranged by author, but also listed briefly under broad subject headings. Books, journal articles and reports are all included.

555 **Classified catalogue of books, section VII: Tibet, in the Tokyo Bunko, March 1968.**
Tokyo: Tokyo Bunko, 1968. 126p.
The collection of books on Tibet in the Tokyo Bunko is a strong one and this list includes a number of works not found elsewhere. It includes a particularly good collection of works in German and Russian, but it is worth remembering that it is a library catalogue rather than an exhaustive bibliography and therefore has a number of important lacunae.

556 **Catalogue of the Library of Tibetan Works and Archives Reference Department.**
Compiled and edited by Gokey Dekhang. Dharamsala, India: Library of Tibetan Works and Archives, 1981. 328p.
This unannotated bibliography of around 2000 books on Tibet and the Trans-Himalayan civilization is arranged according to the Dewey decimal classification with author and title indexes. As the catalogue of one of the principal library collections of material on Tibet it is invaluable and has been of considerable help to the compiler of this present volume.

557 **Tibetan books and newspapers: (Chinese collection): with bibliographical notes.**
Josef Kolmas. Wiesbaden, Germany: Harrassowitz, 1978. 131p.
bibliog. (Asiatische Forschungen, Bd. 62).
This catalogue lists 191 Tibetan publications and textbooks covering the period 1952–59. They include linguistic works, original literary works, translations and newspapers. There are title and name indexes.

558 **Britain and Tibet 1765–1947: the background to the India–China border dispute: a select annotated bibliography of printed material in European languages.**
Julie G. Marshall.   Bundoora, Australia: La Trobe University Library, 1977. 372p. (Library publication no. 10).
An extensive annotated listing of 2874 titles, books and periodical articles, including a brief section dealing with the post-1947 Sino-Indian border disputes. British relations with Ladakh, Nepal, Sikkim, Bhutan, Assam and other Himalayan hill states are also covered. A particularly useful feature is that book reviews of important works are listed immediately following the main entry of the work concerned. The bibliography covers works published up to 1974.

559 **A selective survey of literature on Tibet.**
Beatrice D. Miller.   *American Political Science Review*, vol. 48, no. 4 (Dec. 1953), p. 1135–51.
This bibliographical essay, although old, is still a useful introduction to the literature of Tibet, covering sources of interest to the political scientist, historian or sociologist. Analytical works of history and anthropology and travellers' works form the majority of the references, and it is particularly useful that so many Chinese sources are included. It is important to note that items concerned exclusively with religion or philosophy are not covered at all.

Indexes

There follow three separate indexes: authors (personal and corporate); titles; and subjects. Title entries are italicized and refer either to the main titles, or to other works cited in the annotations. The numbers refer to bibliographical entries, not to pages. Individual index entries are arranged in alphabetical sequence.

Index of Authors

A

Addy, P. 162
Ahmad, Z. 434
Allen, C. 45
Allione, T. 258
Amar Kaur Jasbir Singh 549
Amipa, S. G. 283
Anderson, W. 310
Andersson, J. 235
Arakeri, A. V. 259
Aris, M. 154
Ash, N. 108
Atisa 311
Avedon, J. F. 242, 394
Aziz, B. N. 263

B

Bacot, J. 164-5, 296, 496
Bailey, F. M. 80-1
Baktay, E. 55
Barber, N. 196
Bass, C. 109
Batchelor, S. 39, 312
Beall, C. M. 272, 462
Beckwith, C. I. 15, 142
Beer, R. 515
Béguin, G. 502
Bell, C. 129, 166, 374
Bernard, T. 82
Berry, S. 83
Berzin, A. 541
Beyer, S. V. 313
Bishop, P. 46
Bleicksteiner, R. 314

Bloomfield, A. 284
Booz, E. B. 40
Boulnois, L. 455
Bower, H. 56
Brar, B. S. 243
Brewster, P. G. 378
Brook, E. 110
Brooke, B. A. 201
Brown, C. W. 464
Brunt, M. H. 551
Buchi, E. C. 264
Buckley, M. 41
Bull, G. T. 367
Bullert, G. 197
Burman, R. B. 471
Burrard, S. G. 23
Bu-ston 315
Byron, R. 84

C

Cammann, S. 155
Campbell, A. 456
Candler, E. 167
Carey, W. 57
Carrasco, P. 395
Cassinelli, C. W. 396
Cathcart, R. B. 552
Chakrabarti, P. N. 156
Chakravarti, P. C. 436
Chalon, J. 86
Chand, A. 553
Chang, Y. 397
Chapman, S. 85
Chattopadhyaya, A. 317
Chaudhuri, S. 554
Chen Rinong 457

Chimpa, Lama 317, 472
China: Population Census Office 234, 239
China: State Council 454
China: State Statistical Bureau 454
Chinese Academy of Science, Institute of Geography 239
Chiu, H. 398
Choeden, D. 198
Chogyam, N. 209, 318
Chophel, N. 279, 285, 533-4
Chung, G. C. C. 332
Clarke, G. E. 458
Clifford, T. 385
Cloud, S. 199
Committee to Voice the Aspirations of the Tibetan People 423
Conway, J. S. 244
Cordier, H. 79
Corlin, C. 245
Cosson, C. 92
Cox, S. 212
Crossley-Holland, P. 528-9
Csoma de Kőrös, A. 58, 280
Curzon, G. N. 438
Cutillo, B. 489
Cutting, S. 87

D

Dakpa, R. 201
Dalai Lama, 1st 340

Dalai Lama, 2nd 341
Dalai Lama, 3rd 342
Dalai Lama, 5th 339
Dalai Lama, 6th 486, 491
Dalai Lama, 7th 343
Dalai Lama, 14th 227,
   349-52
Dargyay, E. K. 375
Dargyay, E. M. 319
Das, S. C. 59, 286
Dasgupta, S. B. 320
Dash, V. B. 386-7
Davenport, C. 370
David-Neel, A. 88-9, 499
Davis, S. 75
Dawson, W. 294
Deasy, H. H. P. 60
Deb, A. 459-60
Dekhang, G. 556
Denwood, P. 521
Devoe, D. M. 388
Dhamatrata 357
Dhondup, K. 157, 168,
   391, 486
Donden, Y. 389
Donnet, P.-A. 202
Dorje, R. 542
Dorjee, T. 473
Dowman, K. 42, 260, 321
Dreyer, J. T. 398, 401-2,
   474
Driver, J. E. S. 21
Drysdale, H. 111
Duncan, M. H. 265, 487,
   492-3
Duo Fen 481
Dutt, S. 439

E

Ekvall, R. B. 90, 119,
   266-9, 300, 396, 497
Ellingson, T. 530-1
Ennals, Lord 425
Epstein, I. 203
Evans-Wentz, W. Y.
   355-6, 358

F

Fei Hsiao Tung 270
Felippi, F. de 61

Finck, E. 390
Fingestein, P. 488
Fisher, J. B. 271
Fisher, M. W. 130
Fleming, P. 169
Fletcher, H. R. 120
Ford, R. 205
Freeberne, M. 236

G

Gedun Chomphel 144
Gedun Drub see Dalai
   Lama, 1st
Gedun Gyatso see Dalai
   Lama, 2nd
Gelder, R. 206
Gelder, S. 206
Gelek, S. W. 461
Ghersi, E. 106
Ginsburgs, G. 207
Gold, P. 1
Goldstein, M. C. 173, 237,
   272, 281, 287-8, 376,
   404-5, 462-3
Gooch, C. R. L. 246
Goodman, M. H. 208
Gopal, R. 440
Gordon, A. K. 488
Gore, F. 368
Gould, B. J. 174
Greenhut, F. A. 441
Griswold, A. B. 503
Grunfeld, A. T. 131
Guenther, H. V. 322
Guibaut, A. 264
Guise, A. 518

H

Haarh, E. 145
Hadfield, C. 112
Hadfield, J. 112
Han Suyin 113
Hannah, H. B. 289
Harrer, H. 2, 91, 114, 219
Harris, N. 24
Hawkins, J. N. 475
Hayden, H. H. 23, 92
Heaton, W. R. 406
Hedin, S. 25, 93-5
Held, S. 3

Hengtse Tu 442
Herber, T. 407
Heron, A. M. 23
Heyu 4
Hicks, R. 5, 209
Hoffmann, H. 6, 301
Holdich, T. 47
Hopkins, J. 323-4, 329,
   347, 359-61, 389
Hopkinson, H. 456
Hopkirk, P. 48
Houser, F. M. 390
Houston, G. W. 146, 491
Hsi Chang-hao 377
Hu, C. T. 476
Hua Zi 408
Huc, Abbé 62
Human Rights Watch: Asia
   Watch Committee 427
Hummel, S. 378
Hutheesing, R. 210
Hyde-Chambers, A. 535
Hyde-Chambers, F. 425,
   498, 535

I

Imaeda, Y. 506
International Commission
   of Jurists 229

J

Jackson, D. P. 515
Jackson, J. A. 515
Jin Zhou 379
Josayma, C. B. 536
Joshi, M. P. 464

K

Kaldhen, J. 465
Kao Yuan-mei 377
Karan, P. P. 26
Karmay, H. 504
Karmay, S. G. 306, 339
Kaul, P. N. 211
Kawaguchi, E. 96
Kelsang Gyatso 326
Kemp, R. 518
Kesang Gyatso see Dalai

Lama, 7th
Khangkar, L. D. 391
Kim, C. 503
King, Mrs L. *see* Rin-chen
  Lha-mo
Klafkowski, P. 158
Klein, A. C. 324, 327
Kling, Kevin 7
Kolmas, J. 443, 557
Kőrösi Csoma S. *see*
  Csoma de Kőrös,
  A.
Kuloy, H. K. 522
Kunga, Lama 489
Kuznetsov, B. I. 307
Kvaerne, P. 308

L

Lai, W. 328
Lamb, A. 159, 444
Lancaster, L. R. 328
Landaw, J. 365
Landon, P. 175
Landor, A. H. S. 63
Lang-Sims, L. 247, 409
Laufer, B. 273, 297
Launay, A. 369
Ledger, W. P. 428
Lee, D. Y. 445
Levenson, C. B. 212
Levine, N. E. 274
Lhalungpa, L. P. 19, 291
Li, T.-T. 132
Li Yongzeng 477
Liao, H. 410
Lipton, B. 49
Lipton, M. 523
Lister, M. R. 326
Lister, R. F. 326
Liu, S. 185
Lloyd, Percy 501
Lo, B. L. C. 478
Lobsang Gyatso *see* Dalai
  Lama, 5th
Lokesh Chandra 316, 482,
  512
Loup, R. 370
Lowry, J. 505
Lu, C. H. 446
Luhan, J. M. 411

M

Macdonald, A. 506
Macdonald, A. W. 147,
  483
Macdonald, D. 8-9
McGovern, W. M. 97
MacGregor, J. 50
Majupuria, I. 43, 261, 543
Majupuria, T. C. 43
Malik, I. L. 133
Maraini, F. 98
Markham, C. R. 64
Marshall, J. G. 558
Mathos, M. 207
Mehra, P. 176-7, 447
Michael, F. 412
Migot, A. 99, 494
Milarepa 332, 488-9
Miller, B. D. 559
Miller, L. 51
Miller, R. A. 298
Miller, R. J. 466
Millington, P. 178
Misra, R. C. 248
Mitter, J. P. 213
Mojumdar, K. 160
Montgomerie, T. G. 65-7
Moraes, R. 214
Mount Everest Foundation
  35
Mukherjee, H. N. 68
Mullin, C. 429
Mullin, G. H. 333-4,
  340-3
Murphy, D. 249

N

Napper, E. 323, 330
Narkyid, N. J. 290
Nebesky-Wojkowitz, R. de
  275, 302-3, 309
Neterowicz, E. M. 215,
  413
Newark Museum
  Association 507
Norboo, S. 144
Norbu, D. 216-17
Norbu, J. 218
Norbu, N. 335, 539
Norbu, T. J. 10, 219, 497
Normanton, S. 11

Nowak, M. 250

O

Obermiller, E. 315
O'Connor, F. 179
Olivier, G. 264
Olschak, B. C. 251, 508
Olsen, E. 509
Orleans, L. A. 238
Ottley, W. J. 180

P

Pal, P. 509-10, 516
Palakshappa, T. C. 252
Paljor, S. 321
Palmieri, R. P. 121
Patterson, G. N. 100,
  221-2
Paul, D. Y. 336
Peissel, M. 223
Pelliot, P. 148
Perdue, D. 479
Petech, L. 161, 414
Peter, Prince 276, 527
Pfandt, P. 337
Phunrabpa, T. P. 326
Pilarski, L. 134
Pott, P. H. 503
Pranavananda, Swami 101,
  122

R

Rahul, R. 417
Ralston, W. R. S. 500
Rao, S. K. R. 338
Rapgay, L. 182, 392
Rawling, C. G. 102-3
Rayfield, D. 70
Reiter, E. R. 27
Richard, R. 115
Richardson, H. E. 135,
  138, 149, 163, 183,
  277, 448-9
Rigzin, T. 282
Rijnhart, S. C. 71
Rin-chen Lha-mo 381
Robson, I. S. 72
Rockhill, W. W. 13, 73

Roerich, G. N. 150-1, 291
Rose, L. E. 130
Royal Geographical
    Society 35
Rupen, R. A. 450

S

Sacks, H. C. 430
Saklani, G. 254
Samuel, G. 305, 418
Sandberg, G. 52
Sanders, R. 75
Sandhutsang, R. T. 524
Savitsky, L. S. 484
Schary, E. G. 104
Schiefner, F. A. von 500
Schlagintweit, E. 344
Scientific Buddhist
    Association 431
Scott, A. M. 184
Sedlacek, K. 292
Sen, C. 136
Sen, J. 467
Senanayake, R. D. 224
Seth, V. 116
Sha Zhou 419
Shakabpa, W. D. 137
Sharma, S. L. 451
Shelton, F. B. 372, 490,
    537
Shen, T. 185
Sherburne, R. 311
Sherring, C. A. 14
Shih Hung-lin 186
Shu-hsing, L. 468, 480
Sierksma, F. 304
Simon, B. L. 357
Sinha, N. C. 187, 469
Skorupski, T. 163, 525
Snellgrove, D. 138, 143,
    345-6
Snelling, J. 53, 194
Somerville-Large, P. 117
Sonam Gyatso see Dalai
    Lama, 3rd
Sopa, G. L. 347
Sparham, G. 357
Sperling, E. 278
Stael-Holstein, A. von 348
Stein, R. A. 16, 152, 485
Still, D. S. 490
Stoddart, H. 188-9

Strauss, R. 41
Strong, A. L. 225-6
Sun, J. T.-S. 295
Suo Wenqing 140
Swift, H. 44
Swinson, A. 105
Sydney, V. 499
Synge, M. see Millington,
    P.

T

Tada, T. 190
Talbott, H. 353
Taring, J. 123
Taring, R. D. 191
Teague, E. H. 520
Teichman, E. 192
Tenzin Gyatso see Dalai
    Lama, 14th
Thinley, K. 325
Thomas, L. J. 228
Thonden, L. 293
Thondup, T. 353
Thurlow, C. 538
Thurman, R. A. F. 354
Tibetan Homes
    Foundation 255
Topping, A. 20
Toscano, G. M. 373
Tsangyang Gyatso see
    Dalai Lama, 6th
Tsarong, T. J. 393
Tseten Dolkar 257
Tsonawa, L. N. 536
Tsong-ka-pa 359-61
Tucci, G. 21, 106, 153,
    305, 512, 517, 539
Tung, R. J. 22
Turnbull, C. 10
Turner, S. 75

U

United States: Board of
    Geographic Names 34

V

Van Walt Van Praag, M.
    139

Vandor, I. 532
Vaurie, C. 124
Vause, W. G. 432
Vesci, U. M. 512
Vitali, R. 513
Vocca, V. 517

W

Waddell, L. A. 193, 362
Walker, J. M. 29
Waller, D. 76
Wang Fujen 140
Wang Peng 433
Wang Yao 495
Wangyal, G. T. 508
Ward, F. K. 107, 125-7
Warren, S. 233
Waterfall, A. C. 540
Weiner, D. 526
Weiss, J. 422
Welby, M. S. 77
Wessels, C. 78
Wilby, S. 118
Wiley, T. W. 384, 470
Williams, P. 363
Williamson, M. 194
Willson, M. 364
Woltereck, H. 2
Woodcock, G. 54
Woodman, D. 453
Woolf, H. I. 496
Wylie, T. V. 30-1

Y

Yang Xiaobing 433
Yang Xin 481
Yeshe, T. 365
Yeshe Tsogyal 366
Yongden, Lama 499, 501
Younghusband, F. 195
Yule, H. 79

Z

Zhang Rongzu 32
Zhang Tianlu 240-1
Zhijie, L. 33
Zhu Li 379
Zwalf, W. 514

Index of Titles

A

Abominable snowman 122
Account of an embassy to
the Teshoo Lama in
Tibet; containing a
narrative of a journey
through Bootan and
part of Tibet 75
Account of Tibet: the
travels of Ippolito
Desideri of Pistoia,
S. J., 1712-1727 61
Adventures of a Tibetan
fighting monk 163
Almanac of China's
economy 1981, with
economic statistics for
1949-1980 454
Alone through China and
Tibet 111
Altar of the earth: the life,
land and spirit of Tibet
1
Ancient Tibet: research
materials from the
Yeshe De Project 141
Animal style among the
nomad tribes of
northern Tibet 150
Anthropologie Tibétaine
264
Architecture of Tibet: an
introductory
bibliography 520
Aristocracy and
government in Tibet
1728-1959 414
Art of Burma, Korea, Tibet
503
Art of Tibet 509
Articles of Tibet trade, 1784
469
Les arts du Népal et du
Tibet 502
Aspects of the phonology
of Amdo Tibetan:
Ndzorge saeme xora
dialect 295
Atisa and Tibet: life and

works of Dipamkara
Srijnana in relation to
the history and religion
of Tibet 317
Autonoom Tibet 199
Ázsiai levelek és más írások
58

B

Balance between
centralization and
decentralization in the
traditional Tibetan
political system 404
Bayonets to Lhasa: the first
full account of the
British invasion of
Tibet in 1904 169
Betrayal of Tibet 213
Beyond the frontiers: the
biography of Colonel
F. M. Bailey, explorer
and special agent 105
Bibliography of
architecture, planning
and landscape in
China, including
materials on Hong
Kong, Manchuria,
Mongolia and Tibet
551
Bibliography of Asian
Studies 550
Bibliography of Tibetan
studies, being a record
of printed publications
mainly in European
languages 554
Blue annals 151
Books of Tibet 527
Boundary question between
China and Tibet: a
valuable record of the
Tripartite Conference
between China, Britain
and Tibet held in
India, 1913-1914 435
Brief study of the

Bhutan–Tibet
relations 439
Britain and Tibet
1765-1947: the
background to the
India–China border
dispute: a select
annotated bibliography
of printed materials in
European languages
558
British India and Tibet,
1766-1910 159
Buddha mind: an
anthology of
Longchen Rabjam's
writings on Dzogpa
chenpo 353
Buddhism in the Tibetan
tradition: a guide 326
Buddhism in Tibet 344
Buddhism of Tibet 349
Buddhism of Tibet, or
Lamaism with its
mystic cults,
symbolism and
mythology, and its
relation to Indian
Buddhism 362
Buddhist Himalaya: travels
and studies in quest of
the origins and nature
of Tibetan religion 345
Buddhist iconography 316
Buddhist monastic
economy: the jisa
mechanism 466
Bulletin of Tibetology 544

C

Cadre education in Tibet
471
Calling from Kashgar: a
journey through Tibet
115
Captured in Tibet 205
Catalogue of the Library of
Tibetan Works and

Archives Reference
Department 556
Catalogue of the Tibetan
collection and other
Lamaist articles in the
Newark Museum 507
Cathay and the way thither,
being a collection of
medieval notices of
China 79
Cavaliers of Kham: the
secret war in Tibet 223
Central Asia and Tibet:
towards the holy city
of Lassa 93
Central Asiatic Journal 545
Changing face of Tibet: the
impact of Chinese
communist ideology
on the landscape 26
Changing population
characteristics in Tibet,
1959-1965 236
Chants from Shangri-la 490
China and its national
minorities: autonomy
or assimilation 407
China and Tibet,
1708-1959: a résumé
of facts 434
China and Tibet in the
early XVIIIth century:
history of the
establishment of
Chinese protectorate in
Tibet 161
China–Tibet–Assam: a
journey 1911 80
China's forty millions:
minority nationalities
and national
integration in the
People's Republic of
China 401
China's reforms of Tibet
and their effects on
pastoralism 458
Chine . . . Japon . . .
Corée . . . Tibet . . . :
catalogue des
collections de la
Bibliothèque Forney
511
Chinese and human rights

abuses in Tibet,
1959-1982 423
Chinese and human rights
in Tibet: a report to the
Parliamentary Human
Rights Group 428
Chinese occupation of
Tibet: a lesson from
history 197
Chinese presence in Tibet:
a thirty year
assessment 402
Classified catalogue of
books, section VII:
Tibet, in the Tokyo
Bunko, March 1968
555
Communist China and
Tibet: the first dozezn
years 207
Communist China's
difficulties in ruling
Tibet 397
Communist China's policy
toward Tibet 410
Compassion in Tibetan
Buddhism 359
Concerning the question of
Tibet 200
Conquest of Tibet 94
Constitution of Tibet,
promulgated by His
Holiness the Dalai
Lama, March 10, 1963
399
Convention between the
United Kingdom and
China respecting Tibet,
signed at Peking, April
27, 1906 437
Cooch Behar and Bhutan
in the context of
Tibetan trade 459
Corpus of early Tibetan
inscriptions 149
Cult of Tara: magic and
ritual Tibet 313
Cultural history of Tibet
138
Customs and superstitions
of Tibetans 265

D

Dalai Lama: a
biography 212
Dalai Lama of Tibet:
succession of births
133
Dans les marches
tibétaines: autour de
Dokerla: novembre
1906–janvier 1908 164
Daughter of Tibet 191
Death and dying in the
Tibetan tradition 333
Death, intermediate state
and rebirth in Tibetan
Buddhism 329
Debate in Tibetan Buddhis
education 479
Dialogue on Tibet (I). Ou
differences with the
Dalai Lama 400
Dialogue on Tibet (II).
Religion, crime and
citizen's rights 424
Diary of a journey across
Tibet 56
Diary of a journey through
Mongolia and Tibet in
1891 and 1892 73
Dictionary of Tibetan and
English 280
Divine madman: the
sublime life and songs
of Drukpa Kunley 321
Domestication and
exploitation of
livestock in the Nepal
Himalaya and Tibet:
an ecological,
functional, and culture
historical study of yak
and yak hybrids in
society, economy and
culture 121
Dream of Lhasa: the life of
Nicholas Przhevalsky
(1839-88), explorer of
central Asia 70
Dynamics of polyandry:
kinship, domesticity
and population on the
Tibetan border 274
Dzog Chen and Zen 335

E

Early Ch'an in China and Tibet 328

Early Jesuit travellers in Central Asia 1603-1721 78

Early Sino-Tibetan art 504

Early temples of central Tibet 513

L'écriture cursive tibétaine 296

Education among minority peoples 477

Education in Tibet 473

Education of national minorities in communist China 476

Educational development in the PRC: regional and ethnic disparities 480

L'église jaune 314

England, India, Nepal, Tibet, China: 1765-1958: a synchronistic table showing the succession of heads of state and other political and diplomatic personages of importance in these countries 130

Essais sur l'art du Tibet 506

Evolution of India's northern borders 436

Exploration in Tibet 101

Exploration of Tibet: history and particulars 52

Extracts from an explorer's narrative of his journey from Pitoragarh in Kumaon via Jumlah to Tadum and back, along the Kali Gandak to British territory 65

F

Facts about Tibet, 1961-1965 204

Fields on the hoof: nexus of Tibetan nomadic pastoralism 266

Fire ox and other years 87

First railway to the "Roof of the World" 457

First Russia, then Tibet 84

Flights of the wind horse: a journey into Tibet 108

Folk culture of Tibet 533

Folk tales of Tibet 534, 537

Food in Tibetan life 542

Formulary of Tibetan medicine 386

Foundations of Tibetan medicine 390

Four lamas of Dolpo: Tibetan biographies 143

Freedom in exile: the autobiography of His Holiness the Dalai Lama of Tibet 227

From heaven lake: travels through Sinkiang and Tibet 116

From liberation to liberalisation: views on 'liberated' Tibet 403

From the land of lost content: the Dalai Lama's fight for Tibet 196

Frontier callings 211

Function and status of the Dalai Lama in Tibet 409

Further papers relating to Tibet 170, 172

Further papers relating to Tibet. No. III 171

G

Games of the Tibetans 378

Geography of Tibet according to the 'Dzam-gling-rgyas-bshad 30

General Huang Mu-sung at Lhasa, 1934 183

General survey of Tibet 4

Girl from Tibet 257

Government and politics of Tibet 417

Government, monastic and private taxation in Tibet 461

Grammar of the Tibetan language: literary and colloquial 289

Great ocean: an authorised biography of the Buddhist monk Tenzin Gyatso, His Holiness the Fourteenth Dalai Lama 209

Great plateau, being an account of exploration in central Tibet, 1903, and of the Gartok Expedition, 1904-1905 102

Great Tibetologist: Alexander Csoma de Kőrös, hermit-hero from Hungary 68

Growth of China's minority population 240

Guide to source materials in the India Office Library and Records for the history of Tibet, Sikkim and Bhutan 1765-1950 549

Guide to Tibet 40

Gyantse and its monasteries 512

H

Handbook of traditional Tibetan drugs: their nomenclature, composition, use and dosage 393

Harvest festival dramas of Tibet 492

Health through balance: an introduction to Tibetan medicine 389

Heat beneath Tibet 33

Heritage of Tibet 514

Hidden Tibet: the land and its people 5

Hidden treasures and secret

lives: a study of Pemalingpa (1450-1521) and the Sixth Dalai Lama (1683-1706) 154

Highest deities of the Bon religion 307

Highlights of Tibetan history 140

Himalayan anthropology: the Indo-Tibetan interface 271

Himalayan frontiers: a political review of British, Chinese, Indian and Russian rivalries 453

Himalayan triangle: a historical survey of British India's relations with Tibet, Sikkim and Bhutan 1765-1950 128

Histoire ancienne du Tibet 148

Histoire de la mission du Thibet 369

History of Buddhism in India and Tibet 315

History of modern Tibet, 1913-1951: the demise of the Lamaist state 173

History of the early relations between China and Tibet: from Chiu tang-shu: a documentary survey 445

History of the sixteen Karmapas of Tibet 325

Hong Kong, Macao, Sinkiang, Taiwan and Tibet: official standard names approved by the United States Board of Geographic Names 34

How the Chinese rule Tibet 411

How Tibet's climate affects other countries 27

Human rights in Tibet: Hearing before the Subcommittees on Human Rights and International Organizations, and on Asian and Pacific Affairs of the Committee on Foreign Affairs, House of Representatives, 100th Congress, First Session, October 14, 1987 426

Hundred thousand songs of Milarepa 332

Hundred thousand songs: selections from Milarepa, poet-saint of Tibet 488

I

Impact of China's reform policy on the nomads of western Tibet 462

In exile from the land of snows 242

In haste from Tibet 201

In praise of Tara: songs of the saviouress 364

In search of the Mahatmas of Tibet 104

In Tibet and Chinese Turkestan, being the record of three years' exploration 60

India and Tibet 195

India–China–Tibet triangle 440

Indian influences in Tibetan music 530

India's trade with central Asia via Nepal 467

Indo-Tibetan Buddhism: Indian Buddhists and their Tibetan successors 346

Inside story of Tibet 224

Inside the treasure house: a time in Tibet 109

Interest rates in Tibet 465

Into Tibet: the early British explorers 54

Introduction to Tantra: a vision of totality 365

Introduction to Tantric Buddhism 320

Introduction to the grammar of the Tibetan language 286

Introduction to Tibetan astronomy and astrology 541

Introduction to Tibetan folk medicine 388

J

Jewel in the lotus: a guide to the Buddhist traditions of Tibet 312

Jewell in the lotus: recollections of an Indian political 174

Journal of the Tibet Society 546

Journey across Tibet 118

Journey into vastness: a handbook of Tibetan meditation techniques 318

Journey to Lhasa and central Tibet 59

Journey to Shigatze in Tibet, and return by Dingri-Maidan into Nepaul in 1871 66

K

Kindness, clarity and insight 350

Knowledge and liberation: Tibetan Buddhist epistemology in support of transformative religious experience 327

L

Lama: a novel of Tibet 498

Lama and the jumbo-jet: report on a Tibetan meditation group in

Switzerland 245
Lamaist art: the aesthetics of harmony 510
Lamp for the path and Commentary 311
Land and polity in Tibet 395
Land of a thousand Buddhas: a pilgrimage into the heart of Tibet and the sacred city of Lhasa 82
Land of the blue poppy: travels of a naturalist in eastern Tibet 125
Land of the lama: a description of a country of contrasts & its cheerful, happy-go-lucky people of hardy nature & curious customs 8
Land of the snow lion 110
Language planning for China's ethnic minorities 474
Last Dalai Lama: a biography 208
Lectures on Tibetan medicine 391
Legal aspects of land tenure in Tibetan society 384
Lhasa: an account of the country and the people of central Tibet and of the progress of the mission sent there by the English government in the year 1903-04 175
Lhasa and its mysteries, with a record of the expedition of 1903-04 193
Lhasa street songs: political and social satire in traditional Tibet 405
Lhasa: the holy city 85
Lhasa, the open city: a journey to Tibet 113
Life and liberation of Padmasambhava: Padma bKa'i Thang 366

Life and teachings of Tsong Khapa 354
Life in the Red Flag People's Commune 198
Life story of Drowa Sangmo 536
Light from Tibet 552
Love songs and proverbs of Tibet 487
Le lumineux destin d'Alexandra David-Neel 86

M

Macro exchanges: Tibetan economics and the role of politics and religion 470
Magic and mystery in Tibet 88
Mahayana Buddhism: the doctrinal foundations 363
Mahayana texts translated into western languages: a bibliographical guide 337
Making of modern Tibet 131
Mandala of sound: concepts and sound structures in Tibetan ritual music 531
Martyr in Tibet: the heroic life and death of Father Maurice Tornay, St. Bernard missionary to Tibet 370
Materia medica of Indo-Tibetan medicine 387
Materials for a history of Tibetan literature 482
Matériaux pour l'étude de la littérature populaire tibétaine 483
Matrix of mystery: scientific and humanistic aspects of rDzogs-chen thought 322
Meditiation on emptiness 323

Meine Tibet Bilder 2
Memoirs of a political officer's wife in Tibet, Sikkim and Bhutan 194
Le mendiant de l'Ambo 189
Merciless repression: human rights abuses in Tibet 427
Military report on western Tibet, including Chang Tang and Rudok 103
Mind in Tibetan Buddhism 330
Minorities and the military in China 406
Mipam: the lama of five wisdoms: a Tibetan novel 501
Miraculous journey: further stories and songs of Milarepa, yogin, poet and teacher of Tibet 489
Modern spoken Tibetan: Lhasa dialect 287
Modern Tibetan language 293
Monasteries of the Himalayas: Tibet, Bhutan, Ladakh, Sikkim 3
Mongols of the twentieth century 450
More harvest festival dramas of Tibet 493
Mount Qomolangma: highest in the world 32
Mountain in Tibet: the search for Mount Kailas and the sources of the great rivers of India 45
Mountains of central Asia: 1:3,000,000 map and gazetteer 35
La musique du bouddhisme tibétain 532
My journey to Lhasa 89
Mystic art of ancient Tibet 508
Myth of Shangri-la: Tibet,

travel writing and the
western creation of
sacred landscape 46

N

Narrative of an exploration
of the Namcho or
Tengri Nur Lake in
Great Tibet made by a
native explorer during
1871-2 67
Narrative of the mission of
George Bogle to Tibet,
and of the journey of
Thomas Manning to
Lhasa 64
National-minority
education in the
People's Republic of
China 475
Nepal–Tibet war, 1855-56
160
New English–Tibetan
dictionary 279
New general collection of
voyages and travels 69
New perspectives on
Tibetan fertility and
population decline 237
1959 Tibetan rebellion: an
interpretation 216
1982 population census of
China: major figures
234
No passport to Tibet 81
Nomads of western Tibet:
the survival of a way
of life 272
North-eastern frontier: a
documentary study of
the internecine rivalry
between India, Tibet
and China 447
Note on Tibet's population
238
Une note sur les mégalithes
tibétains 147
Notes sur le théâtre tibétain
494

O

Old age in the Tibetan
context 278
On negotiations with the
Dalai Lama 408
On the frontier and
beyond: a record of
thirty years' service 179
On the weather and climate
of Tibet 29
On top of the world: five
women explorers in
Tibet 51
On trade between Calcutta,
Darjeeling, Bhootan
and Tibet (and
between Assam, Tibet
and west China) 456
On two Tibetan pictures
representing some of
the spiritual ancestors
of the Dalai Lama and
the Panchen Lama
348
Open secrets: a western
guide to Tibetan
Buddhism 310
Opening of the wisdom-eye
and the history of the
advancement of
Buddhadharma in
Tibet 352
Opening of the eye of new
awareness 351
Oracles and demons of
Tibet: the cult and
iconography of the
Tibetan protective
deities 302
Origin of the Tibetan
Pioneer Mission,
together with some
facts about Tibet 371
Origin of Tibetan writing
297

P

Panchen Erdeni:
Vice-Chairman of the
Standing Committee of
the Fifth National
People's Congress 22
Papers relating to Tibet 18
Path of the Bodhisattva
warrior: the life and
teachings of the
Thirteenth Dalai Lama
334
Peace and war among the
Tibetan nomads 267
Peking's "peaceful
liberation" of Tibet in
retrospect 186
People of Tibet 374
Phallic symbols in Tibet
277
Pilgrimage for plants 127
Place of women in Tibetan
society 259
Plant hunter in Tibet 126
Population atlas of China
239
Portrait of a Dalai Lama:
the life and times of the
great Thirteenth 166
Portrait of lost Tibet 22
Postal history of Tibet 540
Potala of Tibet 518
Potala palace of Tibet 519
Poudre d'or et monnaies
d'argent au Tibet
(principalement au
XVIIIe siècle) 455
Power places of central
Tibet: a pilgrim's guide
42
Practice and theory of
Tibetan Buddhism 349
PRC occupation of Tibet
422
Presence of Tibet 247
Present policies for Tibet
415
La prima missione cattólica
nel Tibet 373
Proceedings of the Csoma
de Kőrös memorial
symposium held at
Mátrafüred, Hungary,
24-30 September 1976
12
Proceedings of the
Symposium on
Qinhai-Xizang (Tibet)
Plateau: abstracts 28

Pundits: British exploration of Tibet and central Asia 76

Q

Quest for universal responsibility: human rights violations in Tibet 430

Quest of flowers: the plant explorations of Frank Ludlow and George Sherriff told from their diaries and other occasional writing 120

Questions and answers on the Lhasa riots 416

R

Random notes from Tibet University 481

Real Tibet 233

Recherches sur l'epopée et le barde au Tibet 485

Red star over Tibet 217

Refugee problems in Vietnam, India, and Hong Kong, British Colony 253

Rélations de divers voyages curieux qui n'ont point esté publiées ou qui ont esté traduites d'Hacluyt, de Purchas et d'autres voyageurs 74

Religions of Tibet 301, 305

Religious observances in Tibet: patterns and functions 300

Report from Tibet 380

Requiem for Tibet 221

Research guide to education in China after Mao, 1977-1981 478

Return to Tibet 114

Revolt in Tibet 214

Riddle of the Tsangpo gorges 107

Rise of esoteric Buddhism in Tibet 319

Ritual music of Tibet 528

Role of the dog in Tibetan nomadic society 119

Rule by incarnation: Tibetan Buddhism and its role in society and state 412

Russia in central Asia in 1889 and the Anglo-Russian question 438

S

Sacred mountain: travellers and pilgrims at Mount Kailas in western Tibet and the great universal symbol of the sacred mountain 53

Say it in Tibetan: conversation in colloquial Tibetan 285

Secret deliverance of the sixth Dalai Lama 158

Secret doctrines of the Tibetan Book of the Dead 331

Secret Tibet 98

Secret visions of the Fifth Dalai Lama: the Gold Manuscript in the Fournier Collection 339

Secrets of Tibet, being the chronicle of the Tucci Scientific Expedition to Western Tibet (1933) 106

Selected works of the Dalai Lama I: bridging the sutras and tantras 340

Selected works of the Dalai Lama II: the tantric yogas of Sister Niguma 341

Selected works of the Dalai Lama III: essence of refined gold 342

Selected works of the Dalai Lama VII: songs of

spiritual change 343

Selective survey of literature on Tibet 559

Serfdom and mobility: an examination of the institution of "human lease" in traditional Tibetan society 376

Seven years in Tibet 91

Shelton of Tibet 372

Short history of Tibetan script 299

Silent war in Tibet 228

Silver on lapis: Tibetan literary culture and history 15

Simla Convention 1914: a Chinese puzzle 187

Sino-Indian border dispute: a legal study 446

Sketch of the geography and geology of the Himalaya mountains and Tibet 23

Sky dancer: the secret life and songs of the Lady Yeshe Tsogyel 260

Some aspects of divination in Tibetan society 268

Some dynamics of Indo-Tibetan trade through Uttarkhnada (Kumaon-Garhwal) India 464

Songs of the Sixth Dalai Lama 486

Sources for a history of the bSam yas debate 146

South-central Tibet; Kathmandu–Lhasa route map 36

Southern Tibet: discoveries in former times compared with my own researches in 1906-1908 25

Splendour of Tibet 20

Sport and travel in the highlands of Tibet 92

State of research in Tibetan folk music 529

Status of Tibet: history, rights and prospects in international law 139

Stories from beyond the clouds: an anthology of Tibetan folk tales 538
Stranger in Tibet: the adventures of a Zen monk 83
Study of polyandry 276
Study of the treaties and agreements relating to Tibet: a documentary history of international relations of Tibet 442
Superhuman life of Gesar of Ling 499
System of monastic education in Tibet 472

T

Tales from Tibetan opera 495
Tantra in Tibet: the great exposition of secret mantra 360
Tantric distinction: an introduction to Tibetan Buddhism 324
Taxation and the structure of a Tibetan village 463
Ten years in exile: an appraisal of the resettlement of Tibetan refugees in India 246
Textbook of colloquial Tibetan: dialect of central Tibet 291
Textbook of colloquial Tibetan language 283
Thirteenth Dalai Lama 182, 190
Three Tibetan mysteries: Tchrimekunden, Nansal, Djronzanmo, as performed in Tibetan monasteries 496
Three years in Tibet 96
Through unknown Tibet 77
Tibet 7, 9, 17-18
Tibet: carte routière 38
Tibet: a chronicle of exploration 50
Tibet: continents in collision 24
Tibet: the facts 431
Tibet: the forbidden land 63
Tibet: a geographical, ethnographical, and historical sketch, derived from Chinese sources 13
Tibet: a guide to the land of fascination 43
Tibet: a handbook 6
Tibet: heart of Asia 134
Tibet: its history, religion and people 10
Tibet: land of snows 21
Tibet: the lost civilization 11
Tibet: mort ou vif 202
Tibet: myth vs. reality 421
Tibet: past and present 129, 398
Tibet: past and present: a select bibliography with chronology of historical events 1660-1981 553
Tibet: a political history 137
Tibet: self-determination in politics among nations 451
Tibet: the sacred realm: photographs, 1880-1950 19
Tibet: today and yesterday 132
Tibet: a travel survival kit 41
Tibet, 10th March 1959 420
Tibet after Mao Ze Dong 413
Tibet and adjacent countries 37
Tibet and Bengal: a study in trade policy and trade pattern 460
Tibet and her neighbours: a presentation of the historic facts of Tibet's relations with neighbouring states 448
Tibet and imperial China: survey of Sino-Tibetan relations up to the end of the Manchu dynasty in 1912 443
Tibet and its birds 124
Tibet and its history 135
Tibet and the Chinese People's Republic: a report to the International Commission of Jurists by its Legal Inquiry Committee on Tibet 229
Tibet and the Tibetans 185
Tibet as a stateless society and some Islamic parallels 418
Tibet at the United Nations 449
Tibet Bon religion: a death ritual of the Tibetan Bonpos 308
Tibet, China and India, 1914-1950: a history of imperial diplomacy 444
Tibet disappears: a documentary history of Tibet's international status, the great rebellion and its aftermath 136
Tibet fights for freedom: the story of the March 1959 uprising as recorded in documents, despatches, eye-witness accounts and world-wide reactions: a white book 210
Tibet from Buddhism to Communism 189
Tibet guide 39
Tibet in China: a report for International Alert 425
Tibet in revolt 222
Tibet in the United Nations 1950-1961 452
Tibet is my country 219
Tibet Journal 547
Tibet leaps forward 377

150

Tibet News Review 548

Tibet no longer mediaeval 379

Tibet on the imperial chessboard: the making of British policy towards Lhasa, 1899-1925 162

Le Tibet révolté: vers Nepemako, la terre promise des Tibétaines 165

Tibet revolution and the free world 230

Tibet the mysterious 47

Tibet to Tiananmen: Chinese human rights and United States foreign policy 432

Tibet today 382

Tibet today: current conditions and prospects 394

Tibet transformed 203

Tibet under Chinese Communist rule: a compilation of refugee statements 1958-1975 231

Tibetan amulets 525

Tibetan and Himalayan woodblock prints 526

Tibetan art 505

Tibetan Book of the Dead, or the after-death experiences on the Bardo plane 355

Tibetan Book of the Great Liberation, or the method of realizing nirvana through knowing the mind 356

Tibetan books and newspapers: (Chinese collection): with bibliographical notes 557

Tibetan Buddhist medicine and psychiatry: the diamond healing 385

Tibetan carpet 521

Tibetan civilization 16

Tibetan community in exile 244

Tibetan cooking: a pioneer book on the food and cookery of the well known mysterious and one time forbidden land 543

Tibetan deputies and "human rights" 433

Tibetan Dhammapada: sayings of the Buddha 357

Tibetan dogs 123

Tibetan Empire in central Asia: a history of the struggle for great power among Tibetans, Turks, Arabs and Chinese during the Middle Ages 142

Tibetan–English dictionary of Buddhist terminology 282

Tibetan–English dictionary of modern Tibetan 281

Tibetan folk tales 535

Tibetan folk tales from Gyantse and western Tibet 539

Tibetan foothold 249

Tibetan for beginners and travellers 288

Tibetan frontier families: recollections of three generations from Ding-ri 263

Tibetan frontiers question from Curzon to the Colombo Conference: an unresolved factor in Indo-Sinic relations 441

Tibetan Homes Foundation report 1966-67 255

Tibetan interviews 225

Tibetan journey 100

Tibetan language: three study tools 290

Tibetan literature of the eighteenth century 484

Tibetan marches 99

Tibetan meditation: theory and practice 338

Tibetan newspaper reader 292

Tibetan nomadic pastoralists: environments, personality and ethos 269

Tibetan painted scrolls 517

Tibetan paintings: a study of Tibetan thangkas eleventh to nineteenth centuries 516

Tibetan phonology 294

Tibetan phrasebook 284

Tibetan polity, 1904-37: the conflict between the 13th Dalai Lama and the 9th Panchen Lama: a case study 176

Tibetan porcelain 524

Tibetan principality: the political system of Sa sKya 396

Tibetan refugees: youth and the new generation of meaning 250

Tibetan religious dances: Tibetan text and annotated translations of the 'chams yig 303

Tibetan rugs 522

Tibetan skylines 90

Tibetan social philosophy 383

Tibetan system of writing 298

Tibetan tales 367

Tibetan tales derived from Indian sources 500

Tibetan thangka painting: methods and materials 515

Tibetan therapeutic massage 392

Tibetan tradition of geography 31

Tibetan village communities: structure and change 375

Tibetan women, then and now: a faithful and vivid account of the status and role of Tibetan women who lived in ancient Tibet

as well as those who
are living today in and
outside Tibet 261
Tibetans 429
Tibetans: a dwindling
population: a
comparative study 235
Tibetans in Bhutan:
problem of
repatriation 248
Tibetans in exile,
1959-1980 256
Tibetans in India: a case
study of Mundgod
Tibetans 252
Tibetans in migration 251
Die tibetische Bon-Religion
309
Das tibetische Staatsorakel
275
Tibet's economic reforms:
an analysis 468
Tibet's great yogi Milarepa:
a biography from the
Tibetan 358
Tibet's population develops
241
Tibet's terrifying deities: sex
and aggression in
religious acculturation
304
T'ien Pao: Chairman of the
People's Government
of the Tibetan
Autonomous Region
232
Tiger rugs of Tibet 523
Timely rain: travels in new
Tibet 206
To Lhasa in disguise: an
account of a secret
expedition through
mysterious Tibet 97
To Lhassa at last 178
To the navel of the world:
yaks and unheroic
travels in Nepal and
Tibet 117
Tombs of the Tibetan kings
153
Toward a people's
anthropology 270
Trade through the
Himalayas: the early

British attempts to
open Tibet 155
Traditional Tibetan
organization in the
Himalayas and the
problem of integration
243
Tragedy of Tibet 215
Trans-Himalaya:
discoveries and
adventures in Tibet 95
Trans-Himalayan trade: a
retrospect
(1774-1914): in quest
of Tibet's identity 156
Travels and adventures in
Tibet, including the
diary of Miss Annie
Taylor's remarkable
journey from
Tau-Chau to
Ta-Chien-Lu through
the heart of the
forbidden land 57
Travels in Tartary and
Thibet 62
Travels of a consular
officer in eastern Tibet,
together with a history
of the relations
between China, Tibet
and India 192
Treasury of good sayings: a
Tibetan history of Bon
306
Trekking in Nepal, west
Tibet and Bhutan 44
Trente ans aux portes du
Thibet interdit 368
Trespassers on the roof of
the world 48
Les tribus anciennes des
marches
sino-tibétaines:
légendes, classification
et histoire 152
Truth about Tibet 184
Two lady missionaries in
Tibet 72

U

Unveiling of Lhasa 167

Uprooted Tibetans in
India: a sociological
study of continuity a
change 254
Use of human skulls and
bones in Tibet 273

V

A világ tetejen: Kőrösi
Csoma Sándor
nyomdokain nyugati
Tibetbe 55

W

Warriors of Tibet: the sto
of Aten and the
Khampas' fight for t.
freedom of their
country 218
Water bird and other yea
a history of the 13th
Dalai Lama and afte
168
Water horse and other
years: a history of 1.
and 18th century Ti
157
We Tibetans: an intimate
picture, by a woman
Tibet, of an interesti
and distinctive peop
381
Western experience in
Tibet, 1327-1950 49
Western Tibet and the
British borderland:
sacred country of
Hindus and Buddhi
14
What is it behind the Da
Lama's 'plan'? 419
When serfs stood up in
Tibet: report 226
White annals 144
Wings of the white crane
491
Winter in Tibet 112
With the Tibetans in tent
and temple: a narra
of four years' reside

*on the Tibetan border,
and of a journey into
the far interior* 71
*With mounted infantry in
Tibet* 180
Women and Tibet 262
*Women in Buddhism:
images of the feminine
in the Mahayana
tradition* 336
Women of wisdom 258

Y

*Yar-lun dynasty: a study
with particular regard
to the contribution by
myths and legends to
the history of ancient
Tibet and the origin
and nature of its kings*
145
Yoga of Tibet: the Great

*Exposition of Secret
Mantra: 2 and 3* 361
*Younger brother Don Yod
. . . being the secret
biography from the
words of the Glorious
Lama, the Holy
Reverend Blo bZang
Ye SHes* 497
Younghusband Expedition
177

Index of Subjects

A

Abominable snowman 122
Administration 14, 135,
    175, 395-6, 404, 412,
    414, 417
Ambans 130, 161
Amulets 525
Anthropology 73, 263-78
    bibliography 559
Archaeology 141, 147, 150
Architecture 2, 502,
    512-14, 518-19
    bibliographies 520, 551
Aristocracy 191, 374,
    395-6, 404
Art 2, 16, 21, 379, 502-16
    bibliographies 511, 551
Astrology 473, 541
Astronomy 541
Atisa 317

B

Bailey, F. M. 80-1, 105
Beggars 374
Bhutan 194, 321
    relations with Tibet 439,
    459
    Tibetan communities in
    248, 256
Birds 124, 265
Birth 8, 265, 533
Bishop, Isabella Bird 51
Bogle, George 54, 64
Bonism 300-1, 303, 305,
    306-9
Books 527, 557
Borders 435-6, 440-2, 444,
    446-7, 452
    bibliography 558
Britain
    relations with Bhutan
    128
    bibliography 549
    relations with Sikkim
    128
    bibliography 549
    relations with Tibet

128-9, 135, 156, 159,
    162, 434-5, 437-8,
    441-4, 447, 453
    bibliographies 549,
    551, 553-4, 558
    Tibetan communities in
    548
Buddhism 53, 300-5,
    310-66, 399, 402, 412,
    418, 466
    and art 503, 506, 510,
    512-14
    and medicine 385,
    389-91
    and music 528, 531-2
    education 472-3, 479
    history 138, 146, 149,
    151, 301, 305, 315,
    319, 344-6, 351,
    362-3
    terminology 282
    texts 311-12, 315, 317,
    321, 323, 327, 329-30,
    332-4, 337, 340-3, 347,
    349-61, 364, 367
    women in 258, 260-1,
    336
    see also Atisa;
    Compassion; Dalai
    Lama; Death;
    Emptiness; Festivals;
    Jisa; Jokhang;
    Karmapas; Mahayana
    Buddhism;
    Meditation; Milarepa;
    Monasteries; Mount
    Kailas; Mystery plays;
    Nuns; Padma
    Sambhava; Panchen
    Lama; Reincarnation;
    Tantra; Tara; Tsong-
    ka-pa; Yeshe Tsogyel;
    Zen Buddhism;
    Zogpen

C

Carpets 521-3
Censuses 234, 239-40

Central Institute for
    Nationalities 477
Children 374, 381
China
    and education in Tibet
    471, 474-8, 480
    and Lhasa riots 416
    and material progress in
    Tibet 379-80, 458, 462,
    468
    and national minorities
    in Tibet 186, 401, 407,
    480
    at United Nations 449,
    452
    claims to sovereignty in
    Tibet 128, 131-2, 183
    colonization 411
    fighting with Tibetans
    164-5, 368, 372
    frontier disputes 192,
    440-1, 453
    human rights abuses
    423-33
    integration of Tibet by
    force 406
    liaison office in Lhasa
    183
    negotiations with Dalai
    Lama 397-8, 407-8,
    419
    1959 uprising 420
    policy towards Tibet
    113, 161, 402, 421, 451
    since Cultural
    Revolution 413, 415,
    422
    relations with Tibet 6,
    135-6, 139, 146, 156,
    400, 410, 434-7, 443-8,
    450
    present-day 394
    since 1951 196-233,
    402-3
    Residents in Tibet 130
    Simla Convention 187
    strategic interest of Tibet
    397
    treaties 442
    821/822 149

China *contd.*
view of Tibet 13, 140,
377
Chinese population in
Tibet 207, 234, 236,
394, 411, 426
Christian missions 50, 52,
61-2, 72, 74, 78,
367-73
Climate 25, 27, 29
Clothing 2, 8, 261, 506, 514
Coins 8, 17, 455, 507
Communes 198
Communism 26, 189, 198,
207, 214, 231-2, 394,
397, 410
see also China, relations
with Tibet; Politics
Compassion 311, 359, 365
Constitution 204, 399
Csoma de Kőrös,
Alexander 55, 58, 68
Cultural Revolution,
1966-76 198, 203, 217,
380, 474

D

Dalai Lama 130, 157, 301,
348, 409
Dalai Lama, 1st 340
Dalai Lama, 2nd 341
Dalai Lama, 3rd 342
Dalai Lama, 5th 339
Dalai Lama, 6th 154, 158,
484, 486, 491
Dalai Lama, 7th 343
Dalai Lama, 13th 166, 168,
176, 182, 190, 194, 334
Dalai Lama, 14th 208-9,
212, 227, 242, 312
Dalai Lama, 14th
Address to European
Parliament, 1988 202
Five Point Plan, 1987 202
David-Neel, Alexandra 19,
51, 86, 88-9
Death 8, 265, 329, 331,
333, 355
Debate 479
Demonstrations *see* Riots
Derge 99
Desideri, Ippolito 61, 78

Dictionaries
English–Tibetan 279,
287
Tibetan–English 280-2,
287, 292
Divination 268, 300, 302,
325
Divorce 261
Dob-dob *See* Fighting
monks
Dogs 119, 123, 464
Dolpo 143
D'Orville, Albert 74, 78
Drama 492-7, 536
Drathang 513
Drugs 393
Dzog Chen *see* Zogpen

E

Economic history 375,
455-6, 459-61, 463-7,
469-70
Economic reforms 380,
415, 458, 462, 468
Economy 17, 135, 368,
375-6, 379, 395, 454-70
role of women 259, 261
Education 135, 239-41,
256, 379, 394, 471-81
bibliography 478
Electric power
bibliography 552
Employment 239, 241, 394
Emptiness 311, 323-4, 326,
349
Ethnology 13-14, 103, 135,
152, 263-78
Exploration 45-107
bibliography 559

F

Farming 375, 379
Fauna 28, 32, 43, 81, 119,
121-4, 175
Fertility 237
Festivals 265, 305, 492-3,
497
Fighting monks 163
Flora 28, 32, 43, 60, 80-1,
120, 125-7, 175

Folk songs 539
Folk music 529
Folk tales 98, 381, 534-8
Folklore 175, 313, 533-9
Food 8, 374, 533, 542-3
Foreign relations 434-53

G

Games 374, 378, 381
Gartok Expedition, 1904-5
102, 105
Gazetteers 34-5
Gedun Chompel 188-9
Geography 6, 13-14, 17,
23-33, 101, 103, 135
bibliography 551
Geology 23-5, 28, 92, 101,
141
Gerontology *see* Old age
Gobi Desert 93
Gold 455, 464
Grammars 283-93
Grueber, John 74, 78
Guerrilla movement 218,
223, 242
Guidebooks 39-44
Gyantse 1, 78, 102, 110,
117, 512, 539

H

Harrier, Heinrich 91
Health 379, 394
Hedin, Sven 19, 45
Herdsmen 374
History 6, 8-17, 21, 39-40,
43, 128-40
bibliographies 549-51,
553-6, 558-9
early and medieval 141-
53
16th to 19th centuries
154-61
1900 to 1950 162-95
since 1951 196-233
political 398, 414, 434-8,
441-5, 447-8, 453
see also Archaeology;
Buddhism, history;
Cultural Revolution,
1966-76; Economic

history; Gartok
Expedition, 1904-5;
Gedun Chomphel;
Huang Mu-sung;
Kings; Museum of the
Revolution;
Nepalese–Tibetan
War, 1788-92;
Nepalese–Tibetan
War, 1855-56; Politics;
Simla Convention;
Tibetan uprising,
1959; Treaties;
Yar-lun dynasty;
Younghusband
Expedition
Huang Mu-sung 183
Human rights 204, 423-33

I

Immigration *see* Chinese
population in Tibet
India
relations with Tibet 136,
146, 192, 271, 436,
440-1, 444, 446-7, 451,
453
Tibetan communities in
242-4, 246-7, 249-50,
252-6, 271
Industry 379
Interest rates 465

J

Jesuits 45, 50, 52, 61, 74,
78, 373
Jewellery 261, 507, 514
Jisa 466
Jokhang 20, 108, 411, 506,
513
Jyekundo 99

K

Kachu 513
Kantze 99
Karmapas 325
Kawaguch, Ekai 83, 96
Kham 218, 223, 381

Khampas 218, 223
Kings 141, 144-5, 151, 153,
315
tombs 145, 153
Kumbum 99, 219

L

Land tenure 375, 384,
395-6
Language 12, 15, 135,
279-99, 474
see also Dictionaries;
Grammars;
Phrasebooks;
Phonology
Law 135
Lhasa 1, 20, 91, 113, 201,
211, 219
anti-Chinese
demonstrations 394,
408, 413, 416
Bell's mission 129
Chinese colonization 411
continuing inaccessibility
97
first Western woman 86,
89
guidebooks 39
maps 36
memoirs 174, 194
1936 expedition 85
Potala Palace 518-19
recent travellers 116-17
street songs 405
temple 513
under 13th Dalai Lama
96
Younghusband
Expedition 167, 169,
175, 178, 193
see also Jokhang; Potala
Palace
Literature 6, 12, 16, 21,
482-501
see also Drama; Folk
tales; Milarepa;
Mystery plays; Opera;
Poetry

M

Mahayana Buddhism 324,
351, 356, 363
bibliography 337
Manning, Thomas 54, 64
Maps 25, 35-8, 239
Marriage 261, 263, 265,
539
Massage 392
Mazuchell, Nina 51
Medical psychiatry 385
Medicine 15, 242, 385-93,
473
Meditation 318, 323-4, 338,
347, 351, 359-60
Megaliths 147
Milarepa 312, 332, 358,
488-9
Monasteries 3, 305, 396,
466, 473, 512-13
Money 455, 465
Mount Kailas 14, 45, 53,
101, 115, 117-18
Mount Qomolangma
[Everest] 32
Museum of the Revolution
20
Music 303, 528-32
Musical instruments 273,
507, 532
Mystery plays 492-7

N

Natural energy 33
bibliography 552
Nepal
Tibetan communities in
256
Nepalese–Tibetan War,
1788-92 75
Nepalese–Tibetan War,
1855-56 160
Ngapo Ngawang-Jigme
225
Nomads 90, 150, 266-7,
269, 272, 462
Norbu, Thubten Jigme 219
Nuns 262, 336

O

Odoric, Friar 50, 79
Old age 278
Opera 495, 536
Oracles 242, 271, 275, 302

P

Padma Sambhava 335, 356, 366
Painting 502-10, 514-17
Panchen Lama 130, 348, 497
Panchen Lama, 9th 176
Panchen Lama, 10th 220, 225, 380
Pandits 45, 59, 65-7, 76
Pastoralism 266-7, 269, 272, 458, 462
Pemalingpa 154
People's Liberation Army 394, 406
Periodicals 544-8
Phallic symbols 277
Philosophy 12, 15, 472
Phonology 294-5
Photographs 2-3, 5, 7, 11, 18-20, 22, 382
Phrasebooks 39, 43, 283-5, 287-8, 291
Poetry 343, 358, 484, 486-91
Political satire 405
Politics 6, 8, 368, 394-422
Polyandry 259, 274, 276
Population 234-41
Porcelain 524
Postage stamps 507
Potala Palace 20, 518-19
Pranavananda, Swami 53
Prostitution 261
Przhevalsky, Nicholas 70

R

Railways 457
Rape 261
Refugees 211, 242-57, 271
Reincarnation 326, 329, 355
Religion 3-4, 6, 8-10, 12, 14, 16, 21, 39-40, 43, 135, 300-73, 424, 426
and art 503, 506, 510, 512-14
and music 528, 531-2
in literature 483
see also Bonism; Buddhism; Christian missions; Jesuits
Rijnhart, Susie Carson 71-2
Riots 212, 394, 408, 411, 416, 426, 428
Robbers 374
Rubruck, William of 50
Russia
relations with Tibet 96, 434, 438, 450-1, 453

S

Sa sKya 396
Sculpture 502-9
Serfdom 376, 383
Shalu 513
Shelton, Albert Leroy 49, 372
Shigatse 1, 66, 78, 110
Sikkim 194
Simla Convention 187, 435, 452
Skulls 273
Sky burials 108, 111
Smoking 374
Social conditions 6, 8-10, 14, 16, 21, 374-84
Social customs 98, 265, 374
Social satire 405
Statistics 234, 454
Street songs 405
Superstitions 533
Switzerland
Tibetan communities in 245, 251

T

Takla-Makan Desert 93
Tantra 320, 334, 340-1, 343, 346, 360-1, 365
Tara 313, 340, 364
Taring, Rinchen Dolma 191
Taxation 384, 395-6, 461, 463, 470
Taylor, Annie 51, 57, 72, 371
Thangkas 503, 505, 515-17
Tibet University 481
Tibetan Pioneer Mission 371
Tibetan script 296-9
Tibetan uprising, 1959 163, 196, 201, 205, 207, 210, 214, 216, 218, 221-6, 228-30, 233, 242
T'ien Pao 232
Tiger rugs 523
Tornay, Maurice 370
Trade 8, 155-6, 456, 459-60, 464, 467, 469
Transport 379, 457
Travellers' accounts
before 1900 55-79
1900 to 1950 80-107
since 1950 108-18
Treaties 437, 442, 452
Trekking 44
Tribes 152
Tsangpo river 45, 80-1, 102, 107
Tsong-ka-pa 312, 354
Turner, Samuel 54

U

United Nations 136, 430, 442, 449, 452
United States
relations with Tibet 432, 451

V

Villages 375, 463

W

Western perception of Tibet 46
Women 8, 51, 258-62, 336, 374, 381

Woodblocks 504, 526
Workman, Fanny Bullock 51

Y

Yaks 121

Yar-lun dynasty 145
Yemar 513
Yeshe Tsogyel 260, 262
Yeti, *see* Abominable snowman
Younghusband Expedition, 1903-4 48, 50, 105, 159, 162, 167, 169-72, 175, 177-81, 184, 193, 195, 437-8

Z

Zen Buddhism 328, 335
Zogpen 322, 335, 353

Map of Tibet

This map shows the more important towns and other features.

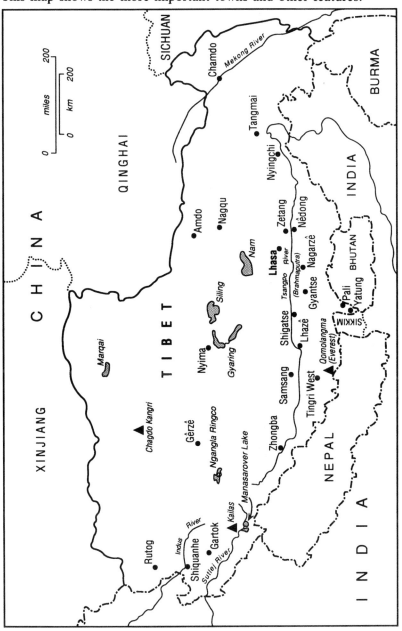